Ethics, Religion,
and the
Good Society

Ethics, Religion,
and the
Good Society

New Directions in a Pluralistic World

Joseph Runzo,
Editor

Westminster/John Knox Press
Louisville, Kentucky

TO JEAN

pour un renouveau

Except where noted, scripture quotations are from the New Revised Standard Version of the Bible, copyright © 1989 by the Division of Christian Education of the National Council of the Churches of Christ in the U.S.A., and are used by permission.

Scripture quotations marked REB are taken from *The Revised English Bible*, © The Delegates of the Oxford University Press and The Syndics of the Cambridge University Press, 1989. Used by permission.

Book design by Kevin Raquepaw

First edition

Published by Westminster/John Knox Press
Louisville, Kentucky

This book is printed on acid-free paper that meets the American National Standards Institute Z39.48 standard.♾

PRINTED IN THE UNITED STATES OF AMERICA

9 8 7 6 5 4 3 2 1

Library of Congress Cataloging-in-Publication Data

Ethics, religion, and the good society : new directions in a
pluralistic world / Joseph Runzo, editor. — 1st ed.
    p.   cm.
  Includes bibliographical references.
  ISBN 0-664-25285-0 (alk. paper)

  1. Religion and ethics. 2. Religious pluralism. 3. Religions.
I. Runzo, Joseph, 1948–
BJ47.E84 1992
291.5—dc20   91-48260

Contents

III. ETHICS AND RELIGIOUS PLURALISM

Contributors

ROBERT M. ADAMS (B.D. Princeton Theological Seminary, M.A. Oxford University, Ph.D. Cornell University) is the author of *The Virtue of Faith and Other Essays in Philosophical Theology* as well as many articles in moral philosophy, metaphysics, history of philosophy, and the philosophy of religion. He has served as President of the Society of Christian Philosophers and is a member of the Board of Trustees of Princeton Theological Seminary and of The Charlotte W. Newcombe Foundation. He has taught at the University of Michigan and has been a Visiting Professor at Yale Divinity School. He is currently Professor of Philosophy at the University of California, Los Angeles.

BHIKKHU CHAO CHU serves as a member of the World Buddhist Sangha Council Executive Committee. Ordained a Theravada and Mahayana monk, he has done extensive international missionary work in Hong Kong, Japan, and other areas of the Far East. He served as official Buddhist chaplain and counselor for the 1984 Olympics in Los Angeles. He is currently Director of the Los Angeles Buddhist Union and the Center of Buddhist Development.

ALAN DONAGAN (M.A. University of Melbourne, B.Phil. University of Oxford) is the author of *Spinoza, Choice: The Essential Element in Human Action, The Theory of Morality,* and *The Later Philosophy of R. G. Collingwood* in addition to numerous articles in philosophy. He served as President of the American Philosophical Association, Central Division, A Fellow of the American Academy of Arts and Sciences, and a Member of the Institut International de Philosophie. He taught at the University of Western Australia; University College in Canberra, Australia; the Universities of Minnesota, Indiana, Illinois at Urbana, and Chicago; and was Doris and Henry Dreyfuss Professor of Philosophy at California Institute of Technology until his death in 1991.

BRUCE C. HALL (Ph.D. Harvard University) has published articles on Indian and Tibetan Buddhism, Indian Philosophy, and Hinduism. He organized the largest collection of Tibetan Buddhist Canons in the West, at the Harvard-Yenching Library. He has been a Visiting Assistant Professor at the College of William and Mary and at the University of Michigan, and a Lecturer in Philosophy and Religion at Claremont McKenna College as well as Lecturer in Religion at the University of Southern California and Visiting Assistant Professor of Religion at Pomona College.

BRIAN L. HEBBLETHWAITE (M.A. Oxford University, M.A. Cambridge University, B.D. Cambridge University) is the author of *Evil, Suffering and Religion, The Adequacy of Christian Ethics, The Problems of Theology, The Christian Hope, The Incarnation,* and *The Ocean of Truth.* He is editor of *Divine Action: Studies Inspired by the Philosophical Theology of Austin Farrer, The Philosophical Frontiers of Christian Theology,* and *Christianity and Other Religions,* and has published numerous articles in philosophy of religion and theology. He serves as Canon Theologian of Leicester Cathedral and President of the Society for the Study of Theology. He is a Fellow and Dean of Chapel at Queens' College, Cambridge and University Lecturer in Divinity at Cambridge University.

JOHN HICK (D.Phil. Oxford University, D.Litt. Edinburgh University) has published twenty books including *An Interpretation of Religion, Problems of Religious Pluralism, God Has Many Names, Death and Eternal Life, Evil and the God of Love, God and the Universe of Faiths, Arguments for the Existence of God,* and *Philosophy of Religion.* He has published numerous articles and lectured throughout the world. He has taught at Cornell University, Princeton Theological Seminary, Cambridge University, and Birmingham University (England), and has been a Visiting Professor at Benares Hindu University, Visva-Bharati University, Punjabi University, Goa University, and the University of Sri Lanka. He is Danforth Professor of Philosophy of Religion at The Claremont Graduate School.

CLARK A. KUCHEMAN (Ph.D. University of Chicago) is editor of *The Life of Choice: Some Liberal Religious Perspectives on Morality* and has published numerous journal articles in religion and ethics as well as contributing essays to several anthologies. He has taught at the University of Chicago Divinity School and is currently Arthur V. Stoughton Professor of Christian Ethics at Claremont McKenna College.

JOHN LANGAN, S.J. (B.D. Woodstock College, Ph.D. University of Michigan), has published widely on the morality of nuclear deterrence, human rights, and social justice. He served as a consultant to the U.S. Catholic bishops on their pastoral letter on war and peace, and is co-editor of *Human Rights in the Americas: The Struggle for Consensus* and *The Nuclear Dilemma and the Just War Tradition*. He has spoken extensively in the United States and also abroad at international conferences. He is a founder and has served as Acting Director of Woodstock Theological Center, is a consultant in ethics to the Chemical Bank of New York, and has been a Visiting Professor at Yale University Divinity School. He is currently Rose Kennedy Professor of Christian Ethics at Georgetown University and a Senior Fellow of the Woodstock Theological Center.

JAMES WM. McCLENDON, JR. (Th.M. Princeton Theological Seminary, Th.D. Southwestern Baptist Theological Seminary), is the author of *Biography as Theology, Ethics: Systematic Theology,* vol. 1, and many articles in his field; co-author of *Understanding Religious Convictions;* and co-editor of *Is God GOD?* He has taught at the University of San Francisco and Golden Gate Baptist Theological Seminary and has held visiting positions at Stanford University, the University of Notre Dame, University of Pennsylvania, Temple University, Goucher College, and Saint Mary's College. Formerly Professor of Theology at Church Divinity School of the Pacific, he is now Distinguished Scholar in Residence at Fuller Theological Seminary.

TOVA MELTZER (Ph.D. University of Toronto) has published articles in Assyriology, anthropology, and Semiotic studies. She has chaired the Hebrew Bible section of the Pacific Coast Region of the Society of Biblical Literature. She is Associate Professor of Religion at The Claremont Graduate School and is currently teaching linguistics in the People's Republic of China.

RICHARD J. MOUW (Ph.D. University of Chicago) is the author of *The God Who Commands, Political Evangelism, Politics and the Biblical Drama, Called to Holy Worldliness, Objections to Christianity, When the Kings Come Marching In,* and *Distorted Truth,* as well as numerous articles in religion and ethics. Formerly Professor of Philosophy at Calvin College, he was Visiting Distinguished Professor of Evangelical Christianity at Juniata College. He is currently Provost, Senior Vice President, and Professor of Christian Philosophy and Ethics at Fuller Theological Seminary.

NANCEY MURPHY (Ph.D. University of California, Berkeley; Th.D. Graduate Theological Union) is the author of *Theology in the Age of Scientific Reasoning* as well as a number of articles in philosophy of religion, theology, and philosophy of science. She has held visiting positions at Church Divinity School of the Pacific, Whittier College, the Dominican School of Philosophy and Theology, Berkeley, and the Lutheran School of Theology in Chicago. She is Associate Professor of Christian Philosophy at Fuller Theological Seminary.

LINDA PETERSON (Ph.D. University of California, Irvine) works in the areas of history of medieval and modern philosophy, metaphysics, and philosophy of religion. She is contributor to *Individuation in the Late Middle Ages and the Counter Reformation.* She has held visiting positions at the University of California, Irvine, and the University of California, Los Angeles, and is currently Assistant Professor of Philosophy at the University of San Diego.

PHILIP J. ROSSI, S.J. (B.D. Woodstock College, Ph.D. University of Texas, Austin), has published *Together Toward Hope: A Journey to Moral Theology* and is co-editor of *Kant's Philosophy of Religion Reconsidered.* He is also the author of numerous articles in ethics, religion, and Kantian studies. He is a member of the Board of Directors of Creighton University and has been a member of the Advisory Committee on Medical Ethics for the Archdiocese of Milwaukee. He has been a Research Fellow at the Woodstock Theological Center and at the Institute for Advanced Studies in the Humanities at the University of Edinburgh. He is Associate Professor of Theology at Marquette University and served as Chair from 1985–1991.

JOSEPH RUNZO (Ph.D. University of Michigan, M.T.S. Harvard University) is the author of *Reason, Relativism and God,* editor of *Is God*

Real?, and co-editor of *Religious Experience and Religious Belief: Essays in the Epistemology of Religion*. He has published numerous articles and contributed to several anthologies in philosophy of religion, philosophical theology, and epistemology. He is founder and president of the Philosophy of Religion Society and has been a Visiting Professor at The University of Michigan and The Claremont Graduate School. He is Professor of Philosophy and of Religion at Chapman University.

MUZAMMIL H. SIDDIQI (Ph.D. Harvard University) has published articles in Islamic and Arabic studies and has participated in many interreligious dialogues and lectured worldwide including the Middle East, South Africa, Australia, New Zealand, the Far East, Britain, the U.S., and Canada. He has been Chairman of the Department of Religious Affairs at the Muslim World League Office to the United Nations and U.S.A., and Director of the Islamic Center of Washington, D.C. He is a member of the Supreme Islamic Council of Egypt. He is currently Director of the Islamic Society of Orange County and Adjunct Professor of Islamic Studies at California State University, Fullerton.

KAREN J. TORJESEN (Ph.D. Claremont Graduate School) is the author of *Hermeneutical Procedure and Theological Structure in Origen's Exegesis* and *Sex, Sin, and Woman: Social Histories of Theological Ideas*. She has published numerous articles on women in early Christian literature, Christianity and sexuality, and the history of doctrine. She has taught at Georg August Universitat (Germany) and Mary Washington College and has been a Visiting Professor at Fuller Theological Seminary. She is Margo L. Goldsmith Associate Professor of Women's Studies in Religion at The Claremont Graduate School.

Introduction

We live in a pluralistic age. We are not only aware of the diversity among peoples, but acknowledge this diversity as both natural and enriching for humankind. We also live in a world at once acutely aware of ethical concerns and yet riven by ethical disagreements. This collection of essays focuses on the intersection of these two trenchant issues of our time within the context of our fundamental perspective as religious beings. For as each essay speaks to a salient issue arising from the contemporary interplay between religion and ethics, throughout this volume there constantly recurs the issue of pluralism—pluralism of two distinct, though related, types.

First, there is the pluralism *within* a specific religious tradition, like Christianity. This is largely a modern recognition. While, for example, sectarian division was common in the early Christian church, and later became painfully evident in a public form in the Reformation/ Counter Reformation period, it was not until fairly recently, with the publication of work like Troeltsch's *The Social Teachings of the Christian Churches*, that the pluralism within the church came to be viewed not as a regrettable set of wounds to be sutured, but as a normal and even enriching part of the Christian tradition. Second, projected on a *global* scale, we see this same phenomenon in the collective pluralism of the great world religious traditions. Again, this very notion of global religious pluralism is a modern notion. We need not look far historically to find as the dominant religious categories the contrasting identifications of "the faithful" and "the infidel." As Ambrose Bierce in the late nineteenth century succinctly put this outlook in his *Devil's Dictionary:* "impiety" is *"your* irreverence toward *my* deity." But as transglobal communication and economic interdependence, a recognition of global ecological interconnections, and just simple curiosity about others have made "foreigners"—whom the Greeks called the *barbarians*—into friends, our sense of community has come to include not just neighbors on our street or in our workplace or our nation, but those on other continents. Consequently, today "religious pluralism" has a positive connotation in this global context. We recognize not just that there are other religious traditions, but that each has its own integrity and its adherents their own dignity.

This pluralistic religious awareness, both internal to traditions and global, not only informs the ideas on ethics and religion in these essays but also is concretely represented in the richly diverse viewpoints of the authors. One distinctive pluralist characteristic of the authors is that they are about equally divided between those in religious or theological studies and philosophers. There is a constant dialogue among the ideas in the essays. Sometimes this takes the explicit form of a direct response to one of the articles, where we find philosophers commenting on those in religious studies, and those in religious studies commenting on philosophers. The openness of this philosophic-theological give-and-take would have been rare ten years ago; the success of this dialogue is a mark of the new pluralist perspective of even one of our more provincial institutions, academia. But there are other, important pluralist aspects of the perspectives represented in this collection of essays: included are traditional/conservative and liberal theological viewpoints, feminist and male perspectives, Protestant and Catholic interpretations as well as representations of Buddhist, Islamic, Jewish, and even secular points of view. What is interesting is that a dialogue from these *prima facie* opposing viewpoints on seminal issues of religion and ethics often not only moves on common ground, but moves *to* common ground.

Thus, along with pluralism, a prevalent feature of these essays as a whole is *dialogue:* a dialogue among specific theses and countertheses as well as among broader perspectives and their alternatives. Within this dialogue, the essays in the book fall into three natural groupings by subject, though shared themes, including pluralism, provide a broader, connective dialogue across the three groupings.

The first set of essays serves to map the terrain for new directions in religious ethics in our pluralistic world. These essays deal with the fundamental questions of the nature of the good, and of the good or moral life. And the more specific sorts of questions in religious ethics addressed in the next two sections really presuppose and proceed on the basis of these more foundational questions.

Within the first section on "The Ethical Life and the Good," there is a further grouping among the first four and the last two papers. The papers by Brian Hebblethwaite, Linda Peterson, Robert M. Adams, and Alan Donagan are concerned with sketching out a religious ethics. With these models of religious ethics in mind, the paper by James McClendon and my paper give us a chance to "step back" and consider more methodological questions about the ways in which we should approach religious ethics in the first place.

So there is this inherent dialogue between the first four and the last two papers of section 1 as well as a dialogue *within* the papers themselves. Brian Hebblethwaite suggests an affirmative answer, which Linda Peterson then debates, to the question of whether there is an ideal religious moral life; Robert Adams brings James Gustafson into the discussion by extensively addressing his work as Adams proposes an alternative theocentric ethics, a debate Alan Donagan also joins in; James McClendon introduces the figures of Sarah Pierpont Edwards and Dorothy Day in a biographical approach to religious ethics; while I draw Gordon Kaufman, and especially Don Cupitt, into the conversation, in a dialogical response to their views on the relation between ethics and theological realism versus non-realism.

The second set of papers all address the question of what makes for a good society, vis-à-vis religion, and what ethical problems we confront in attempting to achieve a good society. While exhibiting points of intersection with the first set of papers on the groundwork of religious ethics, here in the second section we get a clear sense of the ebb and flow, the genuine dialogue, necessary for any fruitful consensus on specific ethical issues in a pluralistic society.

Richard Mouw explores the relationship between one's religious commitment, specifically a Christian commitment, and the now much diminished sense of public civility; Karen Torjesen further illuminates this problem of the loss of a public selfhood, and adds another voice by comparing the manner in which both religion *and women* have been relegated to the "private sphere." Philip Rossi, S.J., suggests a significant place for religious ethics in public discourse, especially by reintroducing the importance of considerations of human destiny; Clark Kucheman responds with a Hegelian approach, which suggests the reverse—that moral duty must precede considerations of the *telos* of humankind. Finally, John Langan, S.J., incorporates the thought of Pope John Paul II into the discussion by offering a provocative analysis of the tension in John Paul II's social encyclicals. This tension arises between his emphasis on individual moral responsibility and the actual "structures of sin" which enmesh us in society; Nancey Murphy supports Langan's observations but advances the dialogue in pointing to the role that the church then has as a model for breaking out of the "structures of sin" in society.

The third section of essays clearly *centers* on dialogue, taking up the ethical dimensions of the pressing problem of global religious pluralism. John Hick provides an overview of the possibility of intertradition dialogue by arguing for the universality of the Golden Rule as a basic moral stance among the great world religions. Then, Bhikkhu Chao Chu suggests that Buddhism itself is inherently pluralistic in orientation, at its core an "open tradition that encourages interfaith dialogue." Bruce Hall develops some of the more specific Buddhist views, including ethical views especially in scholastic Indian Buddhism, which can help set the necessary parameters for a genuine conversation among the world religions. Next in this dialogue, from an Islamic viewpoint, Muzammil Siddiqi suggests that Islam "strongly advocates a global vision" and shows how the Islamic world-view can provide a basis for working out a global ethics. To conclude, and adding another dimension to the perspectives in this dialogue, Tova Meltzer points out that it is not sufficient simply to delineate a structure for an ethical system for society. One must consider "voice"; one must ask *for whom* this is a meaningful ethical system. Her essay contributes a balanced feminist voice to round out these essays on religion and ethics in a pluralistic age.

We noted that this collection of essays is itself pluralistic. In addition, though, a major concern that the essays *address* is the *problem* of pluralism—a theme on which the collection of essays explicitly begins and ends. In the first essay, Hebblethwaite boldly asks whether, in view of the pluralism in our age, the Christian scheme of moral perfection need require conformity, as we would traditionally expect, to a single pattern. Arguing that the Christian moral life is not a matter of imitating a "perfect" pattern, but rather one of relationship to God, he concludes that, given the pluralistic factors in our lives as individuals, Christian ethics can embrace a variety of goodness, that there is a variety of properly good Christian ways of life.

Peterson's incisive essay poses a key question for this pluralistic approach to the Christian moral life taken by Hebblethwaite. While not rejecting Hebblethwaite's sensitivity to the pluralistic demands of our world, Peterson suggests that we do need to be able to "grade" diverse lifestyles. She argues that they should be assessed on the criterion that the goodness of a human life is a function of the natural characteristics of humans. She leaves us with the following challenging query for the religious person in a pluralistic age: If there is no *summum bonum*, then to *what* are the saints closer?

Robert Adams's carefully and powerfully argued paper, "Platonism and Naturalism: Options for a Theocentric Ethics," supports a more Platonic and Augustinian theistic ethics than has been common. Some central features of Adams's view are that God, as the supreme good, has much the same role as the Form of the Good in the "middle" Plato, that this good is intrinsically good, not just good *for* someone, and that our vision of the good in our own lives is a vision, albeit vague, of the infinite good. He concludes that while God is the supreme good, *and* God's purposes go beyond human needs, given our epistemic limitations regarding God's broader purposes, the foundational basis for theistic ethics must be *human* good, not a more generalized good for the planet or universe as suggested on Gustafson's more pantheistic or Whiteheadian conception. It is central to this conception, on which anyone can come to know the good, that exclusivism is inimical to a theocentric ethics. This pluralistic conception is endorsed and further sharpened in Alan Donagan's essay.

Donagan agrees with Adams that on epistemic grounds humans have a weak idea of God's purposes, but he goes on to argue that species are intrinsically good in themselves *because* they participate in God. Indeed, he argues that what marks a creature as an end is not that it is divinely created but that it is in the image of God. Both Adams and Donagan suggest that our moral attitudes and actions toward other creatures should be guided by our vision of them *qua imago dei*. Donagan, though, furthers the direction of Adams's pluralism by emphasizing the importance of recognizing *all* rational species as made in God's image and therefore as ends in themselves, thus extending the scope of religious ethics even to other (possible) extraterrestrial species.

Indeed, as one continues through the essays, it becomes progressively more evident that this theme of the central importance of taking a pluralistic perspective is a foundational element of all the ethical/religious issues assessed. My own defense of theological realism as a better basis for ethics than theological non-realism is based in part on the argument (in agreement with Hebblethwaite's view) that theological realism can account for a pluralistic response by God toward humans, and does not, as non-realists have argued, undermine pluralism. In his essay, "Religious Conviction and Public Civility," Richard Mouw addresses the often-held view that Christian belief is intolerant of the acceptance of diverse viewpoints, therefore making it impossible to reconcile Christian belief with public moral life. Against this, he argues that Christian belief not only need not but should not be relegated, as it has been in American experience, to the private sphere. Thus, the very issue which Mouw addresses— whether religious belief can and should be part of the discussion of civil matters—stems from the pluralism of our current age, with its concomitant, divided, and confused civil visions. Similarly, Philip Rossi addresses the way in which secularization has altered our moral discourse, concluding that religion has much to offer in the public sphere if religious ethics can see *itself* as subject to the challenge of pluralism.

One of the most important aspects of this issue of pluralism vis-à-vis religious ethics is directly addressed in the essays by McClendon, Torjesen, and Meltzer. A fundamental pluralistic aspect of our modern age is the recognition that female perspectives are not necessarily the same as male perspectives; that even in a relatively cohesive society there is not one voice but, at a most elemental level, at least two voices, male and female. Thus Karen Torjesen, in a balanced response to Mouw's analysis of the place of religion in public civility, draws a parallel between the relegation of religious groups and the relegation of women to the private sphere. She argues that the (more) male ethics of justice and the (more) female ethics of love need to be integrated in the public and private domains. Likewise Tova Meltzer, in addressing the role of ethics in the dialogue among the world religions, points out, as we have seen, that "it's not sufficient to delineate a structure for the ethical system of a society, one must ask *for whom* [these ethical structures] are operative." Much like Torjesen, Meltzer argues not only that our understanding of ethics is gendered but that in our contemporary discussion of ethics and religion all the voices, including "male" and "female," must be heard.

These considerations doubly enhance the pluralism of ethical dialogue: with the inclusion of *both* an ethics of justice and an ethics of love, and with the inclusion of the male and female "voices." For as Torjesen and Meltzer observe, these are not rigid pairings and hence not just two perspectives. At different times and places there will be different permutations, and hence a rich pluralism, of the male and the female and the ethics of justice and the ethics of love. As Meltzer neatly illustrates this point, in ancient Mesopotamia—as represented in the Code of Hammurabi—justice largely has to do with human *relationships* and care. This contrasts with our usual "harder" contemporary notions of (either distributive or retributive) justice. And finally, James McClendon, developing an "ethics of delight," gives specific substance to the importance of the inclusion of these different voices by vividly focusing on the lives of Sarah Pierpont Edwards and Dorothy Day. Here, not only do female voices enrich the pluralism of the dialogue, but they are taken as *paradigmatic* of a new direction in ethics, providing an emphasis on what, coming from the underclass, has often been purposely omitted, and allowing for a new emphasis on the "fit" between what is morally right and what feels good.

Of course, one of the most obvious ways in which the importance of a pluralistic perspective has been recognized is represented in the last set of essays on world religious pluralism, essays which return to the question of religious pluralism and ethics raised at the outset by Hebblethwaite, but now in a global context. Here, the essays by Bhikkhu Chao Chu, Bruce Hall, and Muzammil Siddiqi offer internal perspectives regarding specific religious traditions, while the beginning essay by John Hick, and the concluding essay by Tova Meltzer, with its important emphasis on including both female *and* male voices, provide more external, trans-tradition perspectives.

Hick, working from his impressively comprehensive and now well-established theory of Religious Pluralism, argues that the basic criterion for assessing religious phenomena is soteriological, and that moral goodness is one aspect of this. He proposes that the Golden Rule—it is morally good to benefit others and evil to harm them—is universally exemplified in the moral precepts of the great, world religious traditions. Thus in global religious ethics, there is an elemental unity within plurality. Interestingly, Bhikkhu Chao Chu and Muzammil Siddiqi also argue for an elemental religious/ethical unity, though they approach the question from single religious perspectives, namely Buddhism and Islam, respectively.

Bhikkhu Chao Chu starts from the suggestion that all traditions agree about basic prohibitions against killing, stealing, and other acts and suggests that there may be an innate inclination in all people for the same (moral) values. If so, he argues, the reason our religious moral prohibitions reflect an innate human inclination is made clear in the Buddhist tradition. The awakened one, a buddha, possesses direct knowledge into natural laws, and this would include the natural laws of morality. He concludes that Buddhism is "an open tradition that encourages interfaith dialogue" because it points to the ethical universality we all share, and yet insists that there is no absolute truth, held by only one tradition. (In his analysis of the scholastic tradition of Indian Buddhism, Bruce Hall adds support to this when he argues, for example, that the Buddhist ideal of emptiness, which includes the understanding that all conceptualization is ultimately limited, promotes the tolerance which is necessary for a truly pluralistic interfaith dialogue.) Bhikkhu Chao Chu succinctly illustrates this pluralist conclusion using Buddhist teaching. Just as one may need a raft to cross a river, yet the shape of the raft is not important, *and* one does not need the raft once one has reached the other side, so too one's particular religious beliefs are ultimately irrelevant.

Similarly, Muzammil Siddiqi argues that the Islamic world-view is both ecumenical and universal, strongly supporting a global religious/ethical vision. Although, much like Bhikkhu Chao Chu's considerations about Buddhism, Siddiqi allows that others may well not follow Islam, he argues that Islam can provide a basis for working out a global ethics. Again paralleling Bhikkhu Chao Chu's perspective on Buddhism, Siddiqi argues that *Ma'ruf* (goodness) and *Munkar* (badness) are not just religious notions found in the *Qur'an*. Rather, *Ma'ruf* and *Munkar* capture a universal ethical perspective, because religious goodness is in harmony, and religious badness is in disharmony, with human nature. Thus Siddiqi argues for a pluralist understanding, holding that religious dialogue is not just a matter of learning facts about other religions, but its *raison d'etre* is to establish interreligious fellowship based on fairness and good will.

Turning from pluralism, the next two major recurring themes in the essays concern two closely related ethical issues that we must confront in our pluralistic world. First, there is the question of what, if anything, religion can bring to public morality. Put otherwise, *is* there any proper place in the public moral community and public discourse for religious concerns? This issue has, for example, been recently addressed by such authors as Jeffrey Stout in *Ethics After Babel*. The second, related question has to do with the relation between public and *private* morality and the value of religion in addressing this knotty problem in a pluralistic society.

The essays by Richard Mouw, Philip Rossi, and John Langan are all directly concerned with the question of the place of religion in public morality. Mouw, for example, argues that in the face of our present loss of a keen sense of public civility, *worship*—contrary to the intolerance which it is thought to engender—can actually benefit civic responsibility and public selfhood. For the sense of mystery and the consequent humility inherent in worship can help "remind us of the distance between what we are and what we are capable of becoming." Thus public civility can be grounded in an epistemic humility, which comes from the very religious rituals and attitudes that are thought to be intolerant of pluralism. (Note that the same theme of epistemic distance from the divine which Mouw addresses vis-à-vis public morality, Adams sees as a key to developing a proper theistic ethics, and Hick addresses as a salient feature of ethics and interfaith dialogue.) As we have seen, Karen Torjesen sharpens this view by raising the further question of what constitutes public selfhood with respect to male/female differences of perspective and power. Though less optimistic than Mouw about the potential current impact of religion on public civility, Torjesen does conclude that as long as religious values and processes remain relegated to the private sphere, they will not be conducive to the cultivation of a public selfhood. Indeed, turning the tables on those who might ban religious considerations from public morality, she suggests that religious intolerance is itself a symptom of the absence of a healthy and well-developed public selfhood.

In the same vein, Philip Rossi focuses on a seminal concern of religion—human destiny—and suggests that public moral discourse has become anemic by first setting aside and now avoiding this important moral factor. He argues that the very task of a theistic ethics is to become a locus where public discussion of human destiny and its place in the good society is made possible. John Langan draws this theme of the place of religion in public morality to an even finer point in his analysis of John Paul II's primary encyclicals on social teaching. John Paul II directs our attention to "desire for profit" and "thirst for power," suggesting that these attitudes introduce "structures of sin" into our social relations. Thus for John Paul II, social evil is a direct consequence of individual sin. Rather than this one-way relation, Langan sees a reinforcing circle from the public to the private and the private to the public. As Langan points out, we need to recognize that no matter what our intentions, our actions are severely restricted by the social structures of the complex pluralistic society in which we live. His conclusion is that we must not only confront our own sin, but in order to effect a new social and world order, we must explicitly and directly withdraw from the "structures of sin" of the old world.

As we might expect, this unavoidable issue in a pluralistic world, of the proper relation between religion and public morality, also arises in a number of the other essays. For instance, Nancey Murphy, in a response to Langan that can also be seen as paralleling Mouw's considerations, argues that if we do indeed need to pit structure against structure to overcome the endemic "structures of sin" in our social institutions, then the specific role of the *church* is to provide an alternative model in contrast to the world's oppressive structures. More broadly, I argue that any significant new directions in social morality require *shared*, value-centered meta-criteria for a moral community. My key argument for theological realism as opposed to non-realism is that a realist God provides *objective* standards and an *objective* ground for ethics and for taking the moral point of view, which are essential to genuine public moral dialogue. More broadly still, Bhikkhu Chao Chu, directly addressing the role of ethics in interfaith dialogue, begins from the recognition that all the great religions face a common challenge from "materialistic skepticism." Even as the role of religion in the public sphere is now called into question, he suggests that the very ethical sensitivity, which is more important than ever in an interdependent world, can still come from religion.

Related to this pressing issue of the relation between religion and public morality is the question of the relation between public and *private* morality. Mouw sees an intimate relation between the private worship of the believer and its civic benefits, and this notion of an intimate connection between the public and the private forms the core of Langan's essay. Langan agrees with John Paul II that many are guilty of personal sins that maintain the "structures of sin" in society. Yet John Paul II portrays private morality as divided from public morality, so that one can deal with private morality on its own grounds. Rather, the point, Langan suggests and Nancey Murphy agrees, is *not* to accept but to evade the "box" into which we seem forced, between the high moral aspirations of our religious commitments versus the social realities that make the attainment of those ideals impossible. The importance of this relation between public and private morality is vividly forced to the surface in the sorts of considerations Karen Torjesen raises about the parallels between the relegation of women, like the relegation of religion, to the private sphere, and their resultant impotence/infertility in public discourse. And Mc-Clendon's essay, though in a more subtle and implicit manner, moves from the private lives of Sarah Edwards and Dorothy Day to a more public ethic in which not only the right but what is good *for* creatures is godly, concluding that delight makes a moral claim upon us because, as Jonathan Edwards suggested, delight, the good *for* us, is the means by which God guides our lives.

Let us conclude by looking at one other issue which we find interwoven through these papers. This is the question of how to *facilitate* dialogue, now more urgently than ever needed in a pluralistic world. In my essay, I suggest that in order to effect the fundamental ethical changes, which face us in this nuclear and ecological period of human history, we must be able to create a broad moral community in which genuine dialogue is possible. I argue that genuine dialogue involves respecting the other person, that respect for others is fundamental to the moral point of view, and therefore that genuine dialogue in our pluralistic age requires taking the moral point of view, which is best done from a theological realist rather than a non-realist position. Rossi, whose essay is devoted to the question of a public moral community, observes that in our secularized and divided society we must develop the skill to listen, a skill which religious ethics can enhance in the public arena if it can come to see *itself* as subject to the challenge of different points of view. For not only encountering but also appreciating differences with others is an essential step toward being open to authentic conversation. However, the importance of facilitating dialogue becomes most obvious when we move to the global scale.

The whole point of Hick's essay is to show how inter-religious understanding and dialogue *is* possible because of a shared ethics of the Golden Rule. And Muzammil Siddiqi suggests from an Islamic perspective that religious dialogue is a supremely *ethical* enterprise. For the reason to engage in religious dialogue is not to learn *about* other traditions, but to establish fellowship based on fairness and good will. Finally, bringing us again full circle, back to the varieties of goodness raised by Hebblethwaite, Tova Meltzer reminds us of the importance of appreciating distinctive female as well as male voices in effecting genuine dialogue. Though as she notes, one cannot understand ethics and religion simultaneously from more than one perspective, one can understand better—indeed, one can only really understand—in the dialectic of sympathetically listening to different and contrasting, even conflicting, perspectives.

In sum, as religious beings in a pluralistic world, we can no longer evade our responsibility for taking the moral point of view, for promoting a broad moral community, and for working toward the good society for all persons, in all their varieties of goodness.

Introduction

There are many to thank for making a volume like this possible. Ellen Sun provided invaluable support as the Claremont Graduate School Religion Department Secretary for the Eleventh Annual Philosophy of Religion Conference at Claremont Graduate School in the spring of 1990, out of which this volume evolved. Six of my graduate students, Andrew Eshleman, Avery Fouts, Darin Jewell, Tim Musgrove, Bill Rysek, and Cindy Witt, helped make that conference a success with their generous help, creative ideas, and organizational skills. In addition to myself, John Hick (Claremont Graduate School), Steve Davis (Claremont McKenna College), and Bill Whedbee (Pomona College) formed the program committee for the conference and were instrumental in its success. Funds were provided by Claremont Graduate School, Claremont McKenna College, and Pomona College. Anita Storck, Department Secretary for Religion and Philosophy at Chapman University, provided immeasurable support and understanding throughout the editorial process. I am enormously grateful for the generous support of a National Endowment for the Humanities Fellowship for 1990 during which I completed the majority of the work on this volume.

I want to thank each of the authors not only for the quality of their scholarship and hard work, but for the generosity of spirit with which they entered into this dialogue. I also wish to thank all my colleagues and students both at Claremont Graduate School—where I was a Visiting Professor during the time I worked on organizing the Philosophy of Religion Conference for 1990—and at the School of Theology, Claremont. Finally, I am indebted to my wife, Jean, whose companionship for twenty-two years has given special meaning to an academic life, and whose abiding love and support made the completion of this book possible.

JOSEPH RUNZO

I

The Ethical Life
and the Good

1

The Varieties of Goodness

Brian L. Hebblethwaite

The topic of this essay is different from that of G. H. von Wright's 1960 Gifford Lectures, whose title I have borrowed. "By the Varieties of Goodness," said von Wright, "I understand the multiplicity of uses of the word 'good.'"[1] By contrast, I have in mind the multiplicity of ways in which human lives and human communities may be characterized as morally good.

My topic clearly has much in common with what we have grown accustomed to calling "ethical pluralism." In the context of post-Enlightenment humanist ethics, ethical pluralism is thought of first and foremost as recognition and positive affirmation of the varieties of human goodness. The idea that there is a single, paradigmatic ideal of human life, whether personal or social, is rejected. The conception of the highest good, the *summmum bonum*, whether that of classical antiquity, of Augustine, of Aquinas, of Schleiermacher, or even of Kant, is denounced, sometimes vehemently, as Procrustean, by implication totalitarian, or at least failing to do justice to the great value of very different forms of human life. Thus the American pragmatist John Dewey argued that the idea of the highest good was a menace to ethics since it denied the plasticity of human nature and impeded human enrichment and progress.[2]

In the context of comparative religious ethics, a similar interest prevails in the varieties of moral teaching and ideals of life to be found in the different religions of the world. Whereas earlier generations of Christian scholars tended to disparage the moral systems of other faiths and to assume or argue for the ethical superiority of Christianity, now we find not only from students of religion but also from

3

Christian writers a much more positive appreciation of the varieties of religiously motivated human goodness, and a refusal to "grade" religions whether for their moral or for their spiritual power. Thus John Hick argues that, so far as we can tell, all the great religions are "equally productive of that transition from self to Reality which we see in the saints of all traditions."[3]

VARIETIES OF GOODNESS WITHIN THE CHRISTIAN ETHIC

My primary concern, however, is neither with ethical pluralism as valued in "humanist" moral philosophy nor with the different religious value systems studied in comparative religious ethics, but rather with the common assumption that Christian ethics itself is a uniform discipline, that Christianity has one identifiably moral ideal, and that the *summum bonum* can be spelled out as a single paradigm. I want to explore the varieties of goodness within the Christian scheme of things, and to question whether, in Christian ethics, moral perfection should be thought of as conformity to a unitary pattern. At the end I shall return to the varieties of secular and other religious goodness, but still with a view to Christian theological evaluation of those phenomena; for Christian ethics must include a theology of all forms of human goodness.

There are, of course, other forms of human excellence than moral goodness. But I am not concerned here with the varieties introduced into human life by people's different roles in the community or by different forms of creativity and enterprise. Robert M. Adams has rightly pointed out that in Christian ethics, we are not to think that God is interested in moral perfection alone. The vocation to be an artist has a place in Christian understanding.[4] My question, however, concerns not these varieties, but varieties of *moral* goodness. Of course, the pursuit of non-moral excellence raises moral questions. The musician's vocation—or indeed the business person's vocation— does not absolve one from the claims of morality. Indeed, I shall have something to say about the way in which different roles and different vocations affect morality and its different forms. My main concern, however, is with the varieties of *moral goodness* within the overall scope of Christian ethics.

Adams's article, "Saints," raises the interesting question whether sainthood, being primarily a religious notion, should not include exemplary participation in any of God's creative interests, moral or

4

aesthetic.[5] But Adams does not explore the possibility that God's moral interests may be various, giving rise to very different forms of moral sainthood and different forms of Christian moral community. Adams does, however, put his finger on the key factor that will enable us to investigate this possibility, namely, when he stresses that sainthood, moral or otherwise, is not so much a matter of following a pattern as of living in and from an ever deepening *relation* to the God who is the source of all good. It is this factor, the particular relation between the Christian and his God, that yields the varieties of excellence, including the varieties of moral goodness, in people's lives and in the communities they form.

The objection will be raised at once that classical Christian ethics *has* set a single pattern of moral goodness before us—the example of our Lord—and that the imitation of Christ does involve disciplined approximation to a particular revealed and normative ideal of human life. But, as has often been pointed out, the imitation of Christ cannot be thought of as a matter of "uncreative copying." Christ's unique salvific role is of course inimitable and the particular circumstances of his time and place combine with those of his vocation to make him an implausible example simply to follow. Christian discipleship is rather a matter of relation—of growth in faith and love that permits the Spirit of Christ to work through us and build us up into Christian personalities and groups of very different kinds.

Certainly, there are some general features of the Christian life which we shall expect authentic followers of Christ to manifest in their lives. Paul spells these out in terms of the "fruit of the Spirit" (Gal. 5:22). There will indeed be family resemblances between Christians, both as individuals and in community. But despite these characteristic general features, we should not think of Christian men and women as, ideally, clones of Jesus. The saints are striking for their idiosyncrasy as much as for their manifestation of typically Christian qualities. Indeed, an ethic of character should stress not only the type of general qualities and virtues that, when habitual, come to constitute the Christian character—but also the individual personality, the unique "character" in the other sense of that word—which is the product of an individual life story lived in and through a particular and unrepeatable set of interpersonal relations, including, supremely, the relation between that individual and his or her Lord. St. Francis was evidently a Christian character in both senses of that word. So are innumerable lesser figures whom any of us will have encountered in the course of our Christian journey and who will have helped us by their example—their example, that is, not only of general qualities such as forgiveness, patience, and love, but of particular and unique personal excellence and individuality of very different kinds.

It would be a great mistake in Christian ethics for us to follow the early Kierkegaard in restricting the sphere of the ethical to the general characteristics of good interpersonal relations and setting the individual off against that background as the bearer of a particular vocation that transcends or even suspends the ethical. On the contrary, the moral life is as much a matter of growth as a particular personality in relation to others and to God as it is of growth in the manifestation of the virtues. There are many different ways of being a Christian moral individual.

The notion of "works of supererogation" should be mentioned in this connection. One may be inspired and enabled to go beyond the call of duty and dedicate one's life to service of one's fellows in a supereminent way—and in very different ways. When one thinks of Albert Schweitzer or Mother Teresa of Calcutta, one is thinking of unique forms of the moral life that not only transcend ordinary goodness, including ordinary Christian goodness, but result in remarkably idiosyncratic moral characters.

I pointed out that the varieties of Christian goodness include not only very different supereminent examples, but also lesser and more ordinary, though equally individual examples. It is a mistake to expect sainthood of all. (Otherwise the notion of supererogation would be redundant.) As Voltaire observed, the best is often the enemy of the good,[6] and Christian moralists do the good—and the varieties of goodness—a disservice if in the interests of perfection they disparage the less striking forms of moral goodness. When Jesus said, "Be perfect, therefore, as your heavenly Father is perfect" (Matt. 5:48), he was not setting up a quite impossible ideal for everyone to follow. As Keith Ward has shown, for a creature to be perfect (*teleios* in the Greek) is to fulfil one's end or goal.[7] God's unique and infinite perfection is, of course, realized eternally, just by God being God, but ours is temporal, varied, and in any case only fully realized in the end. But what makes for Christian goodness, in both ordinary and extraordinary cases, is the actual relation to God in which the believer stands. As with all personal relations, each case is unique.

Affirmation of the goodness of moral lives at various stages of growth, and in innumerable less-than-perfect forms, helps us to see the point in the older "idealist" teaching about our station and its

duties.[8] Despite the apparently static and uncreative nature of such
teaching, it at least involved the recognition that the moral life of the
artisan, the civil servant, the business person, the scholar, or the artist
entails special claims and obligations that themselves yield varieties of
goodness.

To prevent the discussion from becoming too individualistic, I will
now explore an example from the basic form of human communal
life—the family. Advocates of the imitation of Christ would do well to
consider a good Christian marriage—indeed the variety of good
Christian marriages—as phenomena of the Christian moral life. Jesus
himself, it seems, was celibate. But we no longer think of celibate
Christians as ethically superior to married ones nor of the monastic
life as ethically superior to the family. There are varieties of communal goodness here. There are even varieties within the varieties, for
there is no one ideal pattern of Christian marriage. There exists not
only different, particular, even idiosyncratic, good married relationships (as there are individuals) but also various possibilities outside of
and within those relationships, in part dependent on historical and
social circumstances. It is not clear that there is a single set of ideal
social circumstances in relation to which we should work out what an
ideal Christian marriage should be like. Even if there were such a set,
there might well still be different good possibilities—the extended
family, the small family, the childless family, one partner working,
both partners working, and so on. In each case, the Christian quality
of the marriage would be a function of the partners' actual developing
relation to each other, the other members of the family, society outside the family group, and of course to Christ and his church. For
again, it is believers' actual and specific relations to their Lord that
inform the moral quality of their common life, and these, too, will
surely yield varieties of goodness.

But we cannot restrict attention to ideal social circumstances; most
of the time morality is a matter of how we live in very far-from-ideal
circumstances, although of course it is also a matter of changing and
improving those conditions. This is true of Christian morality as it is
of any other sort. Christians anticipate ideal social circumstances, in
the fullest sense, only in the end. We may well speculate about the
varieties of goodness in the eschaton. But present less-than-ideal circumstances make for even more variety.

Let us stay with the example of family life and consider a question
that came to prominence in the 1988 Lambeth Conference of Anglican
bishops. Some bishops from Africa pleaded with the Conference to

recognize the legitimacy in the prevailing circumstances of polygamy in certain types of African society. It was not only unrealistic, but cruel to the actual women involved to insist on Christian converts renouncing all their wives bar one. No doubt the church would continue to work for social change and for the replacement of polygamy with monogamy as the norm, but in the present less-than-ideal circumstances could not a polygamous marriage and its extended family be regarded as a good?

Not all less-than-ideal circumstances are social, and in principle changeable, conditions of human flourishing. It is widely believed that homosexual orientation is in many human beings a natural—in the sense of genetically based—condition. In these circumstances, it may be argued, a committed and faithful homosexual relationship is a moral good, and not to be condemned as if it were on a level with sexual promiscuity. When the singer Peter Pears refers to his life with Benjamin Britten as "a gift from God" beyond desert,[9] not only the creativity but also the moral goodness of that relationship should be apparent to the Christian as to any moralist.

When we turn to consider wider forms of community life than those of marriage and the family, similar factors making for variety are to be recognized. I have already referred to the goodness of monastic life, not as a paradigm, but as one of the varieties. Indeed there are varieties of monastic life—all of them good. But the church has fostered and encouraged many different forms of community existence and many different ways of contributing to the wider common good. Here, too, these varieties of goodness will in great measure be conditioned by the less-than-ideal circumstances that obtain. Certainly, the ways in which Christians, whether as individuals or as groups, will contribute to the betterment of those conditions are bound to vary greatly.

When Christians in the developed social democracies worry about the extremism and imbalance that seem to characterize many forms of liberation theology, black theology, or feminist theology, it is usually because they are thinking of Christian ethics in allegedly ideal circumstances (often confused with their own!) and not in relation to the actual conditions that have evoked these necessarily one-sided responses. Those who have visited and lived with a Latin American base community and come to appreciate the conditions and predicaments that have called forth these Christian communal responses have no difficulty in affirming their goodness. Of course, such forms of Christian community can constitute paradigms only in relation to extremely unideal circumstances. But, as I say, the ideal circumstances will only be found in the eschaton.

The range of less-than-ideal circumstances is great. Latterly, I have been speaking of extremely negative conditions that call for special, and one hopes temporary, forms of Christian moral response at both the individual and the communal level. We should remind ourselves, however, that positive social and cultural conditions will produce different moral personalities and groups. There is no reason at all why African or Indian Christianity should reflect Western cultural forms. In different cultures Christian contributions to the common good will exhibit diverse characteristics. Much work has already been done toward fostering local theologies rooted in particular historical and cultural situations.[10] Such theologies do not operate solely at the level of theoretical understanding or liturgical expression. Local theology is, in essence, practical theology.

A common feature of the circumstances making for the varieties of goodness in world Christianity is the universal fact of growth, development, and change. As I say, the moral life is a function of the different stages in personal, communal, and social history. A recognition that perfection—itself possibly various—is an eschatological notion, together with a refusal to let the best be the enemy of the good, will undergird our willingness to affirm the varieties of goodness, including the varieties of moral goodness, at every stage of life and history, in their manifold forms. There is much wisdom in Dietrich Bonhoeffer's treatment of the "penultimate" in his posthumously published *Ethics*.[11] But this notion of the penultimate needs to be greatly extended and diversified if it is to do justice to the varieties of goodness.

Christian ethics has the flexibility to embrace and baptize these varieties just because its key category is not imitation but relation. One of the things that makes each individual person unique is the specific set of interpersonal relations that has gone into the fashioning of his or her life history. What makes a person, a family, or a community Christian is their particular relationship to the Spirit of God and of Christ, in which they live and move and have their being. This will differ in each individual case at each stage of life and development, within each cultural context and with respect to each set of circumstances. The point can, after all, be put in terms of imitation. Christ is exemplary precisely because his relation to God was so pure and immediate. Christ's perfection consisted in his dependence on and utter transparency to God's love and will. His commerce with the

Spirit was unadulterated. What that relation meant for him in his situation and with respect to his vocation was very different from what it means to Christian individuals and groups in very different circumstances quite apart from the degrees of imperfection and adulteration that inevitably characterize our feeble approximations to that openness to the divine indwelling.

It may be helpful at this stage in the argument if I summarize the factors making for the recognition of the varieties of moral goodness in the Christian scheme of things. In the first place there is the recognition that morality is not simply a matter of types of action or types of motive, or even types of virtue and formed character. I have stressed the individuality, even idiosyncrasy, not only of the saints, but also of each and every Christian man and woman as a moral personality. Then, secondly, there are the many special interests and vocations both moral and non-moral of particular Christians. I referred to the varieties introduced into the moral life by people's different stations in life. In the third place, we must reckon with the impressive fact of works, indeed of lives, of supererogation. In the fourth place, there are the different circumstances that make for different modes of Christian interpersonal and community life. Some of these are positive, some neutral, and some negative. I referred to the less-than-ideal circumstances, some remediable over time, some not, but all making for varieties of Christian goodness, both individual and communal. But I also referred to cultural differences that yield different forms of excellence in Christian moral lives and groups. Fifthly, I mentioned the different stages in personal growth and historical development, yielding many penultimate forms of Christian goodness. Finally, and most important of all, I stressed the particular, living relation—between Christians and the Spirit of their living Lord—that informs Christians' individual and communal lives in very different ways as they seek to know and do God's will for them.

RELATIONSHIPS AMONG THE VARIETIES
OF CHRISTIAN GOODNESS

Two questions in particular will doubtless occur to those still wedded to the single paradigm of an ideal Christian moral life. The first concerns the possible incompatibilities and conflicts that may arise between the varieties of goodness all claiming the name of Christian.

The second concerns the possibility and desirability of grading these varieties within the Christian fold.

I said that the different forms of Christian goodness will exhibit a family resemblance, recognizable in manifestations of the fruit of the same Spirit and in the effects of personal relation to the same Lord. There can, of course, be no compromise with evil nor any concession to contradictory values such as those of the vendetta or of racial superiority. Even so, there will certainly be incompatibility and conflicts, not only in the obvious sense that one kind of Christian vocation necessarily excludes others, but also in the sense that in the less-than-ideal circumstances in which we find ourselves, some Christianly motivated choices and policies are likely to be at variance with others. Family resemblance is not denied by disagreement amongst members of the family. Some Christians, for example, will embrace pacifism, others will with regret endorse the just war or even tyrannicide. But who will deny the name of Christian either to Dick Sheppard or to Dietrich Bonhoeffer? The family resemblance is not abrogated by the fact of radically different choices. To adapt Sartre's famous example (which, as has often been pointed out, belies his own existentialist philosophy, since both options involve the recognition of objective claims) a young Christian Frenchman might well have been torn between staying to look after his ailing mother and going to work for the Resistance. Simone Weil, for example, took the latter choice. It is no part of Christian ethics to claim that there is always one right answer to such appalling dilemmas.

Christian ethical rigorists tend not only, quite correctly, to affirm that there must be no compromise with evil, but to insist that there must be no concession to the less-than-ideal good. Thus Oliver O'Donovan writes that Christians "are called to accept exclusion from the created good as the necessary price of a true and unqualified witness to it."[12] He says this explicitly with reference to those who may be "ill-endowed psychosexually to enjoy the fulfillment and responsibility of sexual life in marriage." But such rigorism may well be thought to confuse the supererogatory and the moral, and to fall foul of Voltaire's stricture about making the best the enemy of the good. A greater flexibility and compassion will allow us to recognize different kinds and levels of Christian goodness here as in other areas of interpersonal and social life.

The different levels of Christian goodness are not of course fixed or static. Recognition of and rejoicing at the many varieties of ordinary

Christian goodness should be without prejudice to the possibility of extraordinary inspiration and growth—to the possibility, that is, of supererogation. To affirm the value of the good as well as the best does not necessarily mean that we should rest content with the good.

The talk of different levels leads at once to the other question about grading the varieties of goodness within the Christian fold. Clearly, we do and must make such evaluations. The fact that the best should not be made the enemy of the good does not mean that the best is not better than the good. Lives like those of Albert Schweitzer and Mother Teresa are clearly closer to perfection than those of the good Christians we all know and love. To respond to a supererogatory call clearly takes a man or woman beyond the level of ordinary Christian goodness. The facts remain that each level is good and that there are varieties of goodness at each level. I have already insisted that we ought not grade the celibate against the married state or the Latin American base community against, say, a local group of the Society of Friends. Innumerable individual Christians at all levels are plainly incommensurable. So we have to be alert both to different levels and stages of growth toward eschatological perfection—here grading is possible—and to varieties of goodness at every level—here grading is not possible. And if, as I have hinted, perfection in the end is not a uniform concept, then the consummation of all things will include ungradable variety. The pure white of the divine light will forever be refracted in the many colors of created being and goodness.

ETHICAL PLURALISM

I now wish to return to the two subjects which I set aside at the beginning, namely ethical pluralism as valued in *humanist* moral philosophy and the different religious value systems studied in comparative religious ethics. I will consider each of these from the viewpoint of Christian theological ethics and in the light of my reflections on the varieties of *Christian* goodness.

Christian theology, except in its most extreme Protestant forms, has welcomed the fact and extent of ordinary human goodness as a sign and effect of the presence of God's Spirit in creation outside the covenant. It goes without saying that recognition of the varieties of goodness within the covenant will lead us the more easily to recognize the varieties of goodness outside. There should be nothing concessionary or grudging about this. On the contrary, not only are the varieties of secular goodness of great value in themselves—indeed sometimes reaching levels such as that of the secular sanctity portrayed by Dr. Rieux in Albert Camus's *The Plague*—but they also can themselves come to form the basis of critique of distorted or mistaken Christian understandings of allegedly revealed morality. Ideally—in theory, and one hopes, often in practice—the relation between Christ and the Christian (mediated by the Bible and the church), on which I have laid stress in characterizing the roots of the various forms of Christian morality, should enhance and enlarge—and at times correct—the natural goodness of secular humanity. Sometimes, however, the reverse is true. Where Christian understanding has been warped or deceived, natural human goodness, itself the anonymous effect and reflection of God's goodness in creation, may help us to protest, and unmask the deception.

That consideration apart, much the same may be said about incompatibilities and conflicts between secular and Christian morality as was said in the case of the varieties of Christian goodness. Here too we can make no concession to contradictory values. But here too the best must not be made the enemy of the good. The different levels, and the varieties at the different levels, must be positively valued in themselves, but without prejudice to the possibility of further enlightenment and growth, both secular and religious. Certainly the Christian will hope and pray for the opening of a secular friend's eyes to the possibility of the Spirit's conscious indwelling and inspiration, but the Christian will at the same time give thanks for the evident anonymous operation of that same Spirit already.

Finally, I turn to comparative *religious* ethics. There are similar points to be made in this connection. Again, Christian theological ethics cannot endorse contradictory religious *values*, but can and must welcome other forms of religiously motivated goodness. Here it is a question of recognizing the way in which the Spirit has evoked *conscious* response, and of the forms of life, both personal and communal, that have developed in the different religious cultures. We may well speak of complementary values here. The Christian has no monopoly of the ways of God with humankind. There may well be forms of the religious life that encapsulate and manifest values understressed in the Christian traditions. Christianity's historically dynamic and eschatologically oriented moral faith needs to be complemented by Eastern cosmic wisdom.[11]

At the same time, Christian theological ethics, valuing what it finds in other contexts, will want to let the Word of God in Christ be heard in and for those other contexts. We may have learned to look for what the unknown Christ, by his Spirit, has done and is doing already in the contexts of the other faiths; but we shall also want to let explicit forms of Christian life develop and flourish precisely there and in relation to those other histories, cultures, and traditions. An immense range of fresh varieties of Christian goodness is opened up precisely by such processes of "inculturation."

If we ask whether the different forms of secular and religious goodness can be graded, our answer will be as before: some can and some cannot. I do not see how Christian ethics can renounce differential evaluation altogether. For all the wonder and value of the manifested forms of human goodness, some religiously informed, some not, Christianity's christological vision and eschatological hope open up ethical dimensions of personal and communal living, which it can only speak of in terms of enlargement, enhancement, or even sublation (*Aufhebung*). I am deliberately setting on one side the negativities of the moral and religious life—the false values, the corruption, the horrors that human beings and human cultures have spawned throughout world history. Even so, the positive values, whose worth I am concerned to stress, can surely not all be placed on one level. I have already referred to the differences between the good, the better, and the best. To take a religious example, Christian theological ethics must surely give a special place in the hierarchy of values to the Jewish forms of life, which provided the providential context of the Incarnation. As I have argued in another place,[13] Jewish conceptuality, sensibility, family life, and religious faith supplied the context and the vehicle of God the Son's incarnate life. The point has, of course, a key ethical dimension. Jewish morality was the form of life in which alone a perfect human life—that of the incarnate Son—could be lived on earth. The ethics of Jesus supervene upon Jewish ethics, and only very indirectly upon the whole ethical and religious life of humankind. It follows that Jewish morality must be "graded" above all other forms of non-Christian goodness—good though they certainly are. Yet neither Jewish ethics nor the ethics of Jesus would have been possible without the more general ethical and religious background; nor can they be appreciated or appropriated today without that background being there.

This does not mean that non-Christian religion and ethics have merely instrumental value as a preparation for the Incarnation. The history of humanity has come up with innumerable forms of personal, interpersonal, and communal goodness, all of intrinsic worth. But none, Christ apart, has attained perfection. There is always scope for something more. Ordinary morality is good. Works of supererogation are better. We would not have works or lives of supererogatory worth without the background and base of ordinary morality. But that does not make ordinary morality purely instrumental to the supererogatory. Similarly, religious morality, in all its variety, is good. But a truly Christ-centered life is better. We could not have Christ-centered lives without the background and base of religion. But that does not make the history of religions purely instrumental to Christ and his church.

At this present stage in world history, one had better not make too many exalted claims for Christian goodness, even that of the saints. It is enough to say that, in the eschaton, it will be the explicit relation to God in Christ in which we shall stand—namely his conscious indwelling of us by his Spirit—which will sublate all forms of human goodness into the infinitely rich communion of saints (by then all will be saints) in the consummation of all things.

NOTES

1. G. H. von Wright, *The Varieties of Goodness* (London: Routledge & Kegan Paul, 1963), 8.
2. John Dewey, *Human Nature and Conduct* (New York: Modern Library, 1930).
3. John Hick, *Problems of Religious Pluralism* (London: Macmillan Press, 1985), 87.
4. Robert M. Adams, *The Virtue of Faith* (New York: Oxford University Press, 1987), 170f.
5. Ibid., 164–173.
6. Voltaire, *Dictionaire Philosophie*, article on "Art Dramatique."
7. Keith Ward, *The Rule of Love* (London: Darton, Longman & Todd, 1989), ch. 14.
8. See, for example, F. H. Bradley, *Ethical Studies* (New York: Oxford University Press, 1876), essay 5.
9. In a television interview shortly before his death.
10. See, for example, J. C. England, ed., *Living Theology in Asia* (London: SCM Press, 1981).
11. Dietrich Bonhoeffer, *Ethics* (London: SCM Press, 1955).

12. Oliver O'Donovan, *Resurrection and Moral Order* (Leicester: InterVarsity Press, 1986), 95.

13. Brian L. Hebblethwaite, "The Jewishness of Jesus from the Perspective of Christian Doctrine" in *Scottish Journal of Theology*, vol. 42, 1989.

2

In Defense of the Notion
of an Ideal Life

Linda Peterson

In his essay, "The Varieties of Goodness," Brian Hebblethwaite challenges the presupposition that there is a unique format for the exemplary or quintessentially Christian life and that all Christians should aim at conformity to this single paradigm. Following Hebblethwaite's account, what is particularly pernicious about the assumption that an individual's life, or some form of communal life, ought to be judged as better or worse insofar as it more or less approximates *the ideal* is that this way of thinking leads to intolerance of what are perceived as nonconforming lifestyles. It leads us to think that certain extraordinary modes of life are unchristian, hence bad. To avoid this sort of moral mistake, we are advised to give up on the expectation that each person's life should fit the same standardized mold.

Now it is uncontroversial that the celebration of diversity and idiosyncrasy is sometimes good. Yet when one is being admonished to "let a thousand flowers bloom," one wants to reply, "But surely some of them are weeds." It is only fair to point out that Hebblethwaite is concerned to avoid the complaint that he is advocating a posture of indiscriminate acceptance, for he writes: "There can, of course, be no compromise with evil nor any concession to contradictory values such as those of the vendetta or of racial superiority." The claim is, then, that the need to celebrate diversity neither requires, nor even permits, tolerating hideous injustices. Still, I wonder whether it is possible, in his view, to make room for moral disagreement of any sort and for the efforts toward reform, which are often the natural concomitants of such disagreement. Accordingly, I would like to begin by asking some questions about the possibility of genuine disagreement and of justified interference on Hebblethwaite's position. Later on, I will take up the related issues of grading diverse lifestyles and how it is possible to make sense of the notion of supererogation or sainthood on his account.

According to Hebblethwaite, the goodness (specifically, the *Christian* goodness) of any given life is a function of that person's individualized spiritual odyssey—her very distinctive rapport with God—and her particular way of responding to the circumstances and social conditions in which she finds herself. Similarly, the goodness of interpersonal relationships and of forms of community life is held to be a function of the particular ways in which the various members relate to one another, to their social environs, and to God. There is, in this view, no singularly appropriate way to relate to God, to others, or to one's environment. The position, then, is that there is no ideal Christian life and no ideal Christian community. I would like to query this view by considering the following example of community life.

In her autobiography, Dorothy Day presents the details of a community of believers who felt that their mission was to "re-establish the family on the land." These Christians set up a farming commune, and, as Day tells the story, their leader

> made another layman the spiritual advisor of the little community set up and this man imposed penances and insisted on strict obedience. His attitude toward women was that the men were to sit like judges at the gates and the women were to be the valiant women of the Old Testament, hewers of wood and drawers of water, tillers of the field, and clothers of the family. This position was carried to such an extreme on the upper farm that the women were forbidden to speak unless spoken to, and were compelled to knock on the doors of even their own kitchens and dining rooms if there were men present.[1]

Now, it is given that all of the people involved in this situation were in agreement about the character of their living arrangements, and that those community arrangements arose out of their response to the social context in which they found themselves, their special ways of relating to one another, and their peculiar view of what God expected from them. If we suppose, further, that the goodness of these individual lives and of their communal life is simply a function of the foregoing variables, then why not celebrate this form of life for its uniqueness and innovation? It seems that if what constitutes human goodness were really determined along these lines, there could be no possible ground for the opposition, which leads people to urge reform in communities like this. If one abandons the notion of an ideal human life, why call these communities "less than ideal"? But, clearly, one ought not tolerate such practices to the extent that one would refrain from condemnation and protest.

Alternatively, one might think that the position that there are no ideals or paradigms is no more problematic for the possibility of evaluative assessments than is the claim, say, that there is no single way to be a good violinist. Supposing that none of all the excellent violinists fits the description "the ideal violinist," it is still possible to differentiate between good and bad violinists. Correspondingly, one might think that the premise that there is no ideal Christian life does not automatically yield the conclusion that there are no recognizably suboptimal Christian lives. Yet it seems that this analogy breaks down. For human beings, unlike violins, are members of a natural kind. There is not as much room for innovation and creativity in human relations as there is in the relation between artist and artifact. Certain ways of treating human beings are conducive to their flourishing, while others, plainly, are not. Certain modes of life allow for the maximal actualization of natural human potentialities, while others artificially restrict and limit such actualization. The goodness of a human life is a function of what human beings naturally are, that is, it is a function of the possibility of realizing those capacities and potentialities, which are the natural human endowment. What justifies resistance to such oppressive modes of life is that they utterly fail to accommodate natural human capacities. Conditions in South Africa under apartheid are particularly hideous for this same reason, as are conditions in Palestine. Granted, the situation of the farming commune was different in that all of its members were in complicity with oppression, but the evil that all oppressive circumstances have in common is that they render it impossible for their victims to lead flourishing human lives. Our outrage at such oppression is underwritten by our intuitive awareness of what the ideal human life requires, and by our recognition of what is necessary for the possibility of the exercise of characteristically human capacities.

Hebblethwaite's position does receive moral support insofar as it is grounded in the truth that the unreflective intolerance of idiosyncrasy and diversity is a moral failure. Yet, I do not believe he has shown that the notion of an ideal life necessarily leads to intolerance. Further, what the recognition of characteristic human capacities does lead to is the distinction between innocuous and harmful forms of diversity—the distinction between what should and should not be tolerated. One is able to recognize that, underlying the differences in circumstances and personal histories, we all, as human beings, share a common set of needs. It is this recognition that ultimately makes the necessity for reform intelligible.

I will close with some questions about the possibility of grading or evaluating diverse modes of life, and about the coherency of supererogation on Hebblethwaite's account. He maintains that, in one sense, grading is possible, while, in another sense, it is not. It is possible, in his view, to recognize "different levels and stages of growth towards eschatological perfection," but it is not possible to grade the varieties of goodness at each level. I am not clear about what talk of various "levels" signifies here. If I acknowledge that some modes of life are higher than others on the eschatological perfection scale, have I not already graded the diverse forms of life at each level? Yet, he also writes: "And if, as I have hinted, perfection in the end is not a uniform concept, then the consummation of all things will include ungradable variety. The pure white of the divine light will forever be reflected in the many colors of created being and goodness." This latter remark raises a question about the place of supererogation. The supererogatory is set in contradistinction to what can reasonably be expected of all of us. But, on the presupposition that there is no uniform set of expectations, what room is there for this moral category? He observes: "Lives like those of Albert Schweitzer and Mother Teresa are clearly closer to perfection than those of the good Christians we all know and love. To respond to a supererogatory call clearly takes a man or woman beyond the level of ordinary Christian goodness." I would like to know in what sense certain lives are closer to perfection than are others. Is it that they are closer to "eschatological perfection"? But the notion of "eschatological perfection" gets eviscerated in the view that "perfection in the end is not a uniform concept" and "consummation of all things will include *ungradable* variety" (emphasis mine). If there is no final goal or end, no *summum bonum*, no ultimately ideal human life, then the question remains, to *what* are the saints closer than the rest of us? Is it that they are closer to being what God expects *for them* as individuals? But then, again, there is the problem of how to make sense of the category of supererogation independently of recognizing some *universally* applicable standards.

NOTES

1. Dorothy Day, *The Long Loneliness* (New York: Harper & Brothers, 1952), 261–262.

3

Platonism and Naturalism:
Options for a Theocentric Ethics

Robert M. Adams

In recent moral philosophy we have seen much work of Aristotelian and Kantian inspiration, but relatively little of a primarily Platonic character. What is more surprising, to my mind, is that Platonic themes have also not been prominent in recent theological ethics, despite the influence they have historically exercised in Western religious thought by way of Philo and Augustine.

THEISTIC PLATONISM IN ETHICS

I wish to explore the possibility of a contemporary theistic ethical theory that would be broadly Platonic and Augustinian. Such a theory would be characterized by the following features.

1. God would occupy in it much of the role that is assigned to the Form of the Good in the "middle dialogues" of Plato. God, in this view, is the supreme good, a transcendent good, good beyond anything that is found among finite things or adequately understood by us. The goodness of other things consists in their resembling or imaging the supreme Good. There are obvious problems about the nature of this resemblance or imaging, which cannot, however, be explored in this paper.

2. What is thus analyzed is an intrinsic rather than a merely instrumental goodness; and it is also not a beneficial goodness, a goodness *for* some person or other. It is rather the goodness of that which is worthy of love or admiration. In the supreme case it is the goodness of that which is worthy of worship. This is the most natural starting

22

point for a study of ethics that is guided by religious aspiration. I believe also that this sort of intrinsic good is more fundamental theoretically than welfare or beneficial goodness, and that the enjoyment of it should be seen as constituting, at least largely, a person's good. But there is not room to develop here my ideas about welfare.

3. Among the Platonic roles inherited by God, so to speak, is that of the Form of Beauty. The goodness that concerns us here is by no means limited to moral goodness, but also includes the aesthetic (and perhaps other) types of excellence. Again, this is to be expected in a theory of value based on religious aspiration. The divine greatness adored in the Bible, by the mystics, and in the traditions of theistic worship is not exclusively moral.

4. The moral epistemology of theistic Platonism, like that of Plato's middle dialogues, is primarily one of *vision*. Vision is a metaphor in this context, of course. A related metaphor, or perhaps the same, is expressed by the term "intuition," more popular in recent moral philosophy. I prefer the term "vision," however, because its associations link it suggestively with the *transcendence* of the good. Not that the good is not also immanent in the world of our experience. There are things in that world that are good and experienced as good. For the Platonic vision, however, in both its theistic and its nontheistic forms, to apprehend finite things as good is at the same time to glimpse, as in a mirror darkly, a qualitatively transcendent, vastly more excellent Good of which the finite goods are only fragmentary, imperfect imitations.

5. Vision, for Platonism, is closely associated with *love*. One can doubtless regard something as good without loving it, and perhaps without really admiring it. But I think that is a secondary sort of recognition of goodness, an inferential recognition, for the most part. The original vision of the good is inseparable from love and admiration.

6. These views have implications for theological epistemology. We must suppose that most people, in most times and places, and in virtually all cultures, have recognized, albeit imperfectly, the goodness of many things within their experience. For a theory of "goodness" to suppose otherwise is to change the subject. The theistic Platonist holds that recognition of any goodness is recognition of a reflection, dim and fragmentary as it may be, of the divine goodness. It follows from these views that something about the divine goodness is cognitively accessible, at least in part, to people in general. The ethics of theistic Platonism, as I conceive it, is therefore

inconsistent with any theological view that would restrict knowledge of God exclusively to a single religious tradition.

There is more than one possible approach to the development of such a position as I have been sketching. One is to expound it in its own terms. Another approach is to compare the view with alternatives. One such comparison is the subject of the present paper. The alternative I have selected for study is James Gustafson's "theocentric" ethics,[1] and I will contrast it with a theistic Platonist view with specific reference to the treatment of ideas of *nature*. Many reasons can be given for this choice. The importance of Gustafson's multivolume book, *Ethics from a Theocentric Perspective*, and the eminence of its author need no certification from me. His work represents an exceptionally thorough, informed, radical, and comprehensive attempt to think through the foundations of a theistic ethical theory. There are also major points of affinity between Gustafson's views and the sort of theistic Platonism that I advocate. Three of these agreements may be noted at the outset.

1. The most important affinity between theistic Platonism and Gustafson's ethical theory is in the idea of theocentricity. The theistic Platonist must be as insistent as Gustafson that we humans are not the measure of all things, because that role belongs to God, and that what is good *for* human beings is not the most fundamental consideration in ethics—though we shall see that these points receive quite different developments in the two approaches. As I have already noted, the good that measures all things for theistic Platonism is not a merely relative or beneficial goodness *for* someone or something, and it transcends both human understanding and human exemplification of the good. If we are serious in identifying the transcendent Good with God, and thus with the Holy, we cannot altogether deny that the supreme Good has an aspect that is mysterious, alien, even dangerous, in relation to us imperfect creatures. It is a wisdom by which the hawk soars (Job 39:26); a goodness from which the lions also seek their prey (Ps. 104:21). Its terrifying otherness is not easily divorced from its greatness and beauty, or from the greatness and beauty of its works. We do have some vision and understanding of the good, and we cannot be guided by what we do not see or understand; but it is idolatry to identify our own vision and understanding with the good.

2. It is a closely connected point that as a theistic Platonist I must see good, in the sense of resemblance or imaging of God, in the beauty, vitality, and most fundamentally in the being, of creatures

24

nonhuman as well as human. I must therefore agree with Gustafson that nonhuman creatures can have an ethical claim on my respect on account of their own relation to God, and not merely for their service to human needs and purposes.

3. The most fundamental role in Gustafson's ethical and theological epistemology is assigned to states and processes, at once cognitive and affective, that he calls "senses" and "discernment." His account of these, which cannot be reproduced here, is subtle and illuminating; and I agree that partly affective apprehension must play a basic part in ethical thinking. Indeed, Platonic vision of the good is an example of it, involving love as it does. As we shall see, however, I do not agree with the particular way in which Gustafson meshes senses and discernment with more theoretical elements in his ethical epistemology.

TELEOLOGY AND THEOCENTRICITY

I hope it will be clear that I have no wish to join the chorus of critics who have chided Gustafson for heterodoxy, though my own theology is doubtless more conservative than his. He has made his departures from tradition clear enough, and given his reasons for them. His work, like any other intellectual effort, deserves to be evaluated on its own terms.

His official summary of the main principle of theocentric ethics is that "we are to conduct life so as to relate to all things in a manner appropriate to their relations to God" (I, 113). This seems quite open-ended as to what sort of relation might be appropriate. For the most part, however, Gustafson envisages a clearly *teleological* relation as appropriate. He affirms "[a]n understanding of human life in relation to the powerful Other which requires that all of human activity be ordered properly in relation to what can be discerned about the *purposes* of God" (I, 164, my emphasis). The moral question becomes "What serves the divine purposes?" (I, 317) and Gustafson suggests that "the task of ethics is to discern the will of God" (I, 113). This gives rise to what seem to me to be severe difficulties in the carrying through of Gustafson's project.

I will not dwell long on the most obvious of these, which is the difficulty of relating his emphasis on divine purposes to his conception of God, which is resolutely anti-anthropomorphic. Applying even "the analogy of agency" to God is "excessive," in Gustafson's

view, if it "leads us to assert that God has intelligence, like but superior to our own, and that God has a will, a capacity to control
events comparable to the more radical claims made for human
beings" (I, 270). Accordingly Gustafson does not ascribe "intentions"
to God. But it is crucial to his theological program that he does ascribe
"purposes" to God. He says

> we can discern through experience . . . and through our knowl-
> edge of life in the world what some of the divine purposes are for
> creation. . . . I do not find sufficient reasons to move from our
> perceptions of the divine governance to the assertion that these
> imply an intelligence similar to our own, or a capacity of radical
> agency similar to certain claims made for human beings. . . . One
> can acknowledge dependence on ordering powers that sustain
> life and bear down upon it without conceiving these powers as
> gifted with intelligence and arbitrary will. One can be grateful for
> the divine governance, for all that it sustains and makes possible,
> without conceptually personalizing the Governor (I, 270f.).

I have misgivings about the reasonableness or even the intelligi-
bility of speaking about "divine purposes" in such a context. However, any doubts we may have on that score, and any disagreements
we may have with Gustafson's rejection of intelligence and will in
God, may be put aside here in order to concentrate on problems more
internal to his point of view. Some of the main themes of his theology
emerge with great clarity in the passage I have just quoted, and two
of them deserve immediate comment.

1. God is virtually identified, here and elsewhere in Gustafson's
book, with "ordering powers that sustain life and bear down upon
it." As this indicates, Gustafson not only associates God closely with
nature, but regards God as immanent within nature. So far as I can
see, monotheism consists for him chiefly in seeing a unity of purpose
in nature and regarding that unity as an appropriate focus of senses
of dependence, gratitude, obligation, repentance, possibility, and direction (I, 129–136). It is not surprising, therefore, that the interpretation of nature occupies a central place in his theocentric ethics.

Because of its immanentism, Gustafson's thought is strikingly rem-
iniscent of Stoicism in the role that it assigns to nature in relation both
to God and to ethics. The Western tradition contains, and often
mixes, both Aristotelian and Stoic types of naturalism in ethics. In
Aristotelian ethics the primary role of the concept of nature is in
interpreting the good of the individual substances that are the pri-

mary beings of Aristotelian metaphysics. For Stoic ethics, however, the concept of nature directs us first to the good of the cosmos as a whole; and Gustafson's naturalism is decidedly of the Stoic type.[2]

2. The key to a theistic interpretation of nature, for Gustafson, is the ability to "discern . . . what some of the divine purposes are for the creation." That the "ordering" perceived in nature is teleological in this way is essential if our ethics is to be one of "serving the divine purposes." That there is ordering in the cosmos is a datum of science, according to Gustafson (I, 262). Yet, he thinks "the divine purposes" are grasped only by a process of "discernment" that involves broadly religious sensitivities and affections as well as scientific and historical knowledge (I, ch. 7).

Gustafson's commitment to the discernment of teleology in the order of the universe is one of the points at which his position seems to me most liable to criticism. When we regard the order of the universe as a whole with "piety," as Gustafson puts it—with awe and admiration, respect and gratitude—do we indeed perceive it as teleological, as organized by *purpose?* Here we must be careful to distinguish two questions. One question is whether we perceive the order of the universe as something that might well be the *object* of a purpose—perhaps indeed as so eminently suited to be the object of a purpose that it is hard for us not to believe that it was in fact purposely created by a designing deity. That question leads toward the design argument for a theism that Gustafson would reject as anthropomorphic. The question that is relevant to his theology is whether the order of the universe is perceived as an expression of purposes having objects or ends that are *served* by the order. To this question I think the predominant answer at least of the twentieth century is No.

Most of our ancestors in the eighteenth century might have answered otherwise. They saw the machine, created and organized to serve specific purposes, as a model not only for the order of individual living organisms but also for the order of the universe as a whole. It is controversial whether our biological understanding of individual organisms and local systems of organisms has been, or even can or should be, freed entirely from teleological interpretations. But it is no longer natural for us to regard the universe as a whole as a machine organized purposively for the production and sustenance of living things. This is true for many of the same reasons that lead Gustafson to claim that it is no longer reasonable to believe that the whole universe was created, and is maintained, for the sake of human beings (for example, I, 97f.). If we would now compare the universe as a whole to any human product, it might be a work of art rather than a machine; and the value that we see in the order of the whole might be its intrinsic beauty much more than its usefulness for any ends distinguishable from itself.

It might be argued, indeed, that Gustafson's teleological interpretation and evaluation of the order of the universe works against his theocentrism. For what ends can we find it natural to see that order as serving? Is the production of supernovas, or of even bigger bangs, a cosmic purpose? That would yield a childish view of God indeed. If we look for ends that the cosmic order may be seen as serving, we will surely be led, and probably led exclusively, to the generation and maintenance of life, if not exclusively of human life. We will thus have a biocentric, if not an anthropocentric, theology and system of values. I doubt that Gustafson himself escapes this result. For when he comes to summarize his view as to "what can be discerned about the divine governance," he offers the patently biocentric answer, "What can be discerned, to put the matter abstractly, are the necessary conditions for life to be sustained and developed" (I, 339).

A more theocentric view of the universe than that is suggested by the Bible—most majestically in the book of Job—as well as by Stoicism. The cosmos can be seen as manifesting a divine glory that transcends by far its service to life. In order to see it so, however, we must apprehend its value more as beauty to be celebrated than as purposes to be served. Such a view as this will be characteristic of theistic Platonism, for which it is important that God is the supremely Beautiful, and glimpsed in the beauty of finite things.

This does not exclude belief in divine purposes in and for human life.[3] For theistic Platonism, however, the world need not be completely pervaded by purposiveness in order to be pervasively and comprehensively related to God. It is noteworthy also that talk about teleology, in the context of theistic piety, often transforms itself into something quite different. Asking, "What is the chief end of man?" the *Westminster Shorter Catechism* (qu. 1) famously replies, "Man's chief end is to glorify God, and to enjoy him forever." Here no doubt a teleological direction of human life toward its "chief end" is asserted; but the chief end itself is no ulterior divine purpose to be served by human action, but is a more direct relation, of acknowledgement, worship, and enjoyment, to the supreme Good that God is.

Gustafson has strikingly little to say about the beauty of the world, and indeed the beauty of God. This is the more surprising in an

28

avowed disciple of Jonathan Edwards. Gustafson gives us much more of Edwards's moral earnestness than of his rapture. God figures in Gustafson's thought much more as the comprehensive purposer to be served than as the transcendent Good to be admired, loved, and worshiped. Not that materials of worship are entirely absent from what he says about piety, but they receive little emphasis in his work. The emphasis falls overwhelmingly on direction, purpose, teleology.

Those themes may seem the most relevant for the guidance of *action*, and the emphasis on them might therefore be natural for those who see action-guidance as the sole task of ethics. If we conceive the task of ethics more broadly, however, as a study of *living* well, and not just of acting well, then worship and a sense of beauty may be centrally important to a theocentric ethics. Gustafson's teleological emphasis is the more puzzling because there are important points at which he seems to hold the more comprehensive conception of ethics—notably in his endorsement of "the centrality of piety or the religious affections in religious and moral life"—which he takes to be characteristic of the Reformed tradition (I, 164).

DIVINE PURPOSES AND THE GOOD

The role of beliefs about divine purposes in Gustafson's ethical theory may be further illuminated by noting how he parts company with another of his mentors in the Reformed tradition. He objects to Friedrich Schleiermacher's ethics because "it is focused on the agent and the actions that are forthcoming from the Christian God-consciousness far more than on a conformation of action to the objective ordering of life in the world" (I, 176). If I understand the difference to which Gustafson points, it is this. For both Gustafson and Schleiermacher our ethical response is to be to God as experienced in the totality of the universe known to us, and for both it is to be grounded at once in the best science available to us and in an affective sense or appreciation of reality. For Schleiermacher, as Gustafson sees him, one's thinking, feeling, and doing are to be integrated around one's affective religious consciousness, and one's ethical response is to be tested by the (largely expressive) value it has as participating or failing to participate in that integration. For Gustafson himself, on the other hand, the integration of scientific knowledge and affective sense is to issue in beliefs about what God's purposes are in the creation, and ethical response is to be mediated by these beliefs and tested by the (primarily instrumental) value it has as serving or failing to serve the divine purposes.

Gustafson might have done better to accept the view he ascribes to Schleiermacher. In this context, at any rate, he gives no reason for rejecting it. I suspect he would object that Schleiermacher's position is too much an invitation to subjectivity, arbitrariness, and self-indulgence; and no doubt it is attended with dangers of that sort. What I do doubt is that the views they share about God, and about ourselves as part of nature, afford Gustafson any better escape than Schleiermacher has from these dangers. Surely we are liable to subjectivity and arbitrariness in "discerning" (as Gustafson proposes) God's purposes in nature. I suspect that Gustafsonian beliefs about divine purposes in nature are in fact likely to strike both religious and secular readers as less well grounded than the judgments Schleiermacher might make about the aptness or inaptness of particular actions to express piety.

Gustafson and the Sacrifice of Human Aspirations

My opinion may be tested by pursuing the most striking and most obviously challenging theme of Gustafson's work: that there may be "good reasons to believe that some stunting of human aspirations is required by 'the structure of the world'" (I, 266). It is clear that "required" has a prescriptive force in this context. Virtually any ethical theory will hold that a human individual is sometimes morally required to accept, voluntarily, some sacrifice of his or her *individual* goals out of respect for the good, or the rights, of others. Gustafson is suggesting, however, that human beings might be morally required to make some sacrifice of the *collective* good of humanity for "the good of the whole creation." The sacrifice required, he indicates, might be significant enough to amount to "some stunting of human aspirations."

But how could "the structure of the world" impose an ethical requirement of this sort? What could we learn about the cosmos that would make it reasonable for us to accept such a requirement? Gustafson is obviously supposing that it would be something that would enable us to discern a divine purpose requiring a sacrifice of human aspirations. He thinks we already know enough about "the structure of the world" to show that we must take seriously, in a *general* way, the possibility of such a requirement. He argues that "from what we know" in science, "it is very difficult to sustain the belief that the cosmos was made for man" (I, 90). God's purposes in the world embrace, presumably for their own sake, ends more comprehensive than even the most comprehensive human good, or at any rate different from it. This thesis about God's purposes is plausible enough, even apart from the deliverances of modern science; but I think one must skate on rather thin ice to draw ethical conclusions from it.

Gustafson argues that "What is right for man has to be determined in relation to man's place in the universe and, indeed, in relation to the will of God for all things as that might be dimly discerned" (I, 99). The questions "What is good for man? . . . What are the right relations between persons?" may therefore be superseded by the questions, "What is good for the whole creation? What is good not only for man but for the natural world of which man is part? What conduct is right for man not only in relation to other human beings but also in relation to the ordering of the natural and social worlds?" (I, 88).

This certainly is initially plausible, given the assumption that God's purposes in the world are not exhausted by purposes for human life; but it may lose plausibility when we consider the questions, "Can we in fact discern God's wider purposes accurately and reliably enough to be guided by them in ethics?" and "To the extent that we can discern divine purposes more comprehensive than any human good, can we do anything that will reliably and effectively further them?" Even if God's purposes are far from exhausted by human good, it might be that we would do well to take our ethical responsibilities as exhausted, or almost so, by the promotion of human good (and the respecting of human rights). For human good surely has a place in the purposes of any God that we would worship, as Gustafson agrees; and it is an end much better proportioned to our powers, both cognitive and active, than is the good of non-human creatures, not to mention the whole cosmos. Only God is fit to bear responsibility for the good of the whole cosmos; it is one of the main objections to utilitarianism that we are probably not fitted to bear responsibility even for the most comprehensive human good.[4]

In what follows I shall pay little attention to questions about our active capacities—that is, about our ability to serve effectively any divine purposes we may recognize for the whole creation. I shall concentrate rather on our cognitive situation—that is, on whether we can in fact discern any divine purposes that might require "some stunting of human aspirations" for the sake of God's ends in the non-human creation. I shall be asking what, concretely, those divine purposes might be. It is a weakness of Gustafson's work that the most dramatic consequence he claims for a theocentric approach to ethics, the possibility of an imperative to make some sacrifice of human good as such, is given little support except by very abstract reasons. Surprisingly, the question of our ecological responsibilities regarding non-human life, the concrete topic in which a plausible case for some such sacrifice is likeliest to be found, is not one of the concrete moral issues selected for focal attention in the second volume of *Ethics from a Theocentric Perspective*, though it receives peripheral attention from time to time in both volumes. The moral questions Gustafson discusses in most detail rarely carry us beyond considerations of human good.[5]

Let us take ecological considerations as the starting point for the next stage of our present inquiry. Do they really pose the alternative of sacrificing human aspirations for a *non*-human good? Many ecological considerations do not. Rather they pose the alternative of sacrificing a narrow or short-range good, or the good of some people, for the sake of an environment that will sustain a more comprehensive and/or a more enduring *human* good. There are two main exceptions to this. One is in cases in which some net sacrifice of human advantage may be required for the survival of some other species of living thing. Even in these cases it is usually believed that there is some human advantage in the survival of the other species, as the extinction of any species is a loss to the aesthetic richness and biological potentialities of our environment. But we may be surer that the other species ought to be preserved than that there is a *net* human advantage in doing so. The other main exception is that we may be ethically required to give up some human advantage in order to avoid cruelty or unjustifiable harm to living individuals of a non-human kind.

When it comes to non-living things, however, it is much less clear what non-human good there is to be served. Clean rivers are better than dirty ones for human beings and for some other living things (though not for all). But what can it mean to say that it is better *for the river* if it is clean rather than dirty? The clean river may seem inherently more beautiful to us; but that may also be a rather subjective judgment. Certainly, it has been possible for many people to find aesthetic satisfaction in very muddy rivers. And beauty is not one of Gustafson's main categories of evaluation anyway.

Suppose we go farther away than rivers. Is it bad *for a star* when it becomes a supernova? Or is it the crowning glory for the star? The questions seem almost senseless. Similarly, it is not obvious that there is any clear or useful meaning to the question, "What is good for the whole creation?'' which Gustafson asks in his first volume (I, 88). He is more cautious on this point in his second volume. He says, "I take it as axiomatic that no human being can perceive, conceive, and respond to '*the* whole,' that is, to the totality of all things and the interrelationships of each of the differentiable parts" (II, 15). Hence "the good of *the* whole is beyond human ken" (II, 17). He still insists, however, that wholes larger than the human race are to be treated as objects of divine purposes in their own right, and that "the theocentric construal of reality at least presses us to expand the scope of the wholes that are taken into account in any normative proposal for human action" (II, 17).

So perhaps we need not worry about supernovas. But planets may be thought to be closer to "our size." Suppose that the habitability of our Earth is drawing to its close in the distant future—a close that plays an important part in Gustafson's argument. And suppose that at that time the human population is small enough, and technically advanced enough, to transport itself *en masse* in rockets to another planet, a planet on which people are reasonably sure that life exists, but nothing as advanced intellectually and socially as a chimpanzee or a dolphin, let alone a human being. They might raise the question as to whether their invasion would disrupt the hitherto more or less autonomous development of life on that planet, and might quite possibly prevent the development of something as rich, intellectually and socially, as human life but different. How would they go about deciding whether it would be better *for that planet* if it continued its own "autonomous" development as opposed to being "graced" by an ongoing history of the human race?

What sort of identity does a planet, or an "ecosphere" (cf. II, 16) have? Does it have an identity, selfhood, or integrity with such a meaning that its interruption by a major influence from outside could be a tragedy comparable to that of the extinction of the human race? I doubt it. The sort of creatures I am supposing to live on the planet in question do not have ongoing projects such that a *meaning* of continuity through time is an internal feature of something going on there.

Gustafson's theory suggests that we should approach such a case by asking what are the divine purposes for the planet. It is hard to see how this will yield a decision. We could take the presence of life on the planet as a sign of a divine purpose that could be fulfilled only by the continued autonomous development of that ecosphere, without human intervention. On the other hand, it seems that we could equally well take the availability of the planet and the technological possibility of reaching it, together with the predicament and survival motives of the human race, as signs of a divine purpose that would be realized by the preservation of humanity through colonization of the new planet.

Indeed, we need not turn to science fiction to find puzzles about the discernment of divine purposes. Is confirmation of the biological theory of natural selection evidence of a divine purpose that would be fulfilled, in many human situations, by oppression of the weak by the strong? Gustafson (rightly) would not want to draw that conclusion, but what is to keep us from drawing it? Are the problems of human overpopulation evidence of a divine purpose that we have violated through the (perhaps "unnatural") development of our medical techniques? Gustafson (rightly again, in my opinion) does not draw this conclusion in the relevant part of his work (II, ch. 7), but why not? These are hard questions; and it might reasonably be asked who has anything better to say in response to them. I will therefore try to state briefly what might be said about them in the context of a theistic Platonism.

Theistic Platonism and Non-Human Good

Let us begin with an issue about the survival of a species of living thing—say, the peregrine falcon or the African elephant. To clarify our focus, let us suppose that the threat to survival of the species is from some human activity that does not cause the death of individual members of the species, but prevents them from reproducing. The peregrine falcon was subjected to precisely such a threat some years ago, when the pesticide DDT was causing catastrophic thinning of the falcons' eggshells. Apart from the other (very diverse and very significant) harms caused to many living things, including humans, by that chemical, many people would agree that it would be reasonable to make some substantial expenditures and some significant changes in human behavior simply for the purpose of saving the peregrine falcon, or the African elephant, from extinction. No doubt many humans enjoy some benefit or satisfaction, of an at least largely aesthetic sort, from the continued existence of species like the falcon or the elephant. It would, therefore, be reasonable, and could be praiseworthy from an ethical point of view, to preserve them at *some* net cost to human well-being. (Obviously questions of justice arise at this point, which there is not space to explore here—for instance, whether persons interested in the preservation of the endangered species bear a full share of the costs, or rather impose them on other, less fortunate humans.)

Why would it be reasonable to sacrifice at least a little net human good for the preservation of another species? The answer I would give is that there is something beautiful, or more broadly wonderful, about the ongoing life of the species, its vitality, complexity, adaptedness, and role in its ecological setting, that commands our admiration; and that respect for this intrinsic value is good enough grounds for going to some lengths to avoid extinguishing the species. In short, the salient reason for preserving the species is that its continued existence is intrinsically good.

It might seem that this account of the matter would fit nicely into Gustafson's theory. For the goodness of the continued existence of the species might well be a reason for believing that its extinction would be contrary to God's purposes. There are at least two reasons, however, for thinking that this solution is not so available to Gustafson as it might seem.

The first is that the intrinsic goodness that figures in this account as a value of the life of the species, and that plays a central role in the ethics of theistic Platonism, plays no role (that I can see) in Gustafson's ethics. In practice, judgments about what is good do appear to play a part in his judgments about divine purposes. His talk of God's purposes for various wholes is closely associated with talk about the good of those wholes; and in summarizing his discernment of "the divine governance" in terms of "the necessary conditions for life to be sustained and developed" (I, 339), he is obviously guided by considerations about what is good for living things. The good of which he speaks in these contexts, however, is beneficial good or welfare—what is good *for* an individual, community, or larger whole.

This relative concept cannot do the work that is needed here. For whom or what would the extinction of a species be bad? For some humans, no doubt, who enjoy the existence of the other species in some way. But we are looking for reasons of another sort, which might override a net balance of benefits to humans. It is unlikely that we will be moved primarily by consideration of the good of individual members of the endangered species, since we are considering a situation in which extinction would not involve their premature death, but would take place through reproductive failure. It remains that extinction would be bad for the species itself, and for certain ecosystems. But why should that consideration move us? The fact that doing

35

something would be bad *for* some entity or system is not always a reason of any ethical weight for refraining. Being melted down as scrap is doubtless bad *for* a weapon, as it would be for any artifact. But there may be no good reason at all not to scrap a weapon as part of a program of disarmament or crime control. Why is it worse to cause the extinction of a species than to scrap a weapon? The answer, I believe, is that the life of the species is not just good *for* someone or something, but is intrinsically good, and therefore commands our respect, in a way that the weapon is not and does not—unless perhaps it happens to be of significant value as a work of art, and not just a weapon.

The first difficulty I have noted in integrating Gustafson's theory with the reason I have proposed for preserving endangered species at some net cost to humans is that my account turns on a sort of intrinsic goodness to which Gustafson does not normally appeal. Perhaps it will be said that he could and should just appeal to it; but that leaves us face to face with the second difficulty. For if we see that there is something intrinsically wonderful about the ongoing life of a species of living things, that is surely grounds enough for us to respect it and try to avoid extinguishing it. We have reason enough to make some sacrifice to preserve it, without any speculation or discernment regarding a divine purpose that would be served by its continued existence. In other words, our ethical response in this case can have a pattern closer to that which Gustafson ascribes to Schleiermacher than to the pattern that he adopts for himself. It can be grounded directly in a respect aroused by our appreciation of the beauty or value of the natural phenomenon, without having to be justified by a belief about divine purposes discerned through science.

Of course, this is not to deny that our scientific knowledge is important to our response in both Schleiermacher's view and mine. Science will affect our view of what the endangered species is and of the consequences of our actions. But our fundamental value judgments in such a case need not be justified by a belief about divine purposes in nature. On the contrary, in the absence of revelations of a sort that play no part in Gustafson's theology, it seems that the value judgments must be presupposed for the justification of the belief about God's purposes.

What becomes of theocentricity, or more broadly, the theistic character of our ethics, if we can base our ethical judgments directly on apprehensions of the intrinsic value of natural phenomena, without inferences running through a theory of divine purposes? The most obvious answer, for theistic Platonism, is that the intrinsic goodness perceived in creatures is an image, fragmentary and imperfect as it may be, of the goodness of God; and respect for the intrinsic goodness of creatures has religious significance as respect for an image of God. But I do not propose to rest in that answer alone. Theistic Platonists are, after all, theists. The supreme Good they worship is not an impersonal Form, but an agent, who may be conceived as more capable of voluntary action in the world than is Gustafson's deity. Theistic Platonism therefore does not exclude, from ethics or from the interpretation of the world, such categories as those of divine purpose, gift, command, and vocation. Some of these categories ought to have a role in theists' thinking about the sort of ethical issues we have been discussing, though I am inclined to give the concepts of gift and vocation precedence here over those of purpose and command.

Actuality and the Good

These categories can be used, for instance, to illuminate the science fiction case discussed above. If our descendants have to choose between the extinction of the human race and its resettlement on a new planet, where human intervention would preempt the autonomous further evolution of indigenous forms of life, we can hardly doubt what they will do. Almost certainly they will occupy the new planet. They will do that because they will care much more, and in a more personally engaged and committed way, about the future of humanity than about the indeterminate evolutionary future of the indigenous creatures of the new planet. In my opinion they will act rightly and manifest an appropriate piety in so caring and so acting. There are at least two reasons for thinking so. First, the potentialities of humanity, in the example as described, are much more fully actualized, more clearly *given* by God, than any possibly comparable goods that would be precluded by human settlement of the planet. Second, humanity, and its potentialities for the future, are given *to us* to care about in a way that the future a strange planet will have if we do *not* control it is not. That God gives us humanity and its potentialities to love and respect may be seen as defining a major part of our *vocation*. We may have more distant respect, but hardly a love, for the mere potentialities of the alien reality not involving humanity. If we act on our love for that which is given us to love, rather than on the more distant respect, surely we do not act impiously. I do not mean, of course, that our love for humanity would justify us in expropriating the property and life-possibilities of creatures that we could recognize as persons having *rights* against us; but that is not what is at issue in the example described.

In this talk about vocation there may well be implications about divine purposes as well as divine commands; but if so, their role here will be different from their role in Gustafson's thinking. In his ethics divine purposes appear primarily as something like plans extending into the future which we have some responsibility for fulfilling. I do not believe that science can enable us to discern that sort of divine purpose for the future. I grant that our perception of the goodness of things that actually exist may be an acceptable basis for thinking in terms of a divine purpose that we should have them, in the sense that we should be able to love them (and perhaps also for speaking of a divine command that we should respect them). Given that we do and should love and respect good things that now exist, the future about which we have reason to care has no clear and definite limit. But we have reason enough to care about that future because of the divine goodness that we can see in existing goods, without needing to trace in our science a scheme of divine purposes for the future.

It is a feature of this type of ethical thinking and motivation that actually existing goods engage our regard in a way that merely possible goods do not. This preference for actual goods is one that no ethics that is to deal with reality can happily do without. Possibility, even the possibility of good, is so vast and illimitable that we will be hopelessly at sea if we do not in some way accept actual structures of life as defining in part a vocation for us. One of the contributions to ethics that we are apt to seek from religion is an illumination of the ethical significance of what appear to be actual structures of life, which may help us to understand how we have more reason to care for existing goods than for merely possible ones.

This is also one of the ethical functions of the idea of the "natural" as it appears in conceptions of "natural rights." Consider the inalienable right that most of us think we have to the vital organs of our own bodies, a right that cannot be overridden by the mere consideration that other persons (perhaps younger, healthier, or more talented) could make better use of them; or the right we think parents have to bring up their own children, a right that may be forfeited by negligence, abuse, or gross incompetence, but that does not yield to the mere consideration that alternative parents would probably do a better job. These rights seem curiously *contingent*. It is clear that they are important to structures of human relationship that we rightly value; and that is a reason for thinking it is good that we have them. But alternative arrangements can be imagined that from an abstract point of view may seem as good or better. These rights are often not respected in fictitious utopias. We think we do have these rights, but there is some plausibility to the hypothesis that other creatures outwardly similar to us might differ from us in this respect.

An explanation of our having these rights may be attempted by saying that it is part of our "nature" to have them. This use of the concept of the natural confronts a notorious difficulty, however. For suppose we adopted a system in which these rights were not respected; how would that be shown to be unnatural? It would be no miracle. By doing it we would show, insofar as we are part of the natural world, that we are naturally able to do it. How then would it be contrary to nature? If, as moderns, we have abandoned Aristotelian conceptions of natural teleology, it will not be easy for us to answer this question. This is among the reasons that attempts that have been made, for example, to establish that one or another actual sexual practice is contrary to nature no longer seem plausible to many of us. Replies to this objection may be offered on behalf of ethical naturalism, but I think theistic Platonism can deal better with the problem without relying on the concept of the natural.

An abstract and impersonal conception of a transcendent supreme Good would give us little help in seeing a reason to regard actual goods more highly than merely possible goods. It is different, however, if we conceive of the supreme Good as personal. Then actual goods can be seen as divine *gifts*, and as such can claim a special respect which lends force to certain rights we claim.[6] We can say, for example, that our bodily organs and our relationships with our children, if we have any, have been given us by God, through the divine activity in creating us, and perhaps also, in the case of parent-child relationships, through the providential ordering of the history of human society. And inasmuch as we can say the same about the goods inherent in a system of social relationships in which the medical and parental rights in question are recognized, we have a reason to respect that system and regard the rights as objectively valid. This clearly leaves it open to us to suppose that if we came on creatures, otherwise like us, who lived with evident satisfaction in social arrangements that differed in these respects, we might be persuaded that they had received different gifts, and different rights, from God.

An important advantage of the line of thought I am following is found in its resources for dealing with one of the main difficulties of using actuality as an ethical guide. How can actuality serve that function, given that ethical judgments are supposed to discriminate, among the things that are or may be actual, those that are or would be good? One way of dealing with this problem is to affirm "Whatever is, is right," while rejecting its apparent consequence, "Whatever will be, will be right," by taking the former as a mandate for opposing change. This systematically "conservative" interpretation of the appeal to actuality is historically common, but obviously objectionable.

A better interpretation of the appeal will be one in which actuality is not an autonomous ethical consideration, but is posterior to judgments of value. It is a basis for choosing only among *goods*. The theistic use of the appeal to actuality that I have proposed is of this type, for only good things can claim our respect as divine gifts. If there actually exists something intrinsically good, it may rightly engage our love, or command our respect as a divine gift, in a way that a merely possible good could not. This may provide a reason for preferring it to imaginable alternatives that might in some sense be better. (It *may*; I do not mean to be formulating a universal rule. Discernment is required to determine whether actual goods are to be preferred to merely possible ones in a given case.) The actuality of forms of human life and relationships can contribute in this way to grounding our sense that rights implicit in them must be respected. They can do this only on the assumption that they are good. The actuality of a form of life or social system is of no avail to defend it against a charge that it is unjust, or otherwise bad.

This is clearly analogous to a point that I have emphasized in my critique of Gustafson, namely, that discernment of ethically binding divine purposes, through our knowledge of nature, must presuppose judgments about the good. It is not clear that Gustafson wishes to reject this point, since his judgments about God's purposes do seem to be influenced by his judgments about what is good for living things. However, the role of the concept of good in his theological and ethical methodology is not very clearly articulated; it is noteworthy that he does not include a sense of the good among the "senses . . . on the basis of which theological inferences are drawn" (I, 129ff.).

An objection might be raised at this point by some who share Gustafson's aspiration for a scientific world-view. I do *not* think Gustafson would endorse this objection, but the issue it raises is important enough to claim some attention here. There is a strong tendency in modern thought to reject inferences from beliefs about value to beliefs about the nature of reality—at least when the inferences have been seen in that light.[7] The elimination of final causes from natural science has been the great slogan in this development, but I think it is more general. Inferences from "ought" to "is" have been even more suspect than those from "is" to "ought." This might lead a naturalistic theologian to avoid reliance on a sense of what is good, in her thinking about divine purposes in nature.

This tendency of much modern thought seems inimical to moral realism—not that it is clear that moral realism entails inferences from "ought" to "is," but the idea of moral realism seems to invite them. If moral truths are facts about a reality, then surely our moral consciousness warrants conclusions about a reality. Plato, in the middle dialogues, is an archetypal moral realist at this point, taking our apprehension of value as a clue to the nature of what is most real. The point is also important for theism. The idea of God is certainly the idea of a reality, but it is obviously a dangerous idea for ethics if it is not shaped at least largely by a moral vision. Perhaps it should even be said that if we are not prepared to let our vision of value control in some ways our vision of reality, then we had better not be theists.

NOTES

1. James Gustafson, *Ethics from a Theocentric Perspective*, vol. I: *Theology and Ethics;* vol. II: *Ethics and Theology* (Chicago: University of Chicago Press, 1981 and 1984). Parenthetical references by roman and arabic numerals in the text of this essay are to volume and page of Gustafson's work.

2. That Gustafson recognizes this is suggested by the one reference I have found to Stoicism in his book (I, 91). It is surprising, however, how little mention he makes of Stoicism.

3. In thus qualifying my rejection of the purposiveness of the world as a comprehensive basis for understanding its relation to the Good, I part company, perhaps not with Plato, but with one of the relatively few important Platonists in contemporary moral philosophy. Affirming "the utter lack of finality in human life," Iris Murdoch has stated that "the Good has nothing to do with purpose, indeed it excludes the idea of purpose" [*The Sovereignty of Good* (New York: Schocken Books, 1971), 71]. Readers of Murdoch may notice, nonetheless, some affinities between my views and hers, including the stress on the ethical importance of beauty.

4. To this, Gustafson may object that it is unjustifiably anthropomorphic to think of the divine agency in such a way as to suppose that God could bear responsibility for the achievement of any purpose. However, this assumption of God's incapacity to bear responsibility for the good of the universe as a whole would not establish our capacity to bear it.

5. The closest Gustafson comes to an exception to this generalization is in his extensive treatment of "population and nutrition," where he states that "attention must be given to the conditions of possibility not only for the continuity of human life but also for other forms of life to be sustained and developed." He says, "This does not imply that every endangered species of plant or sea life has to be preserved," but he does see "signals of the necessity to remain within some limits of ordering of life in the world" (II, 243). But his discussion of this topic contains little that goes beyond these rather vague and general statements (cf. II, 247, 249).

6. For this idea I am indebted to James Read's UCLA doctoral dissertation, "The Right Medicine: Philosophical Investigations into the Moral Wrongness of Killing Patients" (Ann Arbor: University Microfilms, 1988). He applies the idea specifically to the case of body parts.

7. It is controversial whether modern science is in fact free of inferences from value-beliefs. But this is not the place to go into that issue.

4

On Developing a Contemporary Theistic Ethics

Alan Donagan

In "Platonism and Naturalism: Options for a Theocentric Ethics,"[1] Robert M. Adams explores how to develop a contemporary theistic ethics that would be Platonic and Augustinian rather than Aristotelian and Kantian. Adams is as balanced and fair as he is timely and provocative. From the moral point of view, my comments on his essay will be Kantian; from the epistemological point of view, they will be neither Kantian nor Platonist—the best description of them I can give is "realist and holist," but those words do not mean the same things to everyone.

The Platonic theocentric ethics Adams explores has six tenets, namely: (1) God is a good transcending all others, and other goodness is a participation[2] in God's goodness; (2) God's goodness is final, and so neither instrumental nor beneficial; (3) God's goodness is also beauty: God is the ultimate aesthetic object as well as the ultimate source of morality; (4) in apprehending finite goods as good we glimpse "as in a mirror darkly" the infinite good in which they participate; (5) the object thus glimpsed is loved; and (6) "something about divine goodness is cognitively accessible, at least in part, to people in general." The first three are doctrines about what God's goodness is in itself, no matter how it is apprehended: they are ontological. Of them, (1) and (2) would be asserted by both Kantian and Aristotelian Christians as essential to their theocentric ethics; and (3) can be denied by nobody who accepts the authority of the Psalms or Job. The second three, however, are epistemological: they are about how finite goods are apprehended, about what accompanies that apprehension, and about to whom that apprehension is accessible.

43

All three have senses in which I think they are true—and in which Aristotelians and Kantians would accept them. But are they the Platonic senses in which Adams asserts them?

Essentially this question can arise as a problem of scriptural interpretation. Consider the passage in the First Epistle of John, which presupposes Adams's three Platonist ontological theses, in which we are told that, although "No one has ever seen God; if we love one another, God lives in us . . ." (4:12), because "those who do not love a brother or sister whom they have seen cannot love God whom they have not seen" (4:20). John, as I understand him here, says two things. First, our reason for loving our brother or sister is not that we *see* God and so see that our brother or sister is God's image; for we do not see God. And secondly, if we love our brother or sister who is in fact God's image, we not only indirectly love God, but can learn directly to love God by learning, through revelation, that God has made us, and "we are his people, and the sheep of his pasture" (Ps. 100:3).

Nor is that the whole of the matter. The core of the chapter from which I have offered my interpretation is the assertion: "In this is love, not that we loved God, but that he loved us and sent his Son to be the atoning sacrifice for our sins" (1 John 4:10). You do not "see" God, and *a fortiori* neither do you see that God loves you, nor do I see that he loves me: we believe it because we accept a long chain of testimony, which includes that of John, whose letter begins, "We declare to you what was from the beginning, what we have heard, what we have seen with our own eyes, what we have looked at and touched with our hands, concerning the word of life" (1:1). We began by loving some people, among them ourselves; and by not loving, even hating, some others. Because we were so taught by some tradition or other (perhaps by that of Moses, the prophets, and the apostles) we learned that God loves us, and hence that even those we hate are lovable. We "see" God in one another only to the extent that we believe what is reported about God.

What of the numerous philosophers, from neo-Platonists like Philo and Augustine to the Aristotelians—Muslim, Jewish, and Christian—who all professed to have proved by natural reason the existence of a being with attributes that belong (according to Jews, Christians, and Muslims) only to the God of Abraham, Isaac, and Jacob? I believe they were mistaken. I concede that some of the proofs they offered are internally valid; but all of them have some premise that can be rationally doubted. God does not appear in the world as God, except by deniable signs—even that of being resurrected from the dead. Nor do we need the hypothesis of divine creation as a foundation for the sciences of nature. As a matter of fact, most of the founders of modern natural science seem to have been sincere theists, like most of their contemporaries; and many natural scientists still are: but nothing of permanent scientific value in their results requires the hypothesis of a divine creator. A self-subsistent realm of nature is all natural science need postulate. And that presents a difficulty for any approach to God similar to Plato's approach to the Form of the Good, which depends on finding that nature is not a true realm of being—of objects admitting of scientific *episteme*—but only the realm of phenomena, which are between being and not-being, such being as they have derived by participation in the inhabitants of the true realm of being, that of the Forms. No monotheist—Jewish, Christian, or Muslim—can deny that the realm of created nature is a realm of being.

Curiously, Adams finds an epistemological difficulty in James Gustafson's non-Platonic theocentric ethics that closely resembles the one I find in his Platonic one. Gustafson's eminence and the distinction of his work, as Adams rightly says, need no certification. The chief points in the ontology underlying Gustafson's ethics seem to me as to Adams certainly true, namely: that ultimately, the end that matters is God, not any human being or all human beings; that non-human as well as human creatures can have ethical claims on us by virtue of their relation to God; and that they do so, not merely as things believed to participate in the divine goodness, but as things loved by virtue of doing so. Gustafson then proceeds to infer not only that the claims non-human creatures have on us have "to be determined in relation to . . . the will of God for all things as that might be dimly discerned" (I, 99),[3] but also that human cognitive-affective powers as a whole enable us, at least dimly, to discern God's will.

Here, like Adams, I distrust my understanding of Gustafson's elaborate and subtle treatment of human cognitive-affective capacities in chapter 7 of *Theology and Ethics*. Gustafson is orthodox in concluding that since intellect, intention, and "radical agency" (that is, free will), as they are ascribed to human beings, can truly be ascribed to God only analogically,[4] the discernment of God's purposes in nature of which human beings are capable is both partial, being confined to a small part of the whole, and dim. It resembles, but is not identical with, a deeply experienced woodsman's discernment of certain things in the course of nature. Such discernment is usually considered to resemble what is sometimes called the "sagacity" of brute animals: it is a matter of perception, memory, and imagination, and the feelings that go with the exercise of those capacities. Just as the woodsman's discernment of nature's course is not simply an anticipation of an ecologist's scientific understanding of it, which depends wholly on systematic causal analysis and theory, so human discernment of God's purposes in nature is not simply an anticipation of what would be good for a given ecosystem. Yet, Gustafson maintains, human beings can sometimes discern God's purposes in nature.

Adams, as a Platonist-Augustinian, voices a deep uneasiness with this which I share: namely, that Gustafson's God seems to be one in whom nature is, rather than a creator transcending nature. If such a panentheism is true, then I am inclined to think that the first modern panenthist, Spinoza, rightly concluded that, while we can truly speak of the intellect and will of God, then God's intellect must be his full understanding of how nature as it is (that is, himself) is completely determined by nature's laws; and his will must be indistinguishable from his recognition that nature cannot be otherwise.[5] In other words, *Deus sive Natura* neither is nor can be anything but itself: it has no ends beyond itself to fulfill, nothing within it can make any difference to what it is, nor is there anything outside it. The rational human attitude toward it is therefore *acquiescentia:* being at peace with what Nature is. It is proper to save whales or elephants from extinction because we care about them. If, *however*, they become extinct because of human actions, even misguided ones, that extinction will no more be against the will of God than when any other species becomes extinct owing to some environmental change, or to a predator exterminating instead of culling a species that supplies its food. If we are simply "in" Nature, what we do is determined by her so far as what happens in her is determined; and if we think that we either cooperate with or oppose Nature, we are deluded by our imaginations. It is as irrational to try to cooperate with Nature as to try to alter her course. Of course, dropping Spinoza's name does not show that Whitehead, whom I take to have influenced Gustafson, was mistaken. However, I am prepared to defend the opinion that, if panentheism is true, then Spinoza was right that human projects for cooperating with God are chimerical, that a theocentric ethics must be an ethics of *acquiescentia:* that is, an analysis of the highest kind of human freedom human beings can attain in view of the laws of human behavior, accompanied by stern advice to be at peace with how

46

things necessarily are, and not to make a fool of oneself by either railing at them or satirizing them.[6]

Setting aside this deep difficulty, like Adams I have a simple epistemological one, namely: that what human beings can discern about God's purposes in nature is a much weaker ground for conclusions about human responsibilities for the non-human creation than others that are readily available. I assume that we agree about what I take to be the grounds that Christians have traditionally given, which are human-centered. All the law (the Mosaic Torah) and the prophets hang on the two principles that we are to love God with our whole heart, and our neighbors as ourselves; and the portion that has to do with God is about worship (for example, the prohibition of idolatry, the institution of the Sabbath). As for the world we inhabit, we are told that its fruits and its non-human inhabitants are ours, to be used for our good, subject to special revealed laws, such as the dietary laws promulgated through Moses for the Jewish people. Although the question of whether we may exterminate a species if that is for our good is not expressly answered in either the Jewish or the Christian scriptures, there seems to be no reason to deny that if it were for our good to exterminate the cockroach or the Argentine ant, and if we could (at present we cannot), it would not be wrong to exterminate either. Of course, it must be for our good to do so; and, in general, Genesis informs us that God found both the non-animal and the animal creation "very good." Yet Isaiah 11:1–9, in declaring that when the Messiah comes there will be no predation among animals (the lion eating straw like an ox), appears to imply that all is less than well in the animal realm as it is. I agree with Gustafson, Adams, and most educated Americans that "it would be reasonable to make some substantial expenditures and some significant changes in human behavior simply for the purpose of saving the peregrine falcon or the African elephant, from extinction" (see Adams, p. 34). However, I also agree with Adams that our wish to save those species is partly sentimental, and that the least disputable reasons for so wishing are that the harm extermination would do, by impoverishing the environment for all human beings indefinitely, would be much greater, perhaps very much greater, than the good extermination would bring to a few people for a short time. To this, Christians traditional enough to believe in original sin may wish to add that, whenever they are moved to "hurt or destroy" (in Isaiah's phrase) any living thing, they have been taught to ask themselves whether they do so from malice—

especially when the reasons that spring to their tongues are political and sanctimonious.

To these traditional lines of thought, Adams adds two that are distinctly Platonic. After stating each, I shall comment on it.

The first is that certain natural phenomena, for example the survival of species as distinct from individuals of those species, are discernibly intrinsic goods, because they each participate in the infinite goodness of God. This seems to me substantially correct and an inescapable deduction from what traditional Christianity adapted from Platonic ontology and bequeathed to those of us who would not describe ourselves as Platonists. Here we must remember Adams's caution that "theistic Platonists are, after all, theists. The supreme Good they worship is not an impersonal Form, but an agent" (see Adams, p. 37). All non-rational species participate in the being and hence the goodness of God. Their good, and even their survival, is a lesser good than the good of rational creatures, but unless their good is incompatible with the good of rational creatures, it has a claim on them. However, I venture one amendment: that not all participated goods should be recognized as ends for action. I shall return to the question of which goods, if any, should be so recognized.

The second line of thought that Adams commends is surprising as well as persuasive: it is a Platonic reason for the place given in Christian ethics to the actual, and in particular to the contingent:

> An abstract and impersonal conception of a transcendent supreme Good would give us little help in seeing a reason to regard actual goods more highly than merely possible goods. It is different, however, if we conceive the supreme Good as personal. Then actual goods can be seen as divine *gifts*, and as such can claim a special respect which lends force to certain rights we claim. We can say, for example, that our bodily organs and our relationships with our children, if we have any, have been given us by God . . . And inasmuch as we can say the same about the goods inherent in a system of social relationships in which the medical and parental rights in question are recognized, we have a reason to respect that system and regard those rights as objectively valid. This clearly leaves it open to us to suppose that if we came on creatures, otherwise like us, who lived with evident satisfaction in social arrangements that differed in these respects, we might be persuaded that they had received different gifts, and different rights, from God (see Adams, p. 39).

48

Although this theory of divine gifts seems to me fruitful, I fear that it may invite the unwary to draw invalid inferences. To explain my qualms, I must remind you of the traditional Christian view of the place of human beings in a theocentric universe.

According to that theory, the reason why actually existing things have a claim on us that possibly existing ones do not is that all things produced by action are produced for the sake of beings already in existence. Aristotle recognized this when he distinguished two senses of the expression "that for the sake of which:"

> That that for the sake of which is found among the unmovables is shown by making a distinction; for that for the sake of which is both that *for* and that *towards* which, and of these one is unmovable and the other is not. Thus it produces motion by being loved, and it moves the other moving things (*Metaphysics* XII, 1072 b1–3, *emphasis added*).[7]

The unmovable *for* which a movable is moved from one state *toward* another must pre-exist the movement brought about for its sake. Duns Scotus later maintained that only that *for* which is strictly the end (*finis*) of the movement; the final stage of the movement—that *toward* which it is a movement—is not properly its *finis*, but its *finitum*, that which is ordered to the end. For Aristotle as for Christians, God is the ultimate end for which all good agents act in their good actions; and Christians, who believe that God is creator of natural things as well as the end for which they act, also believe that certain creatures (those who as such participate in the divine goodness) may also be said to be ends *for* which by participation.

Such creatures are not such ends, however, simply because, as divinely created, they participate in the divine goodness. The survival of every animal species is not as such a divine purpose; for, by processes involving no human action whatever, nature as created by God has brought about the extinction of many animal species. Hence, the scriptural permission to human beings to use animals for their benefit implies that, if it is genuinely for their benefit (as it will be in very few cases), they may exterminate a species if they can. What marks out a creature as an end is not that it is divinely created, but that it is an image of God: that is, that it participates in the divine attributes of rationality and agency, as not even brute animals do, let alone plants or inanimate things. If it is objected that rationality and agency are properties too abstract and empty to make their possessors images of God, it is enough to point out that all thinking is abstract, and that,

49

far from being empty, the properties of rationality and agency are rich in what they imply about their possessors. Nothing can be a rational agent and be incapable of intellectual love, or capable of intellectual love and not be an agent. Brute animals may love in the sense of desire; but not as an act of will elicited intellectually. In short, only rational beings, like God, can be moved by intellectual love of an end *for* which to bring about a change. It is this that makes them, like God, ends *for* which—what Kant called "ends in themselves."

The reason traditional Christian morality holds moral claims arising from certain actualities to outweigh claims arising from any possibilities is that it regards all actual creatures that are images of God, and only those creatures, as being, like God, genuine ends *for* which, and love of whom has moved God himself, the ultimate end *for* which, and may move their fellow rational beings, to bring about various changes for their sake. The only things that are intellectually lovable as ends are actual things capable of love: God first and then rational creatures.

Like Kant, I speak of "rational" beings rather than "human" ones, because, as Adams reminds us, twentieth-century Christians cannot escape the possibility that there are non-terrestrial rational creatures whom they may encounter one day. If there are, they are as much *imagines Dei* as human beings are. C. S. Lewis did well to prepare us for the possibility that non-human beings may be better than we are—even innocents—who have never lost direct communication with God.[8] They may be, of course, as bad as or worse than humans. However, our duties to extraterrestrials, whether we should arrive as strangers on the planets they inhabit or they on the one we do, are identical in kind with those we have to all terrestrial foreigners. Even with fellow humans, we fail to perform these duties. All habitable nature is for all rational beings, even though no human society recognizes this in practice even for its own members.

Given this, what is the consequence for morality? If we see the goods actually present in the environments we encounter as divine gifts (as I agree with Adams we should), what is the consequence for morality in that context? His own chief inference is that we should respect great differences in social relationships as God's different gifts to different societies ("if we came on creatures, otherwise like us [that is, rational animals], who lived with evident satisfaction in social relationships that differed from ours in [respect of the medical and parental rights recognized in them]"). Obviously, if they are nonmammalian, parental relations and the corresponding parent-child rights will necessarily be different. But if they are "evidently" satisfied with counterparts of the Roman institution that a father can put his children to death at will, or of the Carthaginian one that parents should be prepared to sacrifice at least one child as a burnt-offering to a false god, should we regard the goods inherent in their system of social relations as divine gifts, through creation, or the providential ordering of their history?

The strength of Adams's line of thought is twofold: it warns us against the grave moral and mortal religious error of denying either that every rational animal, terrestrial or not, is *imago Dei*, or that the history of every society of such creatures is under divine providence. We must have both the humility to be prepared to learn from extra-terrestrials and the faith to be prepared to teach them; and we must acquire the capacity, possessed by few or no human beings now, to judge uncorruptly with respect to which of our beliefs and practices we must alter or promote. Adams rightly denounces the notion that respect for the actual is systematically conservative, although as a matter of history, it has commonly been so misrepresented. Here I submit a final Kantian thought: that we can obviate such misrepresentations by drawing our moral distinctions with an impartial eye on *all* the *imagines Dei* affected by them, and not on the stability or self-satisfaction of the societies concerned.

NOTES

1. All references to Adams that follow are to Robert M. Adams, "Platonism and Naturalism: Options for a Theocentric Ethics," in this volume.

2. As Adams notes, since the Form of the Good is not God but imparts to a world that is between being and not-being such being and goodness as it has, "there are obvious problems" about transforming the participation of the world in the Form of the Good in God to its participation in God. How Platonic were the [neo-]Platonists who influenced Augustine?

3. This reference to James Gustafson, *Ethics from a Theocentric Perspective*, vol. I, *Theology and Ethics*, vol. II, *Ethics and Theology* (Chicago: University of Chicago Press, 1981 and 1984), like all subsequent ones, is to a passage quoted or referred to by Adams.

4. Perhaps I have impertinently excused Gustafson from an unorthodoxy of which he would prefer to be accused. When he declares it "excessive" to apply the analogy of agency to God, I take him simply to deny that God's will

is any more like a human will than his intellect is like a human intellect. To deny any analogy whatever would empty the phrase "the will of God" of all sense.

5. I have discussed Spinoza's panentheism in *Spinoza* (Chicago: University of Chicago Press, 1989), 89–102.

6. On Spinoza's doctrine of *acquiescentia* see Donagan, *Spinoza*, 200–206.

7. In an earlier version of this paper, the only authority I cited was that of John Duns Scotus, *De Primo Principio* ch. 2, 4th and 5th conclusions, text and translation by Evan Roche, O.F.M. (St. Bonaventure, N.Y.: Franciscan Institute, 1949). However, Professor Charles Young has since suggested to me that "Aristotle very sketchily distinguishes two senses of 'that for the sake of which' at *Metaphysics* 1072 b1–3 and *de Anima* 415 b2–3. Ross, in his note to *Physics* 194 a35–36 (where the distinction is only mentioned) says that it may have been more fully set out in one of Aristotle's lost dialogues."

8. Especially in the two novels, *Out of the Silent Planet* (London: Bodley Head, 1938) and *Perelandra* (New York: Macmillan Co., 1944), and in occasional papers.

5

Toward an Ethics of Delight

James Wm. McClendon, Jr.

Ethics is very often taken to be the rules people make (or *somebody* makes) to keep people from doing what they want to do—from doing what people, deplorably, are going to do anyway. For example, if there is an ethics committee in the university, this means that something is going on that somebody thinks needs to be stopped, or at the very least, slowed down. On this widely shared view, ethics is something negative; it means "don't!" If there were to be an ethics of delight it would have to mean no delight at all, or at least not too much, and not too soon.

Now this is a caricature. Perhaps no one believes exactly what I have just written. But like most caricatures, it contains some truth. Thus the one some have called the greatest moral philosopher since Aristotle, namely Immanuel Kant, taught that the *only* motive for truly moral action was respect for the moral law. In Kant's view, if you are doing this thing (let us say it is feeding a hungry child) because you like to do it, your deed may of course be objectively good, but you deserve no moral credit for doing it, for you do it because you like it. Only when one does what morally one must do out of respect for the moral law (and a good test of that will be doing it against one's own inclinations)—only then can anyone safely say that one has acted out of pure respect for the moral law, for this is the true test of moral motivation.[1] Now Kant's is a great tradition, and many still think as he did, and I do not fancy myself saying anything that would destroy that great tradition of seeking the right way, or the good life, via stern duty. Perhaps it is even our duty to think in such terms, whether we like to or not. At any rate my goal here is not to discourage anyone who does.

Nevertheless, I wish to suggest that that is a very difficult way of ethics for anyone whose religion comes from the Bible. For in the Bible we read (in Gen. 1) that God created everything good. Creation is good; creation is beautiful; creation is a *delight*. God looked, and *saw* that it was good. We might say that it was visibly good. To be sure, as the Genesis story goes on to show, the human creature in such a creation can take wrong turns. There is disobedience (ch. 3), and later murder (ch. 4), and human corruption (ch. 6), and worst of all, there is proud religion that builds a tower of Babel to exalt human pride (ch. 11). Yet none of these mismoves had the power to ruin the story that was still to come in the following chapters, the Genesis saga of divine-human relations in process of redemption (ch. 12 onward). Then should we not expect, even if contrary to Immanuel Kant (yet see his strikingly supportive footnote in *Religion within the Limits of Reason Alone*[2]), to find a correspondence between what is right and what is visibly good, even what feels good? A fit between right conduct and human satisfaction? Between virtue and happiness?

Certainly I cannot prove that this is so. The most I can hope for is to carry you with me in an experiment of thought in which we can ask how far such an approach may be carried without plunging us into fresh difficulties. We must begin, though, by rejecting the assumption that delight as such is naughty or nasty or wicked. I have argued elsewhere[3] against today's neo-gnosticism, urging that embodied existence itself is as such no embarrassment to a biblical thinker. Here I hope to follow up just one thread of that theme by supposing that a capacity for delight is one part of the moral equipment normally possessed by Christian believers, and by asking whether this equipment is something that Christians can be grateful for. Doubtless others are so equipped as well, but a Christian ethicist is pretty fully occupied merely in trying to work out an appropriate ethics for Christians. If anyone else finds that it applies to, or fits, herself or himself, I can only be delighted to hear that.

To continue with Christians and delight, it was no accident that in John Bunyan's great allegory of the progress of the Christian life, the final range of mountains reached by the travelers to the Celestial City was named "the Delectable Mountains." (Now we might note in passing that *delectable, delightful,* and *delicious* are close kin-words, all related to a cluster of Latin terms whose common meaning seems to be allurement, enticement.) From the Delectable Mountains, for the first time, pilgrims who looked through the Perspective Glass could catch sight of the Heavenly City itself.[4] Does Bunyan mean to tell us, then, that earth's delights can be a kind of foretaste or promise of heaven's ecstasy—the best there could be? It is worth asking.

I have already hinted, and now must acknowledge more clearly, that an ethics of delight will certainly have its difficulties. Not only can it, too, be caricatured (as I have, perhaps unfairly, caricatured the deontological ethic), but an ethics of delight confronts internal problems: For one thing, delights are often inconsistent with one another. I cannot at one and the same time enjoy the bliss of quiet and privacy *and* the whirl of society. I cannot be at once delightfully thrifty and delightfully extravagant, blissfully narcissistic and cheerfully self-forgetful, chaste and profligate, intoxicated and sober, sympathetic and self-contained. Some delights make other delights impossible, either for the time being or forever. Superb fitness is canceled by lazy indulgence; playing the field necessarily competes with fidelity to just one lover. Facing these difficulties, how can delight be an asset in the kingdom of God?

I wish to proceed by way of examples, and the examples I have chosen are two women; the first a gorgeous wife and mother, the daughter of old New England stock; the other a rebellious Californian, plain spoken, powerful, and at the end beautiful as well. Both were highly attractive to men and also to women; both broke conventions out of deep conviction; both suffered and both survived. Most important for our thought-experiment, both of these women found delight close to the center of their lives; it made them the human beings they were.

SARAH PIERPONT EDWARDS

First, then, we consider the New Englander, Sarah Pierpont Edwards (1710–1758). Some background information will be useful. Sarah Pierpont's story has been told and retold, but for this background I will follow mainly the colorful account provided by Elisabeth D. Dodds, *Marriage to a Difficult Man*. As that title suggests, marriage was indeed a crux of Sarah Pierpont's history. She met her husband-to-be, Jonathan Edwards, while he was only a tutor at Yale College, much preoccupied with abstruse philosophical problems. She, however, was by then (in Elisabeth Dodds's phrase) "a vibrant brunette, with erect posture and burnished manners," the offspring of stalwart

Hookers and prestigious Pierponts, living in her parents' home in the colonial seaport town of New Haven.[5] She was at once powerfully present in a physical sense and deeply spiritual. A verbal sketch of his intended bride, inscribed in the back of Jonathan's Greek grammar soon after they met, has survived:

> They say there is a young lady in [New Haven] who is beloved of that Great Being, who made and rules the world, and that there are certain seasons in which this Great Being, in some way or other invisible, comes to her and fills her mind with exceeding sweet delight, and that she hardly cares for anything, except to meditate on him—that she expects after a while to be received up where he is, to be raised up out of the world and caught up into heaven; being assured that he loves her too well to let her remain at a distance from him always. There she is to dwell with him, and to be ravished with his love and delight forever. Therefore, if you present all the world before her, with the richest of its treasures, she disregards it and cares not for it, and is unmindful of any pain or affliction. She has a strange sweetness in her mind, and singular purity in her affections; is most just and conscientious in all her conduct; and you could not persuade her to do any thing wrong or sinful, if you would give her all the world, lest she should offend the Great Being. She is of wonderful sweetness, calmness and universal benevolence of mind; especially after this Great God has manifested himself to her mind. She will sometimes go about from place to place, singing sweetly; and seems to be always full of joy and pleasure; and no one knows for what. She loves to be alone, walking in the fields and groves, and seems to have some one invisible always conversing with her.[6]

Well, Sarah's relation to God was one thing she had on her mind; another was Jonathan. Soon they were married, she being seventeen and he twenty-three. He became a pastor and she a pastor's wife. Their gifts were complementary; he apparently all books and thought, she, all poise and presence. Together they set up housekeeping and faced the big church at Northampton in western Massachusetts, where he must preach and she must set an example for all the other women; she and he one *équipe* of witness, one common front against the storms that were about to blow.

Regarding marital pleasures Sarah and Jonathan were forgivably reticent. Yet we do have some evidence of their most intimate life together in the form of the regular arrival of new infant family members in their big parsonage. Now (I quote myself) "there is a comic touch here: New England superstition held that a baby's day of birth disclosed its day of conception—and little Sarah (their first child) was born on Sunday, a day when Christians, and ministers in particular, were supposed to be worshiping God and *resting!* The joke gets richer: of the eleven children Sarah Edwards bore, no fewer than six were born on the Sabbath, and a seventh missed by only half an hour. Blessed day of rest!"[7] However we marvel at the stamina of pioneer women, far from modern facilities, in childbirth, we must marvel still more at Sarah Pierpont, who never lost a single one of her eleven to infant disease and death, but brought each one, flourishing under her motherly care, into maturity. The point of providing these domestic details is to make clear that by all outward signs Sarah Pierpont was no stranger to earthly delights. Quite the contrary.

Our topic is delight, and now we may ask if Sarah Pierpont Edwards's delights were limited to these so far indicated—a fondness for meditation, youthful courtship and engagement, the joy of shared work, the marital bed and board, the painful pleasure of child rearing? In fact, there was for her still another delight, deeper, and by her account more intense, than any of these just mentioned. My aim so far has been to show that it came entwined in her life with these other, earthy ones already mentioned.

A second background element must be noted. In 1742, when Sarah Pierpont was already thirty-two, the spiritual movement we call the Great Awakening arrived in New England, breathing new life (and considerable controversy) into Congregational churches including the church in Northampton. Jonathan Edwards became the champion of the movement, and Sarah supported it also, though there were those in the neighborhood and in their own church who vigorously opposed them. The issues divided all New England, opponents and advocates alike becoming deeply involved in the issue. During the Awakening, Sarah experienced a highly significant turn that might have remained unknown to us, had not her husband encouraged her to write out an account of it. This account survives, Thomas Schafer has told me, in private hands, unpublished. However, it has twice been summarized by careful scholars. First, Jonathan Edwards himself employed the account in one of his writings defending the Awakening against its critics.[8] For Edwards it was a piece of prime evidence of the power of the Awakening to change lives. Subsequently, the account was carefully reported by Sereno Dwight in his *Life of President Edwards.*[9] Thereby we have a cross check on its contents.

When the crucial event occurred, Jonathan happened to be away on a preaching trip, so Northampton Sunday services were conducted by a guest minister, one Samuel Buell. Buell believed in the revivals and was conducting weekday services as well. Following custom, he was also a guest in the parsonage, where Sarah would naturally see him frequently. Imagine then the surprise in that household, and in the town, when it became known that while Buell was there, Mrs. Edwards had been seized in her own sitting room by some sort of transport, had fainted more than once, and had had to be carried to her room. How much greater the excitement had it been known that she then spent in that room (and now I quote her reported account) "the sweetest night I ever had in my life" as she glowed with newfound awareness of Christ's love. This included her awareness of Christ's love for her, coming down, she said, like "a pencil of sweet light" into her heart; it also included Christ's love, as she said, "to all mankind," reaching out through her, making her immediately the lover of every soul who ever lived. A limitless love, from Christ to all, passing right through her!

Did it also include erotic stirrings aroused by attractive, young, visiting preacher Sam Buell? Given the evidence, I think the answer must be Probably. It is no secret that throughout Christian history there has been a close convergence between spiritual and sexual passions. The most recent canvassing of the evidence, in a piece by Garry Wills reviewing the televangelism scandals, is aptly titled "The Phallic Pulpit."[10] And in a more Jungian vein, Ann Bedford Ulanov has recently argued that spirituality *is* sexuality; or (less sensationally) that spirit in human beings possesses gender, so that spirituality must be oriented to gender.[11] On such grounds it seems to me reasonable to suppose that there is a sexual component in Sarah Pierpont Edwards's swoon and her night of ecstasy. If however the question is whether she was engaged in an illicit sexual liaison with Samuel Buell or anyone else, the answer is just as clearly No. The reasons are plain: first, she was a truthful woman, and she has told us the story. And second, she lived in a fishbowl of a house, with others constantly coming and going, and if anything out of the ordinary had gone on, it would have been known and gossiped about and the family enemies would not have let the story die. No infidelity marred this story of delight.

Another dimension: Sarah became, she said, a "lover of all mankind." Did this love include those family enemies just mentioned—her own enemies? The people she really hated? Her testimony, and Jonathan's confirmatory report, assert that it did. In that "sweetest night," Sarah found her life being turned round afresh. Friends and supporters such as Sam Buell were the objects of her new esteem, but so was the abominable Mrs. P . . . as she is called in the documents. Mrs. P . . . was a church member given to gossip and troublemaking. Included as well was the execrable Mr. Williams, a preacher from nearby Hadley and an old family rival. Thus, when Jonathan Edwards came home at the end of his own preaching trip, he found a wife collected and calm yet with a memory of days and nights of bliss including that "sweetest night," *and* with a life profoundly changed. Nothing in Jonathan's own experience seemed quite to equal what had happened to her. And he, too, was the object of this new love which she lavished freely upon him, her pastor-lover.

Now if the task were to investigate the authenticity of religious experience, rather than the ethics of delight, we would pause long at this place to test and question Sarah Edwards's episode. I have not even tried to furnish here all the details of the original true story; far less can we linger to hear all its interpreters. In brief, three explanations of Sarah's experience have been proposed. There is a purely medical explanation: She had been ill; fantasies therefore flitted through her head; but she recovered from the whole thing (so Elisabeth Dodds). Then there is a purely psychological explanation. One version of this treats Sarah's fainting and her ecstasies as psychosexual. Stirred from repression, the theory goes, Sarah's libido fastened upon Buell, but her desires were then sublimated into religious aspirations. And finally, there is a purely spiritual explanation: her conversion occurred as a work of the Spirit of God; everything else is irrelevant.

It seems that the medical explanation (winter fatigue, or a bout of flu) leaves too much unexplained. Most of us do not have visions of Jesus when we come down with the flu. Much the same can be said of the psychosexual hypothesis: granted that sexual imagery suffuses the account of this remarkable week in Sarah's life, is sexual repression and sublimated release really an adequate account of the life story of this healthy, sexually active, *pre*-Victorian colonial woman? Yet if we grant that there can be such a thing as spiritual experience, in which in appropriate times and places the human soul opens wide to God and to divine influence, why may not such influence use as its avenue the human psychic mechanisms, including the role of libido and its imagery? At least, that was the thinking of William James, who in *Varieties of Religious Experience*[12] made his own exploration of

Sarah's conversion. Following him, I reckon that each view—the medical, the psychological, the spiritual—may reflect a part of the truth about what happened, while no one view is able to sustain itself without help from the others.

Our own question, though, is different: How do these delights that Sarah Edwards enjoyed—social, erotic, familial, and as now revealed, spiritual—help answer the ethical question: what have these delights to do with morality, with living the good life, with right and wrong? Kant's answer was: Essentially, nothing. Do we now have material with which to give a different answer?

Let me try this: Delights, episodes of intense or prolonged joy such as those just described in the course of one woman's life, function neither as (extrinsic) motives inciting moral conduct, nor as (extrinsic) rewards for moral achievement. Rather such delights are *intrinsic* to the good life as Christians understand it; they are intrinsic to the pilgrimage of faith. In that life, they serve at a very minimum as authentic clues dropped along the path, reassuring the traveler who asks, "Am I on the right road?" "Yes," say the clues, "yes, you are now within sight of the Delectable Mountains, and yonder, still ahead of you, is the Celestial City to which you are traveling." In more prosaic terms, episodes of delight are signs of grace, disclosing to the eyes of believers the gracious character of the entire journey that she or he takes.

Yet in that case, how are we to distinguish those joys and pleasures that are authentic delights from episodes of pleasure that are only false clues, misleading signs, taking us away from the fullness of life proclaimed by Jesus? Should we think of the latter as counterfeits? Or (within a different world-view) as real joys, mischievously planted in the path by our old Enemy? Leaning to the former view, I have two interpretive suggestions: the first is mine; the second will come from Jonathan Edwards. My own is this: to see which clues to regard, we need to see the longer trail, the whole story of a life. Taken by itself, often we simply cannot tell whether a given pleasure is God's gift of delight or only a counterfeit. Imagine a student trying to distinguish a genuine A on her paper from an A that her roommate has put there to cheer her up. It may take time to find out what's what. *Taken by itself*, Sarah could not have told whether her girlish attraction to Jonathan when they met in New Haven, or even her sweetest night of ecstasy, was or was not part of the good life she was to live. Only in the light of their interconnection with other events, experiences, and actions could she know how to read those delights. When we have lived our own lives awhile, the pattern may begin to come clear. Admittedly, though, waiting till the end of life seems a costly method of learning where we should have been along the way. So here we invoke a central methodological principle of Christian ethics: Attend to others' life stories.[13] Read and study the lives of those said to be saints. And at least occasionally, study the life story of an out-and-out scoundrel as well. In another's story we can track delights and counterfeits right through a life, see their source, observe their outcome in a relatively detached way. In the process, we can learn by analogy how to read the delights in our own life. As Matthew 7:20 (REB) states: "you will recognize them by their fruit."

The other answer to our question comes from Jonathan Edwards himself, and his name occasions my return to record the final chapters of Sarah's life. The revival that flowered in her own life story also grew and flourished all over colonial New England, flourished even in self-satisfied Northampton. There it was fanned by Jonathan's eloquence and was nurtured by the teaching and pastoral care that Sarah and he continued to practice. But in the end, the Edwards's enemies won out. They spread tales about him, mainly false or distorted tales, or such complaints as that he spent too much of his salary on a locket for his wife. And they snubbed her. The couple were forced to move to a frontier outpost, where he could preach to local Indians and in his spare time write books, including *The Nature of True Virtue*. Meanwhile, Sarah could become once again a homemaker and mother, and a spiritual counselor to women and men who came long distances to draw on her wisdom and strength. Then, in six more years, a call came to Jonathan to become president of the College of New Jersey, today called Princeton. Shortly after his arrival there, he was to die of a smallpox vaccination that worked too well, and six months later Sarah, weakened by grief and by dysentery, would be dead as well. She would then be forty-seven years old, and by all the evidence, still in love.

Jonathan Edwards's test for authentic delight—delight that is a clue to the good life—was spelled out in *The Nature of True Virtue*, written while he was reflecting on the revivals and on the true meaning of Sarah's "sweetest night." Put briefly, here is his test: when we delight in or love someone or something in a way that opens into or is continuous with our love for all that is, that love is true love, that delight (Edwards called it "love of complacence") is true delight. But when we love (or delight) in a way that by its very nature shuts us off from loving others as well, we have only a disconnected imitation of the real thing, namely, secondary or private love or beauty. Jonathan's erotic love for Sarah and hers for him were always in one sense private, his love meant only for her, hers meant only for him. But in another sense, a love that is by its very nature exclusive— loving my own race or my own nation or my own family or my own spouse in such a way as to make me despise others, or taking possessive, erotic delight in another so as to close me off from God's cordial consent to being—this *exclusive*, competitive love is not a clue to the good life. Just the contrary. This, Sarah had told Jonathan, was what she discovered on her own "sweetest night" and in the days that followed it: she found there a love that held fast to its own but reached out as well to others, even to enemies—even to the annoying Mr. Williams of Hadley, and to the previously unbearable Mrs. P. . . . This love was Christ's love in her.

Now these two suggestions, about narrative and about love as consent, are not alternative to one another. They work very well together. We are to look for those delight-clues that open us to all there is, including especially clues that open us to God who made all the clues and all else. We need as best we can to locate those clues within the whole story of a life, not just in isolated pro-feelings, pleasure-quanta, tickles of the fantasy. This need drives us to look at lives other than our own, for as Robert Burns's verse reminds us, we can see them as we cannot see ourselves. Ideally, we should consult a number of such narratives. As a gesture toward the ideal, let us next consider just one other.

DOROTHY DAY

Dorothy Day was a woman whose sense of delight pulled her not in one direction but two. She may have been in her lifetime America's best known Catholic figure—a woman whose life work changed the direction of the American Catholic Church. Yet she was a part of no hierarchy or religious order, had no office in the Roman Catholic Church or in any church, was desperately poor most of her life, and exercised her amazing influence only in person or through the pages of a flimsy little newspaper she operated with friends, called *The Catholic Worker*.

She lacked the special advantages and liabilities of a Catholic childhood. Her parents did not go to any church, or bother much about whether their children did. Born in Brooklyn (1897), Dorothy's earliest distinct memories were of the family homes in Berkeley and Oakland, California, where they lived until the 1906 earthquake. She remembered *that* well enough: her brass bed sliding to and fro, and a great rumbling sound that came nearer and nearer like a freight train. Put out of work by the quake, her father sold everything and moved the family to Chicago, where Dorothy finished high school. Then there were a couple of college years at Champaign-Urbana, no degree, and her formal education was ended. She was almost nineteen; she had taught herself to write; it was time to hunt a newspaper job in New York City.

It is at this stage, her twentieth, twenty-first, and twenty-second years, that I want to pick up Dorothy Day's story. By this time, the dominant notes in Day's life seem clearly established. On the one hand, she has become a careerist—one of those pioneering, feminist women who could carve out a career as a reporter and writer in a man's world. On the other, she is a deeply sensuous woman, alive to her sexuality, interested in men and attractive to them, impatiently waiting for unconventional romance to come along, sweep her off her feet, carry everything before it like an earthquake. To some extent, these two drives were in competition: you could not take a career seriously and have time for dalliance; a romance that swept everything before it was just going to make trouble for a working woman.

To be sure, work provided opportunity for eros. Her first job was on a Socialist newspaper, the *Call*, writing stories about how a "working girl" could live on five dollars a week, and living the experiment while she wrote about it. Then there were strikes to cover and rallies for radical causes to attend. At all these concourses of life in the city, she could and did meet men. The editor of the paper who had hired her was the well-known radical, Mike Gold, and he was interested in Dorothy. But they never blew their smoldering romance into flame. Then, through friends in Greenwich Village, she met a man named Gene—an alcoholic but fascinating playwright who loved to recite poetry to her while they drank. Gene (Eugene) O'Neill and Dorothy only became friends, though, never lovers. Finally, Dorothy did meet an ex-sailor named Moise, who to her mind was the romantic find of her life. She moved in with him, wanted to give herself to him in every possible way. Unfortunately, Moise was not interested in high romance—it suited him to have an affair and move on. They had the affair, and he did move on, while she had a pregnancy, terminated with a secret and painful abortion. Afterwards, she was full of suicidal despair. Somehow delight, painted in the romantic colors of her girlhood, was not quite what she had expected.

Still, there was that other delight, her work. She kept on writing, even wrote a successful novel, disguising her own experiences in it (somewhat misleadingly, it was titled *The Eleventh Virgin*).[14] She took up with and this time married another man, Barkeley Toby, and traveled with him in Europe before she discovered that once again she had made a mistake. Still, there were newspapers to work for, articles to write, movie writing jobs perhaps to be secured. She was tough, she was liberated, she would make her way.

All the time that Dorothy Day was living in New York (and later in Chicago and then New Orleans) there was another side to her life—another delight besides the delight of her radical journalism and the delight of erotic excitement. She was a secret churchgoer. Not frequent, not regular, the practice was hardly admitted even to herself. Yet the tough working woman, the sexy Dorothy, would slip away by herself, and appear in the back of some city church; sometimes she wept as she sat there. She was terribly afraid that her radical friends would find out about this conduct: she regarded it as a sign of weakness in herself. So here we have delights in conflict. There were the sensual delights of sex and of romantic love (in themselves conflictive). There were the intellectual and adventurous delights of radical journalism: the joy of defending a righteous cause, the comradeship of fellow radicals, the satisfaction of a well-crafted sentence, of good work that meets deadlines, of a growing reputation as a writer. And finally, there were the vague mysterious and somewhat shameful delights associated with the Bible, with church, and with God. Where delights clash, which must prevail, which give way? The narrative must answer.

We take up Dorothy Day's story in her twenty-ninth year. She has returned from New Orleans to New York, still a journalist, and is living in a little shack down by the beach on Staten Island. She was living with a man again—this time a man named Forster Batterham, from western North Carolina, a gentleman radical and an anarchist. On working days she is busy at her typewriter; in leisure time she is with Forster, down at the beach, living close to sand and water, picking up driftwood, fishing and cleaning the fish, talking with the immigrant neighbor in the shack next door. There is the earthy delight of nature and the natural; later she would write about it as her time of "natural happiness." Still present, too, is the steady gravity of career opportunity with its urgent moral causes: the Sacco and Vanzetti trial, the labor movement, the cry for radical reform. And what about God? By now Dorothy slips away regularly, no longer secretly, to attend services at nearby St. Joseph's-by-the-Sea. There is no resolution of her conflict: Forster, fearing the intrusion of religion into their love, does not want her to go to church; she wants Forster to marry her, but he refuses. There is one new element: Dorothy is pregnant with his child.

She was ambivalent about church for herself, but the baby must have the opportunity that she had not had; Teresa Tamar must be baptized a Catholic, be given a Catholic upbringing. The mother's dream would be fulfilled in the daughter. Even Forster joined in, catching a big mess of fish and frying them for the party back at the shack after the baptism. Then, perhaps jealous of the attention drawn away from himself, he refused to stay, and did not come back for days. Before long Dorothy asked that she herself be received as a candidate for baptism. Only now there was trouble. Church rules said that Forster must either move out or marry. He was an anarchist and did not believe in marriage. Why could they not just be true to one another? He loved her dearly. She said he was stubborn. He said she was too religious. They quarreled, broke up, made up, came together again more than once. But at last the church won out. He left, and when he came back, she locked him out so that she could become a good Catholic. He left for good, and a few days later, Dorothy Day was baptized.

By her own account Dorothy, baptized and living in New York City, knew very little about Christian teaching. Her baptismal instructions were provided by severely limited people—a sweet but superstitious old nun, a busy priest. She knew no lay members of her new church at all—indeed, part of its attraction had been its mysterious separateness from the world she did know. She only knew that there, somewhere, lay a love that was deeper, more intense, more whole, than any earthly love, and she knew that that whole love came from God. It was enough. Then opportunity came in the form of a teacher: a wandering, homeless prophet and social theorist named Peter Maurin. Although a poor son of French peasants, Maurin had gained for himself a thorough, if highly focused, education. The focus was on social teaching—what the church must be like to be the church, and what society would be like if it were Christian. There should be no unemployment; everyone should do productive work. Agriculture lay at the basis of life, so did education; therefore love of the land and love of learning must characterize each citizen. Government was worse than useless unless it was rooted in the common people. War was forbidden. As long as there were poor folk, every church should have next door to it a "house of hospitality," open every night to the homeless and the hungry.

Meeting Peter Maurin was for Dorothy Day like meeting herself made whole; he understood, she thought, what she had always wanted to understand. And he was prepared to act. By now the Depression was on, and the unemployed stood on street corners around the nation. She turned her apartment into a House of Hospitality and began cooking soup daily in a huge pot. Peter said there should be a newspaper ("for clarification of thought"), so she borrowed a few dollars and started one, *The Catholic Worker*. She wrote it, edited it, and sold the first copies herself, one cent each, on Union Square. Here was fresh delight, the delight of religious fidelity, the delight of comradeship in work and in daily living. For indeed there were soon guests in the hospitality house, and they never ceased to come as long as she lived. From these 1933 beginnings grew the Catholic Worker Movement, which at its height in the Depression maintained Houses of Hospitality in American cities by the hundred, guided by the paper with its national circulation.

That seemed to leave only one yearning unfulfilled, only the intimate human side of "the long loneliness" that Dorothy Day said was the story of her life to date. What of those erotic longings that had driven her, before, into the careless arms of Moise and Toby and other men, and had all but blinded her to other goods? For a long time after her conversion, these drives seemed merely suppressed. She still had her daughter, growing now into a lovely woman, whom she loved with a fierce, maternal love. There were no more affairs, though at least once she did consider marriage to another man. But finally, she realized, she was satisfied as she was. The delight that had come sufficed.

It is not easy always to be joyful, to keep in mind the duty of delight.

The most significant thing about *The Catholic Worker* is poverty, some say.

The most significant thing is community, others say. We are not alone any more.

But the final word is love. At times it has been, in the words

of Father Zossima, a harsh and dreadful thing, and our very faith
in love has been tried through fire.

   We cannot love God unless we love each other, and to love we
must know each other. We know Him in the breaking of bread,
and we know each other in the breaking of bread, and we are not
alone any more. Heaven is a banquet and life is a banquet, too,
even with a crust, where there is companionship.[15]

These sensuous words were written by Dorothy Day as the conclusion of her autobiography, *The Long Loneliness*. They depict a woman
who has made costly choices, but who has acted always out of desire
and delight—desire at long last for the true good, delight in the good
that at last she could clearly see.

THE CENTRALITY OF DELIGHT

What do we learn from these two narratives, Sarah Pierpont Edwards's and Dorothy Day's, about the ethics of delight? At the least,
they give us by way of illustration a case for making delight central in
any faithful account of Christian morality. It might be claimed that
delight is just not what we are talking about when we talk in moral
terms, not what we contemplate when we take up the moral point of
view. But such a claim must depend heavily upon stipulation. While
we can grant the possibility of focusing morality in so narrow a way
that delight is excluded from the reckoning, such a narrow focus will
not grow from an examination of richly Christian lives such as those
of Sarah Pierpont Edwards and Dorothy Day. In those lives, delight
is not only present, it is centrally present; to exclude it from account
would mean taking a narrow view indeed of the making of right and
wrong, good and evil, in their lives. For if we thus construe morality
broadly as the shaping of life itself, delight is for these lives a central
component that cannot rightly be omitted.

   Yet aside from mere stipulation in favor of the broad or narrow, the
inclusive or the exclusive view of what constitutes morality (and more
particularly, of what constitutes Christian morality) it is not easy to
know how to choose between these moral theories. An obvious move
might be to widen the circle of biographical studies, making no gen-
eralizations until many life narratives lay open before us. This move
seems to me not only obvious but imperative, and it is one in which
I myself have from time to time been engaged. In a more systematic

fashion, Carol Gilligan has gathered data on childhood moral development from girls as well as boys, and has used the results to challenge the (mainly) Kantian understanding of her senior colleague, Lawrence Kohlberg.[16]

Yet however wide our biographical sweep, a conceptual problem would remain: are we talking here about two different sets of phenomena, two fields of human response called "moral," the one focused perhaps upon duty, law, and prohibitions, the other upon such features as consent, delight, and love? Or are these two aspects of one field, one single sort of phenomenon, so that our question is about the adequacy of delight (or in the contrary case, duty) to comprehend that single field? No gathering of sociological data, or even of life-histories, can by itself resolve this conceptual problem.

My own way of proceeding cannot be fully explored within the limits of the present essay. But perhaps a line of direction can be sketched in. Delight seems naturally to take its rise in that strand of Christian morality that is concerned with our lives in their continuity with the natural environment, our bodies as part of earth's crust, our selves as God's creatures amid God's creation. Duty, on the other hand, takes its rise in another, social strand of the moral life. In it, our primary engagements are not with the natural but with the social order. (This can be seen by observing that duties are duties *to* someone or *under* some law or rule existing in some social setting, and if they are duties to God, then to God as Lawgiver, Father, and Friend—each of these being itself a *social* metaphor for conceiving Divinity[17]). The question to be asked, then, is whether delight is marginalized as a moral factor once we take up the social strand and think within it? To ask the question though, is to answer it. However we construe the nature of Christian social morality and the moral law that gives point to its precepts, delight is no transient stranger there. It is the very stuff of our social existence in biblical perspective. At the very beginning of the Psalms, the author celebrates one whose "*delight* is in the law of the LORD" (Psalm 1:2 REB). And in Jesus his followers found not a canceling but rather a refocusing of that very quality of delight:

> Whole-offerings and sin-offerings you did not delight in.
> Then [Christ] said 'Here I am: as it is written of me in the scroll,
> I have come, O God, to do your will.'
>
> (Heb. 10:6–7 REB)

Here "doing God's will," which I take to be a function of second-strand or social morality, becomes the occasion of delight. And as it is for the Christ, so it is for his followers—see for example Romans 7:22, and note the regular association in New Testament communities of the gift of the Spirit, joy, and rejoicing.

To offer now a theoretical generalization, we could say that in Christian perspective *social practices* (reading the law and keeping it [Ps. 1], accepting costly persecution [Matt. 5:10–11], creating Christian community [Acts 2:41–47]) were in themselves occasions of delight; in them delight is shared and thereby discloses its own social character. And a similar case, omitted here for brevity, can be made for delight as a third, anastatic or eschatological strand of Christian existence.[18]

All this can be concisely illustrated in the present discussion by returning briefly to those flawed accounts of Sarah Pierpont Edwards's "sweetest night." How easy it seemed for commonsensical mid-twentieth century interpreters of Sarah's story to attribute her experience to illness (perhaps influenza?), or for post-Freudian readers to assign her delight to the realm of the psychosexual. There is nothing necessarily erroneous about either attribution; Sarah may very well have been ill, and it seems credible that like other sexually constituted women she was moved by libido. What is defective, indeed pitiable, about these explanations is their reductionism, and here the peculiar reduction that explains everything in terms of the interpreter's context and ethos without sensing any need to discover the context and ethos of the biographical subject. But if Sarah was delighted, and uniquely so on that sweetest night, it makes vast good sense for us to understand her delight in *its own* terms. We need to hear what *she* had to say, to find that the Savior's presence, and the consequent "love to all" that she enjoyed, counted as delights for her precisely because her life was formed in a human and divine milieu in which just such delight was properly and definitively central. If our own lives and our own delights are different, that does not necessarily cast an unfavorable shadow over her and hers. Perhaps instead Sarah Pierpont Edwards's is a normative story of authentic Christian delight in its socially interactive strand.

It is along these lines, then, that I would argue for the wide reach of delight as a possible focus for understanding Christian ethics. A misunderstanding can arise even yet, however, and it is fitting to say a word to avert it before closing. The misunderstanding involves submitting delight (or joy) to a quantitative calculation, so that the ethics of delight becomes no more than one variant of utilitarianism, a variant in which values are assigned to various delights, with the moral life to be guided by a quantified delight-calculus. The ethical task then becomes the impossible one of weighing or grading delight-quotients and summing them up in hypothetical arrays. But this is alien to the way of Jesus, which as noted above leads the disciple into not-at-all-delightful persecution—a leading at which disciples are nevertheless to rejoice. This is not to deny that Jesus' way is *on the whole* a way of greater delight than any other; it is only to say that the final evaluation of that way in those terms remains a heavenly, not an earthly task ("great shall be your reward *in heaven*"). The way Jesus leads is discovered, not by quantified prior calculation, but by uncalculating love that follows its Lord and faithfully submits to Christian practice.

What is finally the issue here is what I have in *Ethics* called "decisionism"—the mistaken belief that people occupy neutral survey posts, located high above life's pathways, from which vantage points they can estimate their own best opportunities and "decide" accordingly. It was not so for Dorothy Day or Sarah Edwards, and it will not be so for us. Rather, what seem to be our choices are made *in via*, along the way; and if we are followers of Jesus Christ, the delight we experience will not be calculated in advance, but will by his promise arise as confirmation of the way already taken. So delight is indeed a crucial component of the moral life, but it is not a computational component. Rather it is an intrinsic, given element in the narrative process of life in Christ.

To return to our own argument in closing, I have sought to show that delight as here understood does not stand alone; as a moral term it cries out for a more full account, for the whole story, which in its turn must embrace other strands of morality than the first, in whose terms my biographical illustrations have largely been cast.[19] In these other strands, the social and the anastatic, delight returns to show the way.

Yet all this is programmatic: it indicates work to be done in this mode, rather than reporting upon work already done. The most that has been shown is that the ethics of delight raises to our eyes a strand of human life that cannot be denied or swept over. It has its own majesty, its own loveliness, makes its own moral claim. To invoke again the name of Jonathan Edwards, for him delight was precisely the means by which God guides all our lives. For, he wrote, the will is as the greatest apparent good is. God has then only to set before us our true good as the greatest apparent good, and appearance and reality must merge; our wills are drawn to our true good, and we to that long home that awaits us.

70

NOTES

1. See Immanuel Kant, *Fundamental Principles of the Metaphysics of Morals,* trans. Thomas K. Abbott, with an introduction by Marvin Fox, The Library of Liberal Arts (Indianapolis: Bobbs–Merrill Co., 1949), 17f.

2. Immanuel Kant, *Religion Within the Limits of Reason Alone,* trans. Theodore M. Greene and Hoyt H. Hudson, cont. J. Silber (New York: Harper & Brothers; Harper Torchbooks/Cloister Library, 1960), 18f.

3. James Wm. McClendon, Jr., *Ethics: Systematic Theology, Volume 1* (Nashville: Abingdon Press, 1986), chapters 3–5.

4. John Bunyan, *The Pilgrim's Progress and Grace Abounding,* ed. and introduction by James Thorpe (Boston: Houghton Mifflin Co., 1969), 170f.

5. Elisabeth D. Dodds, *Marriage to a Difficult Man: The "Uncommon Union" of Jonathan and Sarah Edwards* (Philadelphia: Westminster Press, 1971).

6. Jonathan Edwards, *The Works of President Edwards,* ed. Sereno Edwards Dwight, 10 vols. (New York: Carvill, 1830), vol. 1, 114f. Volume 1 contains Dwight's biography of Edwards.

7. McClendon, *Ethics,* 114.

8. See Jonathan Edwards, *Some Thoughts Concerning the Revival,* ed. C. C. Goen in volume 4, *The Works of Jonathan Edwards* (New Haven, Conn.: Yale University Press, 1957), 331–341.

9. Edwards, *Works of President Edwards,* vol. 1, 171–186.

10. Garry Wills, "The Phallic Puplit," *New York Review of Books* (December 1989): 21.

11. Ann Bedford Ulanov, "'Two Sexes'" in Philip Turner, ed., *Men and Women: Sexual Ethics in Turbulent Times* (Cambridge, Mass.: Cowley, 1989).

12. William James, *The Varieties of Religious Experience: A Study in Human Nature* (New York: New American Library of World Literature, 1958), 219–224.

13. See James Wm. McClendon, Jr., *Biography as Theology: How Life Stories Can Remake Today's Theology* (Nashville: Abingdon Press, 1974), chapters 1 and 7.

14. Dorothy Day, *The Eleventh Virgin* (New York: Albert & Charles Boni, 1924).

15. Dorothy Day, *The Long Loneliness* (New York: Harper & Brothers, 1952), 285.

16. See Lawrence Kohlberg, *Philosophy of Moral Development,* vol. 1 of *Essays on Moral Development* (San Francisco: Harper & Row, 1981) and Carol Gilligan, *In a Different Voice* (Cambridge, Mass.: Harvard University Press, 1982).

17. McClendon, *Ethics,* chapter 6.

18. Ibid., chapter 9.

19. On the several strands, see Ibid., chapter 2.

6

Ethics and the Challenge of
Theological Non-Realism

Joseph Runzo

Theological *non*-realism presents a fundamental challenge to objective theism. Its attraction comes from the fact that the move to non-realism is justified by appealing to ethics. And coming from within the theological circle, in important respects this new challenge supplants even the long-standing challenge of a-theism.

In the nineteenth century, Dostoyevsky enunciated the theist's growing ethical concern about the rise of atheistic nihilism: If God is dead, would not *everything* be permitted? However, contemporary theological *non*-realists, while rejecting nihilism, also reject this idea that the death of (the old) God must lead to moral anarchy. Quite the contrary, as Don Cupitt puts it: "A God out there and values out there, if they existed, would be *utterly* useless and unintelligible to us. There is nothing to be gained by nostalgia for the old objectivism, which was in any case used only to justify arrogance, tyranny and cruelty. People [forget] . . . how utterly hateful the old pre-humanitarian world was."[1] Thus the question today is often less "Why believe in God?" than "Why talk about God at all?" As Gordon Kaufman notes, "Our world is not so much characterized by conscious atheism . . . or even explicit agnosticism, as it is by the utter irrelevance of God."[2]

Even a century and a half ago, when Napoleon asked the great French astronomer and mathematician, Pierre-Simon Laplace, about the place of God in the scheme of things, Laplace responded that he could "find no need of this hypothesis." For the theist, the only answer to this modern sense of the irrelevance of God, must be that talk about God is meaningful, because it makes life, and especially the moral life, meaningful.

While many traditional arguments against objective theism are epistemological, metaphysical, linguistic, or historicist,[3] the most powerful objections are moral, and often undergird these other arguments. For the moral life is elemental to the religious life, and talk of God is supposed to clarify, support, and extend our understanding of the ethical. Theological non-realism poses such a potent challenge to objective theism precisely because ethical considerations provide the fundamental impetus—and the principal attraction—of the emergent non-realism. Don Cupitt, for example, argues from our modern insistence on the necessity for autonomy in moral matters to an anti-realist theology and a "new Christian ethics," and Gordon Kaufman supports a non-realist approach to theology in light of our moral responsibility for the grave nuclear and ecological problems we have created.

I argue that theological realism, rather than non-realism, better accounts for both the basis of normative ethical judgments, and more broadly, for taking the moral point of view. After explaining the putative need for a theologically *non*-realist view to meet the demands of the ethical life, I will suggest five ways in which theological non-realism is self-defeating because it offers an inadequate account of the very ethical considerations for which it was meant to account. Having shown that theological non-realism is internally defective in a way in which realism is not, I will conclude by suggesting several positive reasons for holding to theological realism rather than to non-realism, given the demands of ethics.

THEOLOGICAL REALISM AND NON-REALISM

Theological realism is the view that God exists (in part if not wholly) independently of the human mind. Theological non-realism denies this. In its historically strongest form, theological realism holds that God is a transcendent, self-subsistent entity: God possesses aseity. Traditionally, theologians—whether Augustine or Philo; Aquinas or Al-Ghazali or Maimonides; Karl Barth or Karl Rahner—uniformly have been realists.[4] But being a theological realist is not necessarily tantamount to being a theological traditionalist. Paul Tillich is a theological realist. John Hick, a religious pluralist, centrally holds the "basic religious conviction" that religious experience, including the-istic experience, is not, "a realm of illusory projection but is . . . at least in part, an effect within human consciousness of the presence and pressure of a transcendent divine Reality."[5] The feminist theo-logian, Sallie McFague, argues that "Christian faith is . . . most basi-cally a claim that the universe is neither indifferent nor malevolent but that there is a power (and a personal power at that) which is on the side of life and its fulfillment," and that "God as mother, lover, and friend of the world as God's body is both transcendent to the world . . . and profoundly immanent in the world."[6]

Theological realists most fundamentally hold that unless theism involves ontological reference to such a God, there is little if any point to the religious life. Non-realists, on the other hand, hold that the true significance of the religious (and moral) life can be found apart from any such metaphysical claims and conceptions. As Don Cupitt neatly sums the non-realist position: "What then is God? God is a unifying symbol that eloquently personifies and represents to us everything that spirituality requires of us. . . . the divine attributes represent to us various aspects of the spiritual life, and God's nature as spirit represents the goal we are to attain."[7]

Two principal types of arguments from ethics are used to support non-realism. Gordon Kaufman presents one type of argument in *The-ology for a Nuclear Age*. Emphasizing our full responsibility for the ecological as well as the potential nuclear disasters we face, Kaufman asks what the radically new possibility of self-annihilation in the nuclear age means for humanity's basic self-understanding, and therefore for theology.[8] Viewing theology as "imaginative construc-tion," not merely "handing down" the theological tradition but nec-essarily reinterpreting it for the present community, Kaufman concludes that we must not try to depend on a God "out there," but restrict our talk about God to that which "makes possible all creativity and life."[9]

This turn to language about a completely immanent God stems in part from an underlying Kantian view that God in Godself would be noumenal and transcendently unknowable.[10] More fundamentally, though, it is based on the deeper concern for ethics and the mean-ingful life, rather than these epistemological and metaphysical con-cerns. "The proper criterion for our talk about God," says Kaufman, "is not the postulation of some being or reality beyond the world but rather concern with the relativizing and *humanizing* activity going on within the world."[11] For Kaufman, traditional theological symbolism

74

is "more a hindrance than a help" because it is partially responsible for our blindness to ecological concerns and tends to legitimize our parochial political objectives. Thus on ethical grounds he argues for the non-realist view that God should be understood "as the unifying symbol of those powers and dimensions of the ecological and historical feedback network which create and sustain and work to further enhance all life . . . conditions which have made human existence possible, which continue to sustain it, and which may draw it out to a fuller humanity and humaneness."[12]

In important respects, Kaufman's position is not as radically revisionist as it might seem. His non-realist use of theistic language does not preclude a noumenal God (Kant), and the idea that God should not be thought of as *a* being or individual is shared with many theologians (for example, Tillich). Moreover, the positive thrust of Kaufman's turn to theological non-realism is the prevailing attempt to make theism relevant to, and the theist aware of her or his responsibility for, the pressing ethical issues of our day. Kaufman's call is one for "service and self-sacrifice," a call to see Jesus *not* as the triumphal judge—depicted, for example, in Michelangelo's Sistine Chapel "Last Judgment"—but as, in Bonhoeffer's phrase, "a man for others."

Significantly, this form of non-realism is not reductionist. The religious life and religious belief is more than just the moral life and belief. Kaufman insists that God is the "'ultimate point of reference,' that in terms of which everything else is to be understood, that beyond which we cannot move in imagination, thought, or devotion."[13] He thinks that a "narrowly naturalistic" way of conceiving of God does not do justice to the actual conditions which have created human existence, and hence that in our contemporary conception of God we must posit a "hidden creativity at work in the historico-cultural process."[14] So this non-realist approach retains strong ties with the long tradition of theological realism. This is not the case with a second way of arguing for non-realism, exemplified by the work of Don Cupitt.

Cupitt holds that traditional theological realism is unremittingly destructive of the moral and religious life. In his earlier work, *Taking Leave of God*, he expresses this by saying that "there cannot and must not be any religious interest in any extra-religious existence of God; such a thing would be a frivolous distraction."[15] In his recent book, *The New Christian Ethics*, he declares, taking Dostoyevsky's query head on: "While the old God was about, he prevented Christian ethics from becoming truly creative . . . Only through the death of that God does Christian ethics at last acquire the duty and the authority to create value *ex nihilo*, which marks it as truly Christian and enables it to redeem our life."[16] Hence, like Kaufman, Cupitt begins his theological inquiry with ethical considerations, emphasizing *our* moral responsibility. His rejection of the traditional ontology of realist theology is primarily based on his view of the relation between ethics and theology. But Cupitt's non-realism is more radically revisionist:

> The more "objective" your theology is, the more you will suppose yourself to be in possession of a kind of literal account of God's nature and dealings with men, and the more open your belief will be to severe moral criticism. . . . it is the most highly developed dogmatic theologies which represent God in the most repellent light. And it will not do to say, "It's only symbolism," if the symbolism is in fact morally repellent.[17]

In contrast, Kaufman believes that "there remain depths of meaning and profundity in the central Christian symbols, I am persuaded, which are worth our attention as we face one of the most frightening dilemmas with which history has confronted humankind."[18]

Moreover, unlike Kaufman, Cupitt's revisionist account of religion is also reductionist. For Cupitt, the most fundamental feature of truly ethical action (which creates value) is autonomy.[19] And the insidious—and inextirpable—moral deficiency of the old theological realism, as Cupitt portrays it, is that it promulgates a heteronomous relation with God, where morality is treated as a set of "guide rails" constraining and directing humans from outside.[20] Thus, engendering a sense of one's own worthlessness, theological realism can only lead to pessimism. For Cupitt, then, "The *first* task is to create enough value, to inject enough meaning and weight into our human world to make life worth living at all;" this is "the life that is ethically creative. . . . creat[ing] value where previously there was no value . . ."[21] Therefore, Cupitt offers the reductionist view of religious ethics that we now "have to do what God used to do for us. . . . Our immediate task is to *secularize* and humanize the Christian self . . ."[22]

To see whether non-realism succeeds in the ethical task it sets as its *raison d'etre*, let us look more closely at this latter, thoroughly revisionist non-realism, which Cupitt refers to as "Christian humanism."[23]

DEFICIENCIES OF A NON-REALIST CHRISTIAN HUMANISM

There are at least five internal deficiencies in this non-realist Christian humanism vis-á-vis morality. The first internal problem results from the fact that Cupitt's ethics is non-cognitivist.[24] A purely secular non-cognitivist meta-ethics, whether or not it is correct, is consistent. But a *religious* ethical non-cognitivism of the sort Cupitt proposes is self-defeating. Cupitt argues that Christian humanism is superior to secular humanism because it "explicitly presents itself as a temporalization and humanization of God. Thus the human being acquires a dignity and a status that is directly derived from the ancient holiness and worshipfulness of God. God indeed just was a symbol of the goal towards which our moral development is heading and of the dignity to which we should ultimately attain."[25] But this approach encourages us to engage in self-deception. While acknowledging that God does not exist, we are to continue to use traditional language about God—such as in the Psalms or the Beatitudes—because this will transfer a special holiness and nobility to our ethical striving. However, monotheistic language, and traditional theistic texts, are realist in intent, historically deriving the ethical reverence they inspire from the sense of the presence of a transcendent Thou. This is like suggesting that when we reach the age of reason we should continue to give deference to the moral authority of our parents, because this will enhance the sense of the seriousness of morality, even while recognizing that our parents have no particular moral authority. The trouble here is that self-deception is a character trait we have a moral obligation to diminish as much as possible. So Cupitt's call to Christian humanism is a call, though unintended, to morality based in part on cultivating a morally deficient character trait.

A second internal problem with this non-realist "Christian humanism" is that it provides little check, despite Cupitt's sensitivity to this issue, against moral anarchy. This stems from Cupitt's particular historicist perspective. He argues that "*all* frames—whether we are talking about religion, morality, scientific theory, philosophy, logic or whatever—*all* frames are historical-cultural improvisations. . . . We make truth and we make values."[26] Applying this to theism and ethics, he reaches the non-realist conclusion that "Religion can no longer be defined in terms of belief in God . . . [it is] a continual human creative work. . . . Morality, correspondingly, will no longer be seen as the constraint of human behaviour by some set of invisible but objective, unchanging and very solemn guide-rails. It will be seen

77

as our own continual creative production of new values."[27] Let us grant the general historicist (and even relativist) perspective held by Cupitt, as well as Kaufman and many non-realists, that truth and value are socio-historically conditioned. And surely religion and morality have no value unless they are practical and relevant to present needs and purposes. So far we have a pragmatist-relativism not unlike William James's.[28] Yet James was an objective theist.

Cupitt suggests that "to enhance the authority of the ethical by pretending that it is . . . grounded somewhere beyond the changes and chances of our historical life, is now at an end."[29] But our historicity does not entail that nothing exists beyond our conventions. If nothing else, that would be a parochial homocentrism. Further, though, the fact that we can only understand reality within the limitations of our structuring world-views does not tell us what *is*, only what *is possible* from our perspective, and what we know of the possible. Unless one holds the crassest sort of verificationism, how could we *know* that there is nothing beyond *our* possible knowledge? Hence, our historicity does not, in itself, preclude theological realism from accounting for the present socio-historically conditioned demands of morality.

Cupitt additionally holds the stronger thesis that our human historicity makes our differently enculturated world-views *incommensurate*. While we structure the world we live in, on Cupitt's extreme historicist (and relativist)[30] conception, "just where the lines are drawn doesn't matter."[31] Thus Christianity itself, he says, "has no essence. It is perfectly free to become whatever we can succeed in making it into," and in morality, because the underlying world-views have changed, "we cannot say that we are right and [some earlier view is] wrong; only that we are different from them."[32] If differences of world-view really led to incommensurability, this would obviate dialogue across differing world-views,[33] leaving us subject to the moral anarchy of isolated, idiosyncratic views. Moreover, in one sense, we *can* make Christianity anything we want it to be. This recalls Humpty Dumpty's words in *Through the Looking Glass*: "When *I* use a word it means just what I choose it to mean." As Humpty points out, this shows that *we* "are the master."[34] Of course, we also change the *topic* if we sufficiently change the meaning of a term. In reducing the Christian life to the moral life, it would seem that Cupitt changes not just the significance of religious terms, but the very topic.

Again, to address another way Cupitt puts his point, it *does* matter what we say the world is like. As is evident in Cupitt's own treatment of ethical standards, we need to be able to say that some views with which we disagree are wrong. Recognizing the Dostoyevskian warning that "anything might be permitted," Cupitt attempts to provide a standard for right moral action: "The best Christian life is the life that is dedicated to those who are of the least account, those who are the most victimized—and your own vocabulary will give you a pretty good idea of who they are."[35] Yet surely the vocabulary of a community cannot, in itself, serve as the criterion of what is value-making, and who is victimized. To use an example of Cupitt's, Nazis, with their more developed view, might have a vocabulary—"Jews are an inferior race"—which does indicate who is victimized, and hence whom we should value more highly. Consider, though, the more provincial Ku Klux Klan. The Klansman will often justify his negative treatment of others primarily on the basis of a perceived prejudice against *him*—he is the victim (in his mind). If world-views are incommensurate and there are no shared, cross-schema moral standards, relying on "one's own vocabulary" would count the Klansman right and allow for moral anarchy.

We do not agree with the Klansman. We do not agree because of a standard to which Cupitt himself appeals: "There are a lot of people who think that if you are an anti-realist about morality/science/religion, then you must think it doesn't matter what is believed about morality/science/religion. But . . . I am a Christian humanitarian, and I think it is very important that we should all detest cruelty and try to banish it from our social relationships."[36]

It is just this strong moral stance in Cupitt's non-realism which commands respect. But then some things are paradigmatically wrong, and not just a matter of people thinking differently. To take the moral point of view at the least entails believing that cruelty is wrong. Consequently, there do appear to be some general moral standards—the very standards, it would seem, by which we judge Nazis and Klansmen to have acted wrongly. So the incommensurability of Cupitt's radically subjective non-realism is self-defeating. Trans-world-view standards are the antidote to the moral anarchy of subjectivism.

The third and fourth self-defeating aspects of non-realism are closely related. In his turn to "Christian humanism," Cupitt insists that the importance of ethics in our modern age is to conquer nihilism, not sin. But Cupitt's non-realist imprecation to create value, and his laudable vision and encouragement of the morally transformed self, can be evoked as effectively, it seems to me, without any reference to religion. In "The Creed of a Scientific Humanist," Julian Huxley, starting from the view, not unlike Cupitt's, that "it is among human personalities that there exist the highest and most valuable achievements of the universe," is surely correct to say "many men and women have led active, or self-sacrificing, or noble, or devoted lives without any belief in God."[37] Hence we must ask, "Why be a *Christian* humanist, and not simply a secular humanist?"[38] Cupitt's rejoinder is that a *religious* ethics is important because religion holds that the moral standards of contemporary society are too low. This misses the issue. Thoughtful theological realists, non-realists, and secular humanists all agree that caring about others, charity, and self-awareness among humankind leave much to be desired. The question is why a *religious* call to raise our ethical sights would be any stronger or more motivating than a purely secular appeal.

Bertrand Russell's clarion call in "A Free Man's Worship" to "expel all eagerness of temporary desire, to burn with passion for eternal things" is *prima facie* as inspired and motivating as Cupitt's position; Russell's dedication to disarmament was, in and of itself, as convicting to general society as the proclamation of a Roman Catholic bishop or the pacifist stance of the Mennonites. Once more Cupitt has a rejoinder: Religion, he says, provides a "supportive symbolic and institutional context"[39] for ethics. But again, this appeal to the symbolism of Christianity to retain the positive *affective* aspects of earlier "Christian" ethics without the putatively destructive cognitive aspects, is, from a reductive, non-realist perspective, to appeal to a known fiction; to encourage self-deception. Second, even if religious institutions are demonstrably supportive of a heightened moral awareness, the same is clearly true of purely secular institutions like UNICEF, Amnesty International, and the American Civil Liberties Union. If secular humanitarian institutions are as morally conative and affective as religious institutions, then on the non-realist account itself, the negative metaphysical baggage of Christian symbolism and tradition undermines any reason to be a Christian humanist rather than a secular humanist. In this way, the non-realist attempt to retain a Christian humanism becomes self-defeating.

This brings us to the fourth, related internal difficulty with Cupitt's position. Cupitt holds that theological objectivism is inimical to the essential autonomy of ethical action: "It is a contradiction to suppose that my highest spiritual freedom could be determined for me from without, and by the act of another."[40] He argues that "all reference to any supernatural world or beings or forces must be expunged or, at the very least, given a purely natural interpretation . . .”[41] Thus religion is reduced to naturalistic phenomena and the religious life to the moral life.[42] But does the classic question of whether obedience to God destroys the agent’s autonomy really drive us to this non-realist conclusion?

True, master/slave, parent/young child, and officer/blindly obedient soldier relationships either lack or destroy autonomy and so restrict the moral agency of the second party. But not all obedience is of this sort. Obedience must be not only total, but unquestioning to be destructive of autonomous moral action. As responsible adults, we often obey our parents, our spouses or our close friends. We do so because we love and trust them, have usually found their moral advice sound, and feel free to question a directive which goes against our basic moral sense. We remain autonomous, moral agents. In much the same way, obedience to (a realist) God does not entail the loss of autonomy. For the mature person of faith must not only be obedient, but *committed* to (what they take to be) the divine moral imperatives in themselves. We should not love the disadvantaged, the disenfranchised, and even the disagreeable only because God so wishes it—indeed this would not be love. We should value them for themselves, as well as because God values them.[43] Non-realism, then, is internally defective insofar as it is based on the erroneous assumption that obedience to God necessarily *entails* loss of autonomy.

This brings us to a fifth, and perhaps the most trenchant, deficiency of a theological non-realist framework. The imperative to create value and the “higher” standard of valuing those who are least valued, which Cupitt calls for, requires new directions and even fundamental changes in society. Now, genuine dialogue is essential for resolving any social ethical issue. And the importance of genuine dialogue in ethics is even more evident in a pluralistic society, with its conflicting and not just divergent points of view. Yet genuine dialogue is not possible without mutual respect. Mutual respect among persons is itself basic to taking the moral point of view. So *if* we wish to promote rational dialogue on normative moral issues, we must begin by taking the moral point of view.[44] But *non*-realism fails to explain adequately why we should take the moral point of view in the first place. To see this, we will need to say more about the moral point of view.

In order to form a moral community, though we may disagree about particular moral judgments, we must share *meta-criteria,* whether implicit or explicit, for deciding moral issues. There are certain obvious, standard meta-criteria for rational assessment between any alternative views—whether in science, religion, morality, or everyday affairs. These include *semantic* meaningfulness, consistency, and coherence—the more formal, "logical" standards of rationality. Additionally, there are *value*-centered criteria which we employ (often implicitly) when we take another world-view seriously. For even if the truth-claims of our own or the other world-view do not violate any intellectual obligations, and are therefore *epistemically* justified, the ultimate justification of our beliefs and judgments is our most fundamental value judgment about what best helps us fulfill our goals and gives meaning to our lives. Hence these additional, value-centered meta-criteria include which view is judged better to explain and give meaning to life, which better coheres with and explains one's currently held normative ethical theory, and, most fundamentally, which view best conforms to taking the moral point of view.[45]

Now, Cupitt himself addresses the crucial question: "Why be moral?" (or "Why take the moral point of view?"). He rejects the notion that we should be moral because it is in our self-interest, and argues that "our life is *objectively* worthless . . . it's all up to us and we are entirely free to establish, if we can, the convention that each human life is unique and of infinite worth. . . . The morality that it is rational to prefer is the morality with the greatest power to inject value into life, and that morality is the Christian morality . . ."[46] In the first place, Cupitt's appeal to rationality here just returns us to self-interest as the motive for the moral life. We want to be rational because it is prudent. That aside, why suppose it is "most rational" to prefer a morality which—unqualified—"injects value into life"? Perhaps I cannot rationally choose to act only in my self-interest. But cannot I be perfectly *rational* and sometimes choose to act immorally? Or choose to benefit only a small, select group of people? Here we think of the sort of case which Dorothy Sayers neatly poses in "Dilemma": "If you could get a million pounds, without any evil consequences to yourself, by merely pressing a button which would electrocute a single unknown Chinaman ten thousand miles away— would you press the button? . . . Think of the *good* one could do with a million pounds."[47] The kind of action contemplated here *might* be rational, but it is contrary to the moral point of view. Yet on Cupitt's non-realist account, to take the moral point of view and treat all persons as ends and not means, would seem to be a matter of luck, or if you prefer, natural inclination. There is nothing more to which to appeal. And adding "Christian" to what he refers to as "rational" morality will only change the case if this introduces the *standards* underlying the Christian tradition of humanitarian value. But Cupitt rejects any such appeal to tradition, since there is no essence to Christianity, and no objective value even to human life. We are left with only prudence as a reason for taking the moral point of view.

THE MORAL LIFE AND THEOLOGICAL REALISM

Theological *realism* not only avoids the foregoing internal problems of non-realism but additionally offers a nonprudential, and not merely fortuitous reason, to take the moral point of view. To see this, let us turn to two specific moral issues.

Consider for instance three principal views on the question of nuclear deterrence. One might be a just war theorist, and in our current nuclear age suggest an extremely careful and circumscribed approach to the policy of nuclear deterrence.[48] Or one might be a just war theorist, but a nuclear pacifist. Or one might be a pacifist, and therefore a nuclear pacifist. Secularists, non-realists, and realists could hold any of these three views about nuclear deterrence. Certainly the historicist considerations Cupitt appeals to no more support a non-realist than a theological realist approach, as having a better moral congruence with any of these three views. Indeed, both pacifism and just war theory have been strongly represented within traditional theological realism. In all three contemporary positions regarding nuclear deterrence, there is a moral obligation to avoid war. For the pacifist this obligation is exceptionless. For the just war theorist/ nuclear pacifist there is a *prima facie* obligation to avoid war, and the moral considerations which *could* override this obligation vis-á-vis conventional warfare—for example, to preserve human freedom and a just social order—are themselves overridden in the case of nuclear deterrence by the possibility of violating the *Jus ad bellum* criteria of proportionality and *Jus in bello* criteria of both proportionality and discrimination for a just war.[49] Last, for the just war theorist who allows for nuclear deterrence, the danger of violating proportionality and discrimination can be overridden by a belligerent's nuclear threat to a just social order so that, though lamentable, nuclear deterrence is a justifiable political policy.

In general, whether one dismisses the value of God-talk, thinks of God in non-realist terms, or holds theological realism, does *not* determine one's normative ethical position on questions of broad social issues. This is what we would expect in a pluralistic society. For we have social cohesion in large part because—despite our religious, meta-ethical, and other differences—we frequently subscribe to normative moral views which cut across those differences. On the other hand, to come to a resolution—or achieve a *new* consensus—in a pluralistic society on grave moral issues like nuclear deterrence, requires a concerted dialogue in which we respect the contrary views of others. Yet on Cupitt's incommensurability thesis, such a dialogue between world-views is not possible. However, unless we can respect the ethical views of others, respecting them as persons, we will be prevented from fully taking the moral point of view.

Next, to set the positive support for the moral life which theological realism offers against non-realism, consider the moral issue of sexism. To avoid sexist thought and action and thus to try to reverse a long history of treating half of the human race as intellectual, spiritual, or moral inferiors, will not be just a matter of both males and females *acting* differently than we have in the past. As historical beings, our world-views are importantly determined by our past, and so we must *change our world-views* if we are to fundamentally change our social actions. This is the sort of theological project which Sallie McFague undertakes in *Models of God*. Proposing that we need a new ethic in the face of nuclear threat and ecological disaster, she argues for a more "female" model of "responsibility and care" rather than the traditional "male" model of competing rights.[50] She suggests that whereas king/subject models of God have tended to perpetuate hierarchical sexist (as well as racist and class) language and action, theological models of the world as God's body and God as mother, lover, and friend offer enriching ways to perceive a less divisive interdependence with God, with each other, and with the world. Clearly, many secular humanists (feminists as well as just the morally sensitive) have been leaders in the move to break down the bonds of sexism. But theological *realism* adds a new dimension to this ethical reorientation. As McFague neatly puts it, "to have faith in God . . . is to believe that the universe is neither malevolent nor indifferent but is on the side of life and its fulfillment."[51]

This points to two sorts of meta-ethical considerations which separate theological realists from both non-realists and secular humanists. First, on a theological realist account, there are *objective* standards, apart from what humans happen to think, which in part determine what is moral—such as whether the principles behind engaging in nuclear deterrence, or in employing gender-based pay discrimination, are moral. This gives the theological realist a further reason, unavailable to the non-realist and secular humanist, for utterly opposing sexism and for pursuing policies to avoid war, whether as a pacifist or just war theorist. Whatever humanitarian reasons, and whatever filial feelings of care and nurturing toward others we may have, for the theological *realist* these reasons and feelings find their ultimate *objective* ground in the God who is the source of being.

The second meta-ethical consideration separating theological realists from both non-realists and secular humanists is that the existence of the God who loves and gives life provides a reason to take the moral point of view. As we have seen, Cupitt, and in a like manner the secular humanist, can only appeal to prudential grounds, or happenstantial good fortune, that a person is naturally inclined to take the moral point of view. In contrast, in theological realism, one takes the moral point of view because one is both autonomously committed to this stance toward others *and because* one loves the things that God loves. To fail to take the moral point of view not only vitiates genuine dialogue through lack of respect for the other but also is a failure to respect what God loves.

ADVANTAGES OF THEOLOGICAL REALISM

The non-realist argues that the ethical crisis of our day, and the general demands of the moral life, force us to a responsible, non-realist approach to God. In sum, not only is this view internally defective and so self-defeating, but on practical grounds—precisely the sorts of grounds to which the non-realist appeals—there are better positive reasons vis-á-vis morality to take a *realist* view of God.

The first advantage concerns criteria for choosing between alternative world-views. As we observed, appropriate sorts of ultimate considerations include whether one thinks that the meaning of life, or the significance of morality, or the presence of goodness in the universe can best be explained by one view rather than another. Whereas the non-realist can only point to either inner-subjective or inter-subjective valuations of the moral life and spirituality as criteria for the acceptability of a religious world-view, the realist posits an external, objective state of affairs, namely the existence and acts of God, which grounds the final justification for theistic faith and morality and a religious world-view. This objective grounding for ethical principles provides an objective check on the vicissitudes of ever-changing convention and the insidiousness of our self-deceptive tendency to cloak what we desire in the guise of morality. Of course, the extent to which we correctly *understand* the objective grounding of ethical principles is subject to the vagaries of our inextricably socio-historical perspective and individual desires. This problem of historicity and egocentrism affects realist and non-realist views equally.

Importantly, while ethical principles are objectively grounded within theological realism, they are neither destructive of freedom nor need be rigid and invariant. We have already seen that we need not give up autonomy to follow external, objective standards. The person who trusts (has faith in) God *chooses* to love and do the things that, to his or her best understanding, God loves. There is also considerable latitude for a pluralist view of the moral life within theological realism. Why suppose God would want us all to be precisely alike in our moral values? For the realist, the universe God purposely creates and sustains encompasses a staggering diversity of laudable human moral convictions. Why suppose a realist God would not desire that this continue? As Leibniz suggests, is not variety of goodness, and not just quantity of goodness, what makes for the better (if not the best of all) possible worlds? Though objectively grounded, morality may be pluralistic because God relates to us as *individuals* with irreducible differences.

As a second point in its favor, theological realism supports an objectivist view of ethics in another sense. Cupitt insists that "valuation is just human" and that the value of Christianity is the "attempt to improve the score by loving the worthless and neglected and raising their value-gradings."[52] On a realist view, not only are ethical values objective, people have *intrinsic* value. The theological realist would agree with Cupitt that we should love the neglected. But the neglected are not *ipso facto* worthless. Rather, we are to love our neighbor—that is, every person—because each one has self-worth. For the self-worth of all persons, just as the value of the universe, is objectively grounded in a real God, however difficult this is to comprehend or appreciate fully, given our limiting socio-historical perspective.

Finally, realism offers a *relational* understanding between humankind and God. Non-realism encourages us to be better persons by transcending our self-centeredness; theological realism enjoins us to be better persons by responding to a transcendent Thou. By exercising freedom and will, a person can sometimes transcend his or her present egotistical place in the natural order, but will remain in the natural order. If there is a God with whom we can *interact*, a transformation of our egotistic selves, not just within, but beyond the natural order, becomes possible. Here, even Kaufman's more moderate allowance for the bare possibility of a realist (noumenal) God is inadequate—for even then God would not be causally effective in human morality as an action guide.

The moral life is hardest, and our moral outrage greatest, when we watch friends and loved ones and the innocent brutalized by the world, when our highest ethical aspirations seem pulverized in the crucible of a disinterested universe and the ugliness of human greed. Perhaps this is when we are most aware of the need for help to transcend ourselves. Perhaps this is when it means the most to understand that the source of being is on the side of love. As a personal God, the realist God can enable us to persevere in holding to the moral point of view. No less effort is required of us than the humanist expects; for the theological realist, though, God as parent, lover, and friend both encourages and enhances our moral efforts.

This does not show that theological realism provides the best account and support for the moral life. But among the three views—secular humanism, a non-realist "Christian humanism," and theological realism—one should either be a theological realist or a secular humanist. For within this trichotomy, Christian humanism is self-defeating in its attempt to best account for the moral life. To deny realism yet continue to use theistic language for its evocative symbolism and its historical power to inspire the moral life encourages self-deception. It is better either completely to "take leave" of the historical vestiges of Christianity and turn to secular humanism, or to turn to theological realism with its positive objective reinforcement of the moral life. Of course, if God does not exist, then theological realism will turn out to be misguided. But unlike non-realism, theological realism does not rely on an accepted fiction to further morality. It is both a long story and, given the long history of arguments for and against God's existence, it may be an open question whether God exists.[53] So theological realism may turn out *not* to be the best of all possible choices. But between secular humanism and objective theism, theological *non*-realism fails to possess the best of either choice.

At the heart of his non-realist view, Cupitt holds that the task of Christian ethics is "to inject enough meaning and weight into our human world to make life worth living at all." Either life is already worth living, or we will not be able to make it so, apart from God. The weight of our own human history is against us.[54]

NOTES

1. Don Cupitt, *The New Christian Ethics* (London: SCM Press, 1988), 36.

2. Gordon D. Kaufman, *Systematic Theology: A Historicist Perspective* (New York: Charles Scribner's Sons, 1968), 111.

3. I have in mind such arguments as that a transcendent God is an unknowable God, that the natural order simply is all that exists, that talk of a noumenal God is meaningless, and that given the inextricable enculturation of our experience and thought, what we call God is merely a socio-historical convention.

4. As Brian Hebblethwaite puts the narrower traditional view in his defense of objective theism against non-realism in *The Ocean of Truth* (Cambridge: Cambridge University Press, 1988): "The concept of God involved in such an objective theistic understanding is that of an infinite, absolute, incorporeal, omnipotent, omniscient, perfectly wise and good mind and spirit" (p. 7).

5. John Hick, *Problems of Religious Pluralism* (New York: St. Martin's Press, 1985), 97.

6. Sallie McFague, *Models of God: Theology for an Ecological, Nuclear Age* (Philadelphia: Fortress Press, 1987), x and 183.

7. Don Cupitt, *Taking Leave of God* (New York: Crossroad, 1981), 9.

8. Gordon D. Kaufman, *Theology for a Nuclear Age* (Philadelphia: Westminster Press and Manchester: Manchester University Press, 1985), viii.

9. Ibid., 61.

10. See Gordon D. Kaufman, *The Theological Imagination: Constructing the Concept of God* (Philadelphia: Westminster Press, 1981), for example, chapter 9.

11. Kaufman, *Theology for a Nuclear Age*, 37, italics mine.

12. Ibid., 56 and 42.

13. Ibid., 24.

14. Ibid., 40–41. In the earlier work, *The Theological Imagination*, Kaufman states this even more strongly: "from the point of view of contemporary theological reconstruction, the understanding [of God] in terms of world-historical movement is distinctly preferable. For it provides a way to speak of an independence and otherness and even aseity over against the human—the requisite condition for breaking our narcissism and anthropocentrism and drawing us out of ourselves—without positing a particular existing being (named "God")" (p. 38).

15. Don Cupitt, *Taking Leave of God*, 9.

16. Cupitt, *The New Christian Ethics*, 15.

17. Don Cupitt, *Crisis of Moral Authority* (London: SCM Press, 1972), 27–28.

18. Kaufman, *Theology for a Nuclear Age*, 62.

19. First, Cupitt thinks that "modern people demand autonomy," and, second, he thinks that autonomy is a necessary condition of moral action (and also of the religious requirement to "fulfill our highest possible destiny as spiritual, self-conscious beings"). Don Cupitt, *Taking Leave of God*, ix and 94, cf. 85.

20. Cupitt, *The New Christian Ethics*, 1.

21. Ibid., 6 and 115.

22. Ibid., 4 and 52, italics mine.

23. In our religiously pluralistic world it is important to keep in mind that the considerations here about the relation between theism and ethics extend far beyond Christianity to other great monotheistic traditions. Cupitt explicitly endorses, and so I address, *Christian* humanism, but many of the considerations below more broadly apply to "religious humanism."

24. That is, ethical judgments are not assertions or judgments which ascribe moral *properties* to someone or something.

25. Cupitt, *The New Christian Ethics*, 18–19.

26. Ibid., 3 and 4.

27. Ibid., 126.

28. See, for example, "Pragmatism's Conception of Truth": "We have to live today by what truth we get today, and be ready tomorrow to call it falsehood." (William James, *Pragmatism and Four Essays from the Meaning of Truth* [New York: New American Library of World Literature, Meridian Books, 1955], 145).

29. Cupitt, *The New Christian Ethics*, 102–103.

30. Cupitt seems to hold subjectivism, an extreme version of truth and value relativism. On the difference between conceptual relativism and (the more extreme) subjectivism, see my *Reason, Relativism and God* (London: Macmillan Press and New York: St. Martin's Press, 1986), 49–50.

31. Cupitt, *The New Christian Ethics*, 118.

32. Ibid., 141 and 39.

33. I discuss the thesis of incommensurability and its self-stultification in *Reason, Relativism and God*, 63–64 and 183–191.

34. Lewis Carroll, *The Annotated Alice* (New York: Bramhall House, 1960), 269.

35. Cupitt, *The New Christian Ethics*, 155.

36. Ibid., 36.

37. Julian Huxley, "The Creed of a Scientific Humanist," in *The Meaning of Life*, ed. E. D. Klemke (New York: Oxford University Press, 1981), 68 and 65.

38. Kaufman is also aware of this problem; see *Theology for a Nuclear Age*, 37.

39. Cupitt, *The New Christian Ethics*, 163.

40. Cupitt, *Taking Leave of God*, 96.

41. Cupitt, *The New Christian Ethics*, 51.

42. In his earlier work, *The Leap of Reason*, Cupitt has not yet moved to such a complete reductionist view. While rejecting the attempt to transcend ourselves via a self-subsistent, external God, he does conceive of the religious life as providing a transcending dimension, the dimension of *spirituality*—that is, "the capacity in men for a 'leap of reason'" (p. 65). In *The New Christian Ethics* he says that what he had earlier called "spirituality," he now refers to as ethics—but ethics no longer has this transcending dimension.

43. A rigorous defense of divine command theory ethics against the charge that it must undermine autonomy is offered in Philip L. Quinn's *Divine Commands and Moral Requirements* (Oxford: Clarendon Press, Clarendon Library of Logic and Philosophy, 1978). See Robert M. Adams, "Autonomy and Theological Ethics," in *The Virtue of Faith and Other Essays in Philosophical Theology* (New York and Oxford: Oxford University Press, 1987), 125–126.

44. By "the moral point of view" I am not referring to a specific normative ethics, nor suggesting that there is only one correct view of morality. To fail to take the moral point of view is to be a-moral, not immoral.

45. We can identify at least four characteristics of the moral point of view. First, one must be committed, or at least willing to be committed, to some set of normative ethical principles. Second, one must adhere to the principle of universalizability and treat one's own acts as morally laudatory or permissible only if the actions of others would be equally laudatory or permissible in similar circumstances. Third, one must consider how one's acts affect others, taking into account the good of everyone equally. And, fourth, one must take others into account in one's actions because of one's respect for them as persons.

46. Cupitt, *The New Christian Ethics*, 13.

47. Dorothy Sayers, "Dilemma," from *In the Teeth of Evidence* (New York: Harper & Brothers, 1952), 98.

48. For a clear exposition of these just war criteria, see David Hollenbach, S.J., *Nuclear Ethics: A Christian Moral Argument* (Ramsey, N.J.: Paulist Press, 1983), ch. 4. Hollenbach sets out to "propose a basic theological approach to the moral issues in nuclear policy" (p. 2), but while he explicates the historical theological positions, and contemporary theological grounds for the alternative positions on nuclear policy and deterrence, he does not explain what added dimension *theological* reasons give to these issues which could not be provided by secular considerations.

49. For a thoughtful treatment of this position, see John Langan, S.J., "Between Religion and Politics," in William V. O'Brien and John Langan,

S.J., *The Nuclear Dilemma: The Just War Tradition* (Lexington, Mass.: D.C. Heath & Co., 1986).

50. Sallie McFauge, *Models of God*, 12.

51. Ibid., 152.

52. Cupitt, *New Christian Ethics*, 133–134.

53. Theological realism is epistemically justified, in part, on faith, since we can be epistemically warranted in believing something on insufficient evidence if it will be pragmatically advantageous to do so. I argue for this in detail in "World-Views and the Epistemic Foundations of Theism," *Religious Studies*, vol. 25, no. 1 (March 1989): 31–51.

54. This paper was written with the support of a National Endowment for the Humanities Fellowship. A shorter version responding to the work of Gordon Kaufman was presented at the 1990 Claremont Conference in the Philosophy of Religion. Longer versions were then presented at Cambridge University, the University of London, King's College, and the University of Wales, Lampeter. I wish to thank those faculties for their helpful discussion, especially Nicholas Lash, Keith Ward, and Paul Badham.

II

The Good Society

7

Religious Conviction and Public Civility

Richard J. Mouw

In his book *Twentieth Century Political Philosophy*, Donald Atwell Zoll has insisted that any attempt to show that Christianity and democratic theory are compatible is "fraught with philosophical difficulties, not the least of which is the obligation to show how religious eschatology is reconcilable with the relativistic, appetitive foundations of popular democratic thought."[1] Whatever else Zoll might be getting at in this remark, at least this much is clear: he is convinced that people who believe that their perspective on life will be vindicated in the endtime have problems getting along in the kind of political society that encourages the toleration of diverse viewpoints.

Nor is it difficult to find substantiating evidence for Zoll's claim. Consider these examples from seventeenth-century Scottish Calvinism. One is the testimony offered by the Covenanter martyr James Durham, just before he was executed for his active opposition to any political concessions on the part of Presbyterians to either Anglicans or Roman Catholics. "Toleration," he proclaimed, "doth either account little of errour, as being no hurtful thing, and so there can be no esteem of truth; or it doth account little of the destruction of souls; both which must be abominable."[2]

And while James Guthrie, one of Durham's fellow Covenanters, did not have the disadvantage of facing martyrdom—or the advantage, as the case may be—when he wrote his tract entitled *The Causes of God's Wrath Against Scotland*, he gave expression to a very similar sentiment: "We judge it," Guthrie wrote, "but the effect of wisdom of the flesh and to smell rankly of a carnal politic spirit to halve and divide the things of God for making peace amongst men."[3] People of this sort would be happy to second Zoll's thesis that the attempt to reconcile the possession of strong Christian beliefs with the toleration of diverse perspectives is "fraught with philosophical difficulties."

Martin Marty has a helpful way of describing the challenge which this pattern of thought presents to many religious believers. The question, he says, is whether we can reconcile the apparent conflict between conviction and civility. It is a fact of public life, Marty observes, that when it comes to religion and politics, "the committed lack civility" and the "civil often lack conviction."[4] Marty himself seems hopeful that the tension can ultimately be resolved. He holds out for the possibility that convicted civility may yet be realized. But he also knows that this resolution will not come easily.

No one has pursued the attendant difficulties here with more sensitivity and persistence than the sociologist John Murray Cuddihy, whose writings Marty cites. The tone of Cuddihy's treatment is captured well in the title of the first of his two books on the subject, *The Ordeal of Civility*.

Cuddihy intends no hyperbole in his use of the ordeal image. Civility is public politeness. It demands that we display tact, niceness, moderation, refinement, good manners—all the stuff that the modernization project requires of people who want to be thought of as "civilized."[5] Cuddihy is well aware of those forces that are indigenous to Judaism and Christianity that compel believers to resist this requirement that they divest themselves of any sense of "sacred particularity."[6] He quotes approvingly Rabbi Arthur Hertzberg's observation that "the American experiment" has asked "something previously unknown and almost unthinkable of the religions," namely, that "each sect is to remain the one true and revealed faith for itself and in private, but each must *behave in the public arena as if* its truth were as tentative as an aesthetic opinion or a scientific theory."[7] Like Marty, though, Cuddihy does think that the ordeal can culminate in the attainment of a civility that does not require the sacrifice of conviction. Indeed, in his analysis, a primary biblical resource for successfully surviving the ordeal of civility is the eschatological vision— the very area of theology that Zoll views as the major source of those "philosophical difficulties" that plague any attempt to reconcile Christianity with democratic thought. But more about eschatology further on.

RELIGION IN PUBLIC SPACE

My concern here is to explore the conviction-civility problem from within a Christian context. I do so with the understanding that the "ordeal of civility" is no accidental feature of the Christian life. It is a genuine ordeal that emerges out of the very inner dynamic of discipleship. We do need to be careful, though, about how we characterize the nature of this ordeal. Secularist thinkers are fond of initiating the discussion in such a way that the burden of proof immediately falls upon the Christians to show how their insistence upon strong religious beliefs is compatible with the maintenance of the appropriate standards of public etiquette.

For example, one of the more familiar passages in the Federalist Papers laments the divisiveness caused by "zeal for different opinions concerning religion." Federalist Ten goes on to note that while the causes of this kind of factional divisiveness cannot be eliminated in our society, we can compensate for its presence by maintaining a form of government that will bring "relief" from the effects of such zeal.[8]

Few thinkers, of course, have blamed all factional clashes that occur in the civil arena on religious passions. But religious conviction has regularly been viewed as especially resistant to the kinds of accommodations and settlements that are expected in civil dialogue. Other sorts of factional advocacies lend themselves more easily to being seen as grounded in diverse "interests" or "appetites"—which is to say that they are more easily relativized. Religion, however, is a more stubborn phenomenon. Thus Rousseau's insistence, in *The Social Contract*, that "theological intolerance" must inevitably lead to "civil intolerance"—since "one cannot live in peace with people one regards as damned."[9]

One thing that is at stake here is our understanding of the relationship of religious conviction to public space. For example, Rousseau wanted to establish the conditions that would provide for a broad public arena that is devoted to the give-and-take of polite dialogue among mutually respectful citizens—a space that would inevitably become cluttered and restricted, he was convinced, when religious considerations enter the scene. The impression is given, then, that modernity's "civilizing" project creates room for free-flowing public discourse, and that religious dogma only serves to crowd and cramp that public space.

A very different view of the situation is presented by Robert Bellah and his associates in *Habits of the Heart*. The Bellah team is convinced that it is precisely because public life has lost its grounding in the older religious and civic visions of life that the space devoted to civic dialogue has become cramped and crowded with individual interests. What is needed to correct this situation is the recovery and/or reinforcement of those "communities of memory"—especially the churches and synagogues—where, as the Bellah group puts it, "there are still operating among us . . . traditions that tell us about the nature of the world, about the nature of society, and about who we are as a people."[10]

These traditions—these communal memories—are, according to the case set forth in *Habits of the Heart*, crucial to the health of a society. The Bellah team calls for a public dialogue that is based on the shared assumption

> that the individual self finds its fulfillment in relationships with others in a society organized through public dialogue. The necessary dialogue can be sustained only by communities of memory, whether religious or civic, and it is symptomatic of the present state of American society that this vision remains sporadic and largely local in scope, though the larger implications are clear. These local initiatives may, however, be the forerunners of social movements that will once again open up spaces for reflection, participation, and the transformation of our institutions.[11]

These comments offer a very different picture of the relationship of religious belief to public space than the one often set forth by secularist thinkers. Bellah and his associates see the constrictions and clutterings that inhibit a broad public dialogue today as due, not to religious dogma, but to the fragmenting of interests that occurs when a society loses its vision of what community and citizenship are all about. Thus, the authors of *Habits of the Heart* insist that the recovery of particularized religious understandings of the issues of public life is necessary for a much-needed opening up of our communal "spaces for reflection, participation, and the transformation of our institutions."

It is encouraging for Christians to be told, of course, that we can make a significant contribution to public life by continuing to nurture our sense of religious identity. But it is also important to develop an understanding, from within that particularized framework, of why the project is a significant one, and of what resources can be provided by Christian thought and practice for maintaining the appropriate sense of public civility.

THE SPIRITUAL BENEFITS OF CIVILITY

In his fascinating study, *The Fall of Public Man,* Richard Sennett insists that modern industrial society has lost an appropriate sense of the benefits of public civility. Our obsession with intimate warmth in human affairs has fostered what he labels an "ideology of intimacy," according to which "social relationships of all kinds are real, believable, and authentic the closer they approach the inner psychological concerns of each person." This perspective, Sennett argues, "transmutes political categories into psychological categories."[12]

The result of this transmutation, says Sennett, is a lack of appreciation for the kinds of "bonds of association and mutual commitment which exist between people who are not joined by ties of family or intimate association"; we have lost our sense of the value of "the bond of a crowd, of a 'people,' of a polity."[13] This loss of public selfhood creates, in turn, a private disorientation: "confusion has arisen between public and intimate life; people are working out in terms of personal feelings public matters which properly can be dealt with only through codes of impersonal meaning."[14] In short, what we have lost in all of this is a proper sense of the meaning of the city itself:

> "City" and "civility" have a common root etymologically. Civility is treating others as though they were strangers and forging a social bond upon that social distance. The city is that human settlement in which strangers are most likely to meet. The public geography of a city is civility institutionalized.[15]

A similar perspective to Sennett's on the benefits of civility is offered—albeit in more graphic terms—by James M. Glass in his recent study of psychiatric patients. Glass, a political theorist, spent considerable time with persons classified as mentally ill in order to investigate

> the experience, the phenomenology, of human beings who see themselves as less than human, whose inner worlds force them outside the human community, who face the unequal distribution of power coming from delusion (the internal frame) and the encounter with others, who find themselves tormented and

frightened by what consensual reality offers as participation, community, and belief.[16]

The patients whom Glass studied were each immersed, he sensed, "in the internal flows of an internal nature that leaves the self isolated, sometimes psychotic, and withdrawn from consensual relationship."[17] They lacked a properly developed *public* selfhood; because of this their struggle for health was of necessity a grasping after a firmer hold on "existence-in-common" and "intersubjectivity." Thus, Glass argues, "the discourse between the self and its public field may constitute considerable benefit for a consciousness desperately fighting the entropic pull of tyrannical inner images."[18]

Both Sennett and Glass, then, are convinced of the therapeutic benefits afforded by public selfhood. Where incivility holds sway, says Sennett, each of us must bear the "burden of personality;" civility, on the other hand, "has as its aim the shielding of others from being burdened with oneself."[19] And Glass puts it even more poignantly: our citizenship roles facilitate "the persistent *public* mediation of private hells and inner conflicts."[20]

These analyses are useful, I think, for understanding the relationship between Christian conviction and public civility. For one thing, Christian teaching can be viewed as a means of grounding and/or reinforcing the kinds of public relationships that Sennett and Glass are celebrating. In their search for antidotes to what they view as the pervasive individualism of contemporary life, the authors of *Habits of the Heart* rightly note that Christianity, while utilizing some kinship notions in dealing with social solidarity—"children of God," "brothers and sisters in Christ"—also makes much of "a universal obligation of love and concern for others that could be generalized beyond, and even take precedence over, actual kinship obligations."[21] This understanding of the extra-kinship dimensions of Christian love could be an important reinforcement for civility in public life.

This is to focus on what Christianity can do for the public realm. We must also look at the relationship from the other direction. How can the public realm have a positive impact on the Christian community? What can Christians learn about their own spiritual identity as they wrestle with the challenges of public civility?

Some of the lessons that can be learned are obvious ones—obvious, at least, in the light of what has already been said here. One thing Christians can learn is that kinship itself, and metaphors that derive from a sense of kinship, are not enough to sustain a spirit of civility. A closely related lesson is that they can learn something about a kind of love that relies for its expression on what Sennett refers to as "codes of impersonal meaning."

To be sure, Christians ought not to allow the kind of perspective that Sennett sets forth to lure them into too strong an endorsement of the notion of public impersonality. Sennett's reminder that public selfhood requires a different set of dynamics than do private selves is a crucial one; he is right to insist that our most intimate experiences of interpersonal nurturing do not provide us with adequate codes for our interactions in public space. But sometimes Sennett seems to shift from a rather plausible account of the differences between private and public selfhood to a somewhat more cynical portrayal of the actual contours of social reality. At one point, for example, he suggests that selves who have come to expect trust, warmth, and comfort from others are not equipped "to move in a world founded on injustice." Is it not inhumane, then, Sennett asks, "to form soft selves in a hard world?"[22]

For those of us who believe that this world, with all of its injustice and hardness, is nonetheless the creation of a loving God, the contrast between a "soft" private self and a "hard" public identity is not exactly the right contrast. It is better, perhaps, to think in terms of the soft intimacy of our private relationships versus the soft formality of the public square—or of a humane and trusting kinship versus a humane and trusting public affection. For all of that, Christians still need to explore the proper contours of a civility that is fitted to the unique demands of a public consciousness.

I cannot conduct that full exploration here; but I will look at some of the resources which Christian thought and practice make available for this important project. I am specifically interested in illustrating how—Zoll's contrary opinion on this subject notwithstanding—Christian eschatological yearnings can reinforce a spirit of civility. Before doing that, I will touch briefly on two more mundane areas of theological concern: church polity and worship.

POLITY AND CIVILITY

The comments I quoted earlier from two seventeenth-century Covenanters exemplify Sheldon Wolin's thesis, as he sets it forth in his brilliant study of major themes in Western political thought, that the

Protestant Reformation gave expression to political ideas that threatened "to jeopardize a whole tradition of order and civility."[23] But Wolin would be disappointed to find that it is Calvinists who are in this case expressing such uncivil thoughts, since he is convinced that it was John Calvin himself who "put forward a system of ideas which stemmed that flight from civility" which his fellow Reformers had encouraged.[24] The case that Wolin makes in this regard is not only impressive as a piece of historical analysis; it is also instructive for our attempt to understand the proper shape of a convicted civility.

Wolin sees the impulses that led early Protestantism to flee from civility as arising primarily out of Anabaptist and Lutheran thought. Both the Lutherans and the Anabaptists promoted the ideal of an ecclesial fellowship that was social without being political—a community which, since it was "a voluntary union bound by love, faith, and the worshipped presence of Christ . . . could not generate power, domination, and authority."[25] These latter features were associated with the coercive patterns of political life, a way of ordering human affairs which both Lutherans and Anabaptists viewed with varying degrees of suspicion—sometimes even contempt—and which they certainly took to be completely inappropriate to the texture of ecclesial bonding.

Calvin challenged this perspective on two counts. He took a much more positive view of political life than did Luther and the Anabaptists. He also insisted that the church itself ought to display a kind of political ordering, since all communities required some form of institutionalized structuring if they were to maintain their coherence.

Calvin was not simply observing that the church would do well to learn a few organizational lessons from political life. There is a larger perspective at work in his thought, one in which both the churchly and the political communities, in spite of their very different callings, possess commonalities and continuities that link them together in a broader unity. Calvin wanted this unity to become more visible in human affairs, so that the links between ecclesial virtue and the virtue of the *polis* could be more clearly displayed in a social order that would be, as Wolin puts it, "not a 'theocracy,' but a corporate community that was neither purely religious nor purely secular, but a compound of both."[26]

There is obviously much that could be explored here, both historically and conceptually. For our present purposes, though, we can limit ourselves to two observations about the contemporary applicability of the perspective which Wolin attributes to Calvin.

The first observation is a general one: to see this perspective on church-*polis* relations as relevant to contemporary life does not require that we see it as a desirable way of structuring the church's relationship to the present-day *polis*.

The insistence that there are important continuities between the church and the *polis* does not have to serve as a platform for a Christian takeover of the public arena. Rather, it can provide Christians with a model for role integration, as a guide for putting together a way of life in which believers operate with a sense of clear continuity between their worship and their activities in the public arena—even if that arena is structured so as to allow very different understandings of "sacred" and "secular" to coexist in relative peace.

The second observation is a more specific one: much can be learned from Calvin's insistence that the church can be a place in which we learn how to cultivate the kind of virtue appropriate and necessary for public life.

Calvin saw the church and the *polis* as each having its own unique integrity—neither simply existed for the sake of the other in the divine order. As Wolin observes, Calvin insisted "that there was a kind of virtue attainable only in the political order;"[27] the *polis*, then, "had a unique role to play," equipping human beings "with a type of civility and discipline that could not be gained elsewhere."[28] In Calvin's own words, it is an important task of temporal government "to shape our manners in accordance with civil justice, to create concord among us, to maintain and preserve a common peace and tranquillity."[29]

These public "manners," however, are not an easy thing to come by. Thus, one of the tasks of the church is, as Wolin puts it, "to refashion Protestant man into a creature of order, or more accurately, to make him conform to a Christian image of civility."[30]

How, in more specific terms, is this to be done?

WORSHIP AND PUBLIC CONSCIOUSNESS

No philosopher has struggled more intensely with the problem of public space than Rousseau. Our natural human impulses, as Rousseau viewed things, do not make the consciousness that is necessary for citizenship an easy thing to attain. In the best known passages dealing with this subject in *The Social Contract*, Rousseau makes it clear that the transition from the state of nature into the cooperative social bond requires a radical transformation of the ways in which we experience interpsychic reality.

The question that vexed Rousseau—and which he explored throughout many of his writings—was how this transformation could take place. His most hopeful proposals came when he was imagining the spontaneous emergence of public space—where people are overtaken by that experience of kinship which comes with the psychic overflow that results from an expanded sense of selfhood. At one point, for example, Rousseau thinks about the way in which the experience of citizenship might spring up in the course of a communal festival when, energized by warm sunshine and gentle breezes, the participants "become an entertainment to themselves," so that "each one sees and loves himself in the others, and all will be better united."[31] And in another place he speaks of the experience of a "patriotic drunkenness . . . which alone can raise men above themselves."[32]

It should not surprise us that a pagan thinker like Rousseau would gravitate toward images of summer picnics and drunken parties as he tries to imagine how a civilizing self-transcendence might be attained. At least he is seeking out mechanisms that make use of the festive and the celebrative. In short, Rousseau seems to be pointing in his own way to a link between worship and public space.

This link has been explored in less cryptic terms by Richard Bernstein in a recent essay on the characteristics of a genuinely public consciousness. Bernstein sees the yearning for public space as a very real force in contemporary life. "No matter how frustrated, perverted, muted, and diffused it may be," says Bernstein, "there is a longing for a genuine sense of community"—not some all-encompassing "Great Community" where our unique particularities are cancelled out, but a community that can be realized in "those local *communities* in which our individuality can be realized."[33] Citing Hannah Arendt for support, he sees the search for community as being fulfilled in a *polis* that is not so much a "physical location" as it is "the type of public space that comes into being *in between* human beings"—a "creative power that springs up among them"—in the course of dialogue that will allow them to understand each other as they work to clarify and test their differing perspectives.[34]

This public space cannot be invented or imposed. It can only come into being, says Bernstein, by springing up in our midst. It will do that only where there is an existing sense of community that we bring to our attempts to find this dialogic space. Bernstein is convinced that religion has an important role to play in these efforts.

Here is how Bernstein describes an experience he had in 1964, when he was engaged in a voter registration project:

> The experience I want to relate occurred in the Morningstar Baptist Church, the headquarters [of the Mississippi Summer Project] for the Easton precinct of Forrest County. Many of those who came to Mississippi this summer knew that they would be returning to the safety of their homes at the end of the summer. But no one then knew what would happen to the local blacks who identified themselves with the civil rights movement. It took an enormous amount of courage and risk to participate. After several weeks of voter registration, the moment had arrived when it was up to the local blacks to meet and publicly elect their representatives. That meeting was one of the most impressive political gatherings I have ever attended. . . . As you might imagine this gathering had something of the quality of a religious meeting. And there were two things that deeply impressed me—that I was witnessing the creation of just one of those public spaces that Arendt describes, and that what gave the participants the courage, hope and conviction to participate was informed by their religious communal bonds.[35]

What this experience illustrates for Bernstein is that religion has "a creative contribution to make to American public life," namely, that of giving shape to our "deep aspirations" for public community "by giving them concreteness and specificity, by making them tangible public realities."[36]

The Bellah team likewise points to the civic benefits of the worship experience. Crucial to our attempts to find communal commitment and civic friendship, they tell us, is "common worship, in which we express our gratitude and wonder in the face of the mystery of being itself."[37]

Needless to say, Christian worship is not always infused with a sense of mystery—which undoubtedly has much to do with the fact that Christians have often had difficulty cultivating the humility that seems to be a necessary ingredient of public civility. Where there is little sense of mystery that attends the handling of human realities *within* the Christian community, it is unrealistic to expect that a dialogic space will spontaneously spring up to forge bonds of civic friendship when we enter into the conversations of the *larger* human community. But where experiences of mystery are encouraged, worship—even of a very convicted and particularistic sort—can contribute to the formation of a public consciousness by reminding us of the distance, not only between ourselves and God, but also between our present state of moral repair and what human beings are capable of becoming.

CIVILITY AND ESCHATOLOGICAL DELAY

John Murray Cuddihy bases his proposed Christian strategy for coping with the ordeal of civility on a recognition of the gap between our present imperfection and our future glorification. He recommends the adoption of an "ethic for the interim" that prescribes patience as we await God's future victory over the forces of unrighteousness. Christian discipleship, Cuddihy suggests, "puts a ban on all ostentation and triumphalism *for the time being*, before the Parousiatic return, at which time alone triumphalism becomes appropriate and fitting." For Christians to attempt to claim our glory here and now "is precisely vainglory—it is vulgar, empty, and in bad theological taste. 'Whosoever shall exalt himself shall be abased; and he that shall humble himself shall be exalted' (Matt. 23:12)."[38]

There is a way of reading this "solution," of course, that will see it as a manifestation of an uncaring attitude toward the present, thus grounding civility in a kind of Christian cynicism. There is at least a hint of this in Cuddihy's account. He quotes approvingly, for example, Glenn Tinder's recommendation that Christians look at the present age with a sense of "resignation" that is outwardly indistinguishable from a "Machiavellian" attitude. This is not as cynical as it might seem at first glance. Both Tinder and Cuddihy mean to place the stress here on the outward appearance of a similarity to Machiavellianism. Our Christian resignation, Tinder insists, is only "provisional; and fundamentally it is neither Machiavellian nor ethical, for it is subordinated to a limitless hope."[39]

This is, I think, helpful. But I also wonder whether a little too much is made here of this Christian "resignation" that gives the external appearance of Machiavellianism. Both Cuddihy and Tinder rightly emphasize the fact that the Christian's hope for the future is profoundly communal in nature. If taken seriously, this vision of a glorious future community should invoke in us not a resignation but an active longing—of the sort described in Hebrews 13:14: "here we have no lasting city, but we are looking for the city that is to come."

Christian resignation does not seem to be the most appropriate way of honoring the fact of eschatological delay. Civility is not something we cloak ourselves in because we have nothing better to do while we are waiting for the future consummation. Rather, our civility is grounded in a genuine conviction that we have much to do by way of preparing for the city that is to come. Practicing a calm and steady humility is not merely a way of biding our time until the endtime arrives. It is itself a crucial way of anticipating the final chapter of the narrative that we are living out. The present dispensation of God's patience is a pedagogical necessity for the believing community. Finding occasions where we can apply a hermeneutic of suspicion to ourselves while applying a hermeneutic of charity to others is itself an important *preparation* for the eschaton.

In describing what he sees as a well-formed Christian posture regarding basic epistemic matters, Arthur Holmes has written about the need to articulate a philosophical perspective that holds together both humility and hope: humility, because we have not yet attained the epistemic qualifications that are possible for human beings; and hope, because we know that epistemic improvement is on the way.[40] The application to our present topic hardly needs spelling out. Public civility is grounded in epistemic humility. Public conviction is grounded in epistemic hope.

A true and lasting public space will arrive, to be sure, only with the eschaton. For those of us who embrace a partially realized eschatology, it is not unrealistic to expect signs of the eschaton here and now. In a manner not totally unlike the occurrences that Rousseau hoped for in his picnics and parties, we have found something like a public space springing up in the midst of our eating and drinking together in the Christian community. These first fruits of the end-time serve both to satisfy and to stimulate our hunger for the concretization of that larger story which, as James McClendon puts it, "overcomes our self-deceit, redeems our common life, and provides a way for us to be a people among all the earth's peoples."[41]

This yearning also makes us bold to join others in the larger human quest for a healthy public space, in the hope that on that journey we too will experience those mysterious and surprising inklings of a larger kind of love that can take concrete shape—even in the here and now—in new forms of citizenship and community.

107

NOTES

1. Donald Atwell Zoll, *Twentieth Century Political Philosophy* (Englewood Cliffs, N.J.: Prentice-Hall, 1974), 94.

2. James Durham, *A Dying Man's Testimony to the Church of Scotland*, quoted by J. D. Douglas, *Light in the North: The Story of the Scottish Covenanters* (Grand Rapids: Wm. B. Eerdmans Publishing Co., 1964), 190.

3. James Guthrie, *Causes of God's Wrath Against Scotland*, quoted by Douglas, *Light*, 74.

4. Martin Marty, *By Way of Response* (Nashville: Abingdon Press, 1981), 81.

5. John Murray Cuddihy, *The Ordeal of Civility: Freud, Marx, Levi-Strauss, and the Jewish Struggle with Modernity* (New York: Basic Books, 1974), 235.

6. Ibid.

7. Ibid., 108.

8. *The Federalist Papers*, selected and edited by Roy P. Fairchild (Garden City, N.Y.: Anchor Books, 1961), 18–19.

9. Jean Jacques Rousseau, *The Social Contract*, trans. Willmoore Kendall (Chicago: Henry Regnery, 1954), 160.

10. Robert Bellah et al., *Habits of the Heart: Individualism and Commitment in American Life* (Los Angeles: University of California Press, 1985), 239, 281–282.

11. Ibid., 218.

12. Richard Sennett, *The Fall of Public Man: On the Social Psychology of Capitalism* (New York: Vintage Books, 1978), 259.

13. Ibid., 3–4.

14. Ibid., 5.

15. Ibid., 264.

16. James M. Glass, *Private Terror/Public Life: Psychosis and the Politics of Community* (Ithaca, N.Y.: Cornell University Press, 1989), 3.

17. Ibid., 14.

18. Ibid., 26.

19. Sennett, *Fall*, 264–265, 269.

20. Glass, *Private*, 27.

21. Bellah, *Habits*, 114.

22. Sennett, *Fall*, 260.

23. Sheldon S. Wolin, *Politics and Vision: Continuity and Innovation in Western Political Thought* (Boston: Little, Brown & Co., 1960), 167.

24. Ibid.

25. Ibid., 166–167.

26. Ibid., 168.

27. Ibid., 183.

28. Ibid., 181.

29. *Institutes*, IV, xx, 2; quoted by Wolin, *Politics*, 182.

30. Wolin, *Politics*, 175.

31. Rousseau, *Letter to d'Alembert*, quoted by Marshall Berman, *The Politics of Authenticity: Radical Individualism and the Emergence of Modern Society* (New York: Atheneum, 1970), 215.

32. Rousseau, quoted in Berman, *Politics*, 283.

33. Richard J. Bernstein, "The Meaning of Public Life," in *Religion and American Public Life; Interpretations and Explorations*, ed. Robin W. Lovin (Mahwah, N.J.: Paulist Press, 1986), 47.

34. Ibid., 36–37.

35. Ibid., 48.

36. Ibid., 49.

37. Bellah, *Habits*, 295.

38. John Murray Cuddihy, *No Offense: Civil Religion and Protestant Taste* (New York: Seabury Press, 1978), 202.

39. Glenn Tinder, quoted in *Ibid.*, 211.

40. Arthur Holmes, *Contours of a World View* (Grand Rapids: Wm. B. Eerdmans Publishing Co., 1983), 128.

41. James McClendon, *Ethics: Systematic Theology*, vol. 1 (Nashville: Abingdon Press, 1986), 356.

8
Public Ethics and Public Selfhood: The Hidden Problems

Karen J. Torjesen

In his essay, "Religious Conviction and Public Civility," Richard J. Mouw engages us in an important and serious question, the question of how a public selfhood is formed. He initially describes the problem as an incompatibility between a belief in absolute truth and the negotiation and compromise required for participation in public life and political process. But he quickly reformulates the problem of the intolerance of religious groups, using Richard Sennett's terms, as the problem of the loss of public selfhood. In doing so, Mouw is able to connect the problems of instituting a public ethics of civility posed by sectarian religious groups to the more general problem of the malaise and fragmentation of American political life.

At the end of his essay Mouw returns to the problem of absolute truth with the suggestion that Christian eschatology can foster "an ethic of the interim" which would mitigate the absoluteness of the claim to truth. I agree with him in what I think are the implications of his position, that the fundamental problem is not that of absolute truth. Political concepts such as capitalism and communism also function as absolute truths in the political sphere. They stand as unexamined first principles, held with deep emotional conviction, to be the premises from which political action must spring. The more fundamental problem is the problem of the loss or the absence of a public selfhood.

Mouw is able to make this connection between religious conviction and public civility by using a "medical" model in which he casts the problem of intolerance, grounded in claims to an absolute truth, as a presenting problem, as only a symptom. His diagnosis is the loss of public selfhood, and it is to this ailment that he addresses himself with suggestions for possible remedies. He suggests, in fact, three ways in which the Christian and Protestant churches may help to restore to the nation a lost public selfhood. He suggests that the Christian teaching on the "universal obligation of love" can be viewed as "a means of grounding and/or reinforcing the kinds of public relationships" that create public selfhood. Mouw comes up with a novel remedy in his appeal to Reformed polity as a school for civility. Here he appeals to Calvin over against the Anabaptists and Lutherans because Calvin's church polity was grounded in a vision of the church as a partner in a theocracy and was therefore concerned with political order. The medieval Roman Catholic church was built on a similar vision of a theocracy, and I wonder to what extent Mouw would recognize as legitimate an appeal to Catholic polity as a way of forming public selfhood. Using Rousseau and Bernstein, Mouw suggests that a sense of public selfhood can be generated by the "expanded sense of selfhood" inspired by communal experiences of emotional bonding. Mouw suggests that Christian worship, through the communal experience of transcendence, creates this expanded sense of selfhood and can nurture a public selfhood. I would be interested in Mouw's reflections on why that seems to happen in the Afro-American religious communities and the *Communidades de Base* of Latin America but rarely in the worship of white middle class churches.

As Mouw implies, the dilemma of the relationship of religious groups to public life is not simply one of commitments to absolute truth versus toleration of difference, but rather the lack of a public selfhood. It seems that the processes and mechanisms for the formation of the public self are weak or entirely absent in the communal life of religious groups. I would now like to offer a diagnosis of this problem, using instructive parallels between the position of religious groups in relation to public life and the position of women in relation to public life.

According to the historical memory of the Western tradition, the public/political domain emerged as a separate sphere with its own morality and selfhood as a result of the development of the democratic *polis* or city-state. With the emergence of democratic political institutions, participation in public life was limited to native, freeborn, propertied males who held the status of *polites* or citizen. The ethics of public life, civility—the right to speak and the right to be heard—was extended only to citizen males.

The ethics of public life, civility, and the public selfhood of political life became normative for the male gender role. The public self of the *polites* was rational and capable of reasoned discourse, deliberation, and public speech; capable of rule, mastery, and control of others; and committed to the virtues of justice, courage, and self-restraint. This public self was a male self and could be aspired to only by men of the ruling classes. Greek democratic institutions not only inaugurated a new political philosophy, but they also established new gender roles; public, political life was the domain of men, and private, domestic life was the domain of women. Each of these domains has evolved a distinctive ethic: one an ethic of justice and civility rooted in rational discourse and associated with the public domain; the other an ethic of love and nurture associated with the private domain.

Carol Gilligan's work, *In a Different Voice*, demonstrates how girls make moral decisions based on an ethic of care and boys make moral decisions on the basis of an ethic of justice. Nancy Chodorov's *Reproduction of Mothering* shows how the ethic of love is rooted in a connective and relational sense of the self, fostered by a girl's gender identification with her mother, whereas the ethic of justice is rooted in a sense of the self as autonomous and separate, created by a boy's experience of gender-separateness from his mother, who is the primary caregiver.

The requirements for citizenship and participation in public process in the American republic were no less restrictive than those of classical Athens. Political life was the domain of freeborn, propertied males. In classical Athens religion was integrated into public life through establishing priesthoods as public offices and festival days as public events. The radical experiment of the founders of the American republic broke with all previous political traditions and removed religion from public life. Here we find the parallels between the social location of religious groups in the private sphere and the social location of women. Both are relegated to the private sphere, and both are bearers of the ethics of the private sphere, the ethics of love in contrast to an ethics of justice. In both cases the sense of self is built on notions and experiences of the self as dependent, relational, and connectional. Religious groups, even when they are institutionalized, tend to operate out of an ethics of love rather than an ethics of justice. As a result even religion with the machinery of justice in its institutionalized form is not able to foster a public selfhood.

The domain of the private and the domain of women is not the domain of rationality, but the domain of feeling and emotion, particularly so since eighteenth-century romanticism assigned to women (of the bourgeoise class) the role of cultivating a domestic world rich in feeling. Mouw's suggestion that public selfhood can be created by the expanded sense of selfhood that arises in experiences of communal festivals, community organizing, and in Christian worship, is I think correct. In each of these cases, he is in fact drawing on the emotional resources that had been relegated to the private sphere for creating a sense of public selfhood.

Religious groups in America, for historical reasons, are enmeshed in a larger system, the public/private system. The notion of a public domain, of a public ethic (civility), of a public selfhood (the citizen), and the public good are valuable and important legacies of the Western political tradition. But historically in every century they have been built on the privilege and power of one group and the silence and subordination of other groups. In Athens a sense of public selfhood was constituted by a sense of power and privilege. The notion of the public good needs to be expanded beyond the classical public/private boundaries. There needs to be an integration of the ethics of justice and civility and the ethics of love in both the public and private domains. The integration of the ethics of justice and the ethics of care presupposes the formation of a selfhood that is both autonomous and relational. The intolerance of religious groups is symptomatic of the absence of a public selfhood, but because religious communities have been relegated to the private sphere in American society, the values and the processes they have inherited are not conducive to the cultivation of a public selfhood.

9

Conflict, Community, and Human Destiny: Religious Ethics and the Public Construction of Morality

Philip J. Rossi, S.J.

The history to be written some generations hence will judge whether the scholars who now see the traditions of Western culture in a state of pervasive, systematic, internal crisis have been correct.[1] To alert us to this crisis, they have told us more than one story of the events that are supposed to have brought us to such a state; one of the storytellers has even provided two versions of the story.[2] Stories of crisis, however, are not the only ones told. There are yet other stories—told by those who do not think we have come to a state of crisis—who see the same events, particularly those taken to constitute "the Enlightenment," as episodes in a story still laden with hope, despite the particular failures it contains.[3] On my reading of these stories, different as they may be, there is at least one element of the plot that most, if not all, acknowledge as crucial: the series of circumstances and events, often conceptually clustered under the heading of "secularization," that altered the context and range of moral discourse in Western culture.

Chief among the contexts that these circumstances and events altered was the one in which individuals or groups could appropriately conduct their quest to identify that which serves as a unifying form or focus for the elements constitutive of "the good of human life." This altered context did not require that individuals or groups within society abandon the quest to find such a unifying focus—be it in art, or in the accumulation of wealth, or in the service of humankind, or in devotion to one's God. It did, however, effect a general public silence about such matters: the quest to identify these unifying forms and to articulate their weight and function within the patterns of human life

114

ceased to be a matter central to that public conversation and civic argument which at once determines and expresses the ethos and the ethics of the polity at large. This quest became, instead, a matter to be settled principally on the basis of individual judgment and personal preference.[4]

The precise character of the alteration that shifted the quest to identify that which serves to unify the elements of human good outside the arena of public discourse is controverted; so too are its causes. Even more controverted is the evaluation to be made about the impact this shift has had, even up to our own day, upon the contours of moral thinking and moral life. I do not propose to address these issues directly in this essay; I propose, instead, to examine this shift, particularly as it bears upon the role that religious ethics can take as a party to such public discourse, from a starting point that I hope will prove (relatively) non-controversial. I thus suggest that we view this shift as *a complex set of conditions placed upon the range of public conversation and civic argument in the hope of delimiting those elements of human good concerning which conflict could be resolved without resort to violence.* These conditions, it is important to note, do not require that the resolution of conflict be, in any instance, an agreement upon the content of the particular element of good in question; these conditions, instead, are intended to help us mark out just those elements of good over which we can have differences—and even deep differences—just as long as they are not of a kind to make us either abandon the conversation or listen no longer to our interlocutors.

John Courtney Murray aptly characterized this shift—at least in the particular way it was embodied in the founding documents and institutions of the United States—as constituting "articles of peace."[5] I do intend to claim Murray's sanction for the use to which I shall put this phrase in the rest of this essay; the point that it suggests to me—which may not very well represent what Murray considers central—can be focused by reference to one such element affected by this shift: the matter of human destiny, that is, the final outcome of our individual lives as well as the final outcome of our lives together as a community, as a polity, and as a species.[6] These are matters that, in the language of Christian theology, bear upon "salvation."[7]

Under the "articles of peace," public conversation is expected to be wide-ranging: the public conversation wherein the goals and priorities of our political and socio-economic life are debated and established allows us (and, indeed, requires us) to consider matters of both the immediate and longer-term well-being of individuals, of social groups and institutions, of our society and nation as a whole, and more recently, of the world community and the planet we inhabit. As wide-ranging as this public conversation about these matters may be, however, there is a limit beyond which it may not carry: the "articles of peace" neither require nor expect us to consider with one another, as part of our public conversation, such matters as "human destiny" or "salvation." Conversation upon these matters would allow us to articulate to one another the various inclusive possibilities by which we hope to interrelate and unify each and all of the particular aspects of our human well-being. The "articles of peace" certainly place no limit upon our speculation about such matters "in private;" yet they do not set space aside in the arena of public conversation for us to discuss this larger and inclusive matter—the final destiny and purpose of our lives—to see what bearing the various possibilities that we articulate for it might have upon the goals and priorities of our political and socio-economic life that we must debate with one another.[8]

This limitation is not arbitrary; history has shown that resort to violence is all too readily taken as the sole means to resolve conflict over different understandings of human destiny—or of the destiny of a particular polity—and over who are called to participate in it. As a result, even those who would hold that considerations of human destiny have a fundamental bearing upon the goals and priorities we are to set for political, social, and economic life can acknowledge at least the prudence, if not the wisdom, of placing debate about its character outside the range of the public discourse that is expected to resolve other, more immediate conflicts about the elements that constitute the good of human life.[9] Since considerations of human destiny seem to be most explicitly a concern and focus for human religious belief and practice, this limitation upon the range of public discourse has, at times, been taken to render ambiguous the appropriateness of giving full voice in the conversation to perspectives shaped by religious ethics.[10]

By drawing our attention to the limits that the "articles of peace" place upon public conversation, Murray's phrase thus provides us with what may prove a useful way to interpret many of the stories of crisis which have recently proliferated: these stories enable us to identify various forces which have potential for unravelling—or for reconstituting—the settlement established in these "articles of peace." Chief among these forces are two that challenge, positively and negatively, these "articles of peace" from seemingly contrary directions.

116

There are, on the one hand, forces that would effectively constrict into ever more narrow limits the elements of human good over which public conversation and civic argument can effectively range. These forces often use the language of "rights," particularly as these are taken to inhere in individuals, as the focus for the challenges they pose to the range of elements of human good that may be encompassed within the public conversation that constitutes civic argument. At their best, these forces form one bulwark against potential incursions by a tyranny of the majority bent upon imposing their rendition of what is for everyone's good; at their worst, they become fragmenting forces of privatization and tribalization. There are, on the other hand, forces that seek to make a prime focus of public conversation and argument precisely those elements of "human good" about which agreement has hitherto proved most elusive: the substantive content of the justice, equality, and participation that form essential elements of "the good of human life." At their best, these forces serve as prophetic reminders that, unless we can and do talk with one another about these central matters, the rest of the conversation swiftly becomes Babel; at their worst, they tempt us to think that the alternative to Babel is a monologue, conducted in a monotone, which is to be brought about, if need be, by being the voice so loud that no others can gain hearing.[11]

Identification of these forces is particularly pertinent for delimiting what, in my judgment, is one of the more pressing tasks that faces religious ethics in this last decade of the twentieth century: the reshaping of its own understanding of the role and responsibility it has as an element in the matrix of public conversation and civic argument that gives form to concrete moral practice. There are a number of reasons why I consider this a pressing task; the remainder of this essay will outline that task by articulating the reasons that make it a pressing one—both for religious ethics and for the public discourse that would be better served by successfully accomplishing this task. The task is not an easy one inasmuch as it is to provide a space where public discussion and civic argument can begin to engage even that topic over which conflict has all too often proved violent and deadly: human destiny. Undertaking this task presumes that religious ethics has by now learned a salutary lesson from the silence that the "articles of peace" have up to now enjoined upon it. This lesson is that ways can and must be found to make the articulation of the deepest convictions that lie at the root of religiously shaped ethics into a locus for the sharing of fundamental human hopes rather than a flash point

117

for division.[12] Therefore, the task for religious ethics is to become the locus in which serious and sustained public conversation about human destiny can go on—and can go on in ways that allow deep and even intractable differences in our understandings and hopes about that destiny to confront and interact with each other without resort to violence.

There will be two parts to my argument; in the first, I will show why there needs to be a place within public conversation and civic argument where matters of human destiny can be debated and where the implications these matters have for the well-being of individuals, institutions, society at large, the world community, and the planet we inhabit can be drawn out. The core of this part of my argument will be the claim that diverse considerations regarding human destiny already function as a central, though implicit, moral reference point for participants in the discourse that constitutes public conversation and civic argument. If that is the case, then public discourse is better served by making explicit the various considerations that function as such a reference point for all those who participate in it. The second part of my argument will show how taking up this task is an especially apt enterprise for religious ethics. The core of my argument in this part will be the claim that religious ethics—and, indeed, those communities for which some form of religious ethics provides a reflective articulation of moral vision and practice—stands in need of the challenge this task offers, that is, to serve as a model for public conversation on a matter upon which human differences run deep, and to serve as such a model precisely by sustaining throughout it the "openness to mutual transformation" that David Tracy notes as the mark of authentic conversation.[13]

To make the case for the first part of my argument, I think it helpful to turn to the efforts that have been made, often by the tellers of the story of crisis, to retrieve for contemporary use those ways of understanding "the good of human life" (such as Aristotle's) that see the context in which such good is discerned and pursued as one in which conflict (*agon*), a public community (*polis*), and a specifiable human destiny (*telos*) play constitutive roles. On these points, I find instructive MacIntyre's work both in *After Virtue* and *Whose Justice? Which Rationality?* Particularly useful for my purposes is the notion of a "tradition constituted inquiry," which takes on special prominence in the latter work.[14] MacIntyre's development of this notion modifies, if not substantially alters, the story of fragmentation that he told in *After Virtue*. That first story ended on the fragile hope that the cacophony

118

which has replaced public conversation would someday be stilled by the persuasive quiet voice of a new St. Benedict or St. Benedicta. In the new story we still hear the clamor of many dissonant voices, but the notion of a tradition constituted inquiry allows us to discern several lines of coherent and continuing conversation. It also provides a hope that attends less to the future appearance (as a moment of grace?) of a new Benedict and more to the present necessity of learning the histories of the traditions—including our own—whose voices can be identified through the dissonance.

I do not propose to examine here the most challenging claim that MacIntyre offers on the basis of his notion of tradition constituted inquiry, namely, that the Aristotelian-Thomistic tradition of inquiry, as he has interpretively rendered it, is the one which is best able to render account both of its own understanding of the workings of practical reason and of (all) the understandings of practical reason that have been proffered by "rival" traditions.[15] More pertinent to my purposes is noting how MacIntyre's acknowledgement of a genuine plurality of traditions, by way of the notion of a tradition constituted inquiry, opens the possibility for our seeing the extent to which various considerations and understandings of human destiny already function as a central, though implicit, moral reference point for the public conversation that constitutes civic argument. The notion of a tradition constituted inquiry opens up this possibility in consequence of the constitutive role that MacIntyre assigns to history within this notion.[16] The role is multiple: first, any tradition constituted inquiry has a history; second, knowledge and appropriation of that history by those who stand within it is a condition for their own effective engagement in the inquiry the tradition constitutes; and, finally, MacIntyre's own construction of this notion has itself been made possible by the (historically conditioned) emergence, within the traditions of Western culture, both of a consciousness of history and of its reflective appropriation within the various forms of inquiry.

The multiple constitutive role that MacIntyre assigns to history provides the fundamental basis for making the claim that considerations of human destiny already function as a central moral reference point for public discourse and civic argument. If he is correct to assign this role to history, then history, or more precisely the conscious appropriation of history, requires that consideration be given to questions of human destiny as they bear upon the engagement in the inquiry. This point can be made less abstractly in terms of another notion that MacIntyre develops in conjunction with that of a tradition constituted inquiry, namely, the narrative character of human life which makes for its moral unity. MacIntyre argues that to comprehend the moral unity of a single human life requires not only the placing of past events into narrative relations with one another but also a correlative placing of those events in relation to projections of the future:

> There is no present which is not informed by some image of some future and an image of the future which always presents itself in the form of a *telos*—or of a variety of ends or goals—towards which we are either moving or failing to move in the present. Unpredictability and teleology therefore coexist as part of our lives; like characters in a fictional narrative we do not know what will happen next, but nonetheless our lives have a certain form which projects itself toward our future.[17]

In this view, history has its correlate in the possibility of hope. To the extent that effective engagement in a tradition constituted inquiry depends upon an appropriation of its history, it also involves expectations about the future into which such inquiry is moving. Such correlation is by no means accidental; the narrative that tells the history of the tradition limits possibilities for the future, though it neither exhausts their range nor makes them fully determinate. The narrative may be told in other ways, and through these versions yet other possibilities may be described. An understanding of human destiny—a view of the finality of the human reality to which the inquiry stands in service—emerges from both the narratives and the possibilities they open. This view may be incomplete and perhaps even inchoate, but without it inquiry can only drift. Although the tradition of inquiry gives shape to this understanding, the finality which is envisioned in the course of the inquiry also has power to shape the inquiry: if our tale is of the life and times of *homo economicus*, the player in the marketplace, we may find ourselves not only looking at just the marketplace for the events that make up this tale; we may also find ourselves taking—or rather, mistaking—the whole city as just the marketplace writ large.[18] We may even find ourselves convinced, by hearing it so insistently told, that the tale of *homo economicus* is the only one that can or need be told.

The possibility, in fact, the likelihood, of our making the kind of mistake in which a partial finality, only partially glimpsed, becomes that upon which we base the full range of our human expectations is one reason why, for the sake of its own integrity, public discourse stands under a pressing need to make space in which questions of human destiny can be engaged. This kind of mistake seems to occur most often—or at least most evidently in current discussion—when public conversation and civic argument try to engage issues of the environment. Partial finalities, such as economic development, resource management, protection of endangered species, maintenance of ecosystems, each clamor for the leading role and each would have the drama written differently; the drama each would have written is nothing less than an adumbration of the larger story it has to tell of human destiny. If the stage must be shared—as our "articles of peace" generally require it to be—it is more often in the manner of a variety show that carefully insulates player from player. In the absence of discussion of questions of human destiny, there is little possibility even for rehearsing the range of different dramas in which each of these players could take roles. No one is supposed to tell her story in a way that would make manifest how it just might turn out to foreshadow a full story of human destiny; this, ironically, makes all the more puzzling the partial stories that do get told.

I rest, for now, my case for the need for public conversation and civic argument to find a space where matters of human destiny can be raised. Let me turn now to the second part of my argument in which I will try to show the aptness of assigning to religious ethics the task of clearing such a space.

Public conversation, the "civic argument" wherein the goals and priorities of our political and socio-economic life are debated and established—disharmonious and cacophonous as it may be, as limited as the "articles of peace" sometimes require it to make its range of discussion—is nonetheless the place in which traditions of inquiry into the good of human life are expected to speak out. It is, indeed, the place where such traditions need to speak with one another so that the life of the polity can go on. The stories of crisis suggest that the cacophony has made it all the harder for us to hear patterns of intelligible speech, even our own. That may be one reason why some of the stories of crisis suggest that some disengagement from the clamor of the public conversation that constitutes civic argument may enable participants in particular traditions to learn anew, or learn better, the accents and the syntax of their own speech.[19] That may be a tactically useful move; its long range impact upon the shape of public conversation and argument, however, may be limited if we fail to pay concomitant attention to a far more pressing task: developing the skill to listen, with neither fear nor threat, to those who speak in accents other than our own.

121

This initial point is a crucial step for this part of my argument because preoccupation with properly appropriating our "own" traditions may deflect our attention from the larger conversation for which each tradition of inquiry shares responsibility to participate in and to sustain. This preoccupation, moreover, can make it tempting to think that discourse within a tradition of inquiry is—or ought to be—immune to that which makes the larger public conversation so tumultuous: the disquieting presence of otherness and difference.[20] The challenging presence of otherness and difference is one reason why we have needed "articles of peace" as a condition for the civility of public discourse: these articles represent a commitment to continue the conversation in the face of the kinds of persistent and stubborn difference and otherness in one another with which we have learned to live in peace.

Preoccupation with the proper appropriation of our own tradition may all too easily lead us to believe that there is no room for the challenging presence of otherness and difference in that place where we expect to feel most at home. The "articles of peace," we might think, are not necessary for discourse *entre nous:* after all, we all know that we do think alike—or at least that we ought to. This, I suspect, simply misses the complex ways by which a shared apprehension of truth may—perhaps even must—contain and even depend upon the abiding presence of difference and otherness. We can more easily note the complexity that allows the presence of otherness and difference if we follow MacIntyre's lead and take narrative, rather than theory, to constitute the more fundamental form of the unity and continuity of a tradition constituted inquiry. From this perspective, it comes as no surprise to hear, in converse with others who share with us the reflective appropriation of a particular tradition, other, quite different versions of the narrative we have appropriated as our own. Encountering these differences "within" may serve as a first step for learning the disciplined attentiveness that is a condition for the "openness to mutual transformation" needed for authentic conversation.

Human destiny—the issue of the final outcome of our lives, which can legitimately claim to be the focus of the most fundamental of our human hopes—is a matter over which "openness to mutual transformation" in our converse with one another is particularly difficult to sustain. It is particularly difficult to sustain because, in the matter of our human destiny, otherness and difference are most radically rooted and most radically encountered. Far too much seems to be at stake to allow our stubborn certainties about *our* destiny to be uprooted: better to direct my resistance against you rather than at my own certainty; better, indeed, to do violence against you, not so much because I am right but because you just *might* be; but since the "articles of peace" deny us the resort to violence, perhaps it is better that we not talk about it at all—or talk about it only with those who share like certainties.[21]

If, however, the first part of my argument is correct, that human destiny is a matter upon which we must at least be prepared to converse, then we must not allow "the articles of peace" to be no more than a silent truce. Religious ethics—or, more precisely those communities for which religious ethics provides a reflective articulation of moral vision and practice—could do much to bring about an effective extension of the "articles of peace" to cover the matter of human destiny. Simply by resisting the temptation to see its own discourse as a conversation that is, or should be, exempt from the challenge of internal difference and otherness, religious ethics could do much to clear space in public discourse for engaging the matter of human destiny. By doing so, religious ethics would thereby exemplify a commitment to conversation that retains its "twofold Latin sense . . . of living together and talking together"[22] even in the face of the most intractable differences we might have about the shape of our human destiny.[23]

NOTES

1. The versions of the story told by Robert Bellah et al., *Habits of the Heart: Individualism and Commitment in American Life* (Berkeley: University of California Press, 1985); Richard Bernstein, *Beyond Objectivism and Relativism: Science, Hermeneutics and Praxis* (Philadelphia: University of Pennsylvania Press, 1983); Alasdair MacIntyre, *After Virtue: A Study in Moral Theory*, 2nd edition (Notre Dame: University of Notre Dame Press, 1984); and *Whose Justice? Which Rationality?* (Notre Dame: University of Notre Dame Press, 1988), and David Tracy, *Plurality and Ambiguity: Hermeneutics, Religion and Hope* (San Francisco: Harper & Row, 1987), are my chief concern in this essay, though they each provide different renderings of the "crisis," as well as different prescriptions for dealing with it.

2. MacIntyre, *After Virtue* and *Whose Justice?*

3. This kind of story is told by Jeffrey Stout, *Ethics After Babel: The Lan-*

guages of Morality and Their Discontents (Boston: Beacon Press, 1988), and Michael Walzer, *Spheres of Justice: A Defense of Pluralism and Equality* (New York: Basic Books, 1983), among others. Walzer's version is one that I find particularly compelling in virtue of its breadth of coverage and depth of insight.

4. MacIntyre, *Whose Justice?* 335–338; John Courtney Murray, *We Hold These Truths: Catholic Reflections on the American Proposition*, 1960, reprinted with an introduction by Walter Burghardt (Kansas City, Mo.: Sheed & Ward, 1980), 72–76; William Sullivan, *Reconstructing the Public Philosophy* (Berkeley: University of California Press, 1986), 9–14; and Stout, *Ethics After Babel*, 266–288.

5. Murray, *These Truths*, 45–78.

6. The term "destiny" in this context is intended to include both those elements of the "final outcome" that are under our control and for which we bear responsibility and also those elements that are not under human control. My use of "destiny" in this sense has its roots in my readings of the central issue in Kant's critical project: the relation between the causal workings of nature and the moral ordering of human action in freedom. Kant's own efforts to answer the last of his three famous questions—"What may I hope?"—suggest that the historical path of human cultural, social, and political institutions has been forged through a struggle to gain a firmer prospect upon the human destiny that answers to our hope (Philip J. Rossi, "The Final End of All Things: The Highest Good as the Unity of Nature and Freedom," *Kant's Philosophy of Religion Reconsidered*, Philip J. Rossi and Michael Wreen, eds. [Bloomington: Indiana University Press, 1991]).

7. Walzer, *Spheres of Justice*, 238–248.

8. On a more limited scale, the articulation of "national purpose," which Bellah and his co-authors see as fundamental to the "politics of the nation," has faced a similar difficulty in the context of the fragmenting tendencies that become characteristic of the culture of individualism (Bellah, *Habits*, 200–207). In this case, however, the silence is not imposed by the "articles of peace." It issues from our own engagement and complicity in a culture that persuades us that we stand in isolation from one another even in the face of our human commonalities and that we can therefore decently respect one another only by rendering ourselves speechless about those commonalities.

9. Bellah, *Habits*, 219–249; Murray, *These Truths*, 72–73.

10. John Rawls, *A Theory of Justice* (Cambridge, Mass.: The Belknap Press of Harvard University, 1971), 553–554.

11. Recent discussions that distinguish between "contractarian" and "communitarian" views of ethics and social philosophy provide some help in identifying each of these "forces" and in sorting out the potential they each have for strengthening or weakening the "articles of peace." See Christopher Lasch, "The Communitarian Critique of Liberalism," *Soundings* (1986) 69:

60–76; Michael Sandel, *Liberalism and the Limits of Justice* (Cambridge: Cambridge University Press, 1982), and Sullivan, *Public Philosophy*.

12. I have argued elsewhere that the failure of long years of debate over abortion to yield such a locus for the sharing of common human hope is itself partly a consequence of the silence about matters of substantive human good that has been enjoined upon public conversation (Philip Rossi, "Abortion and the Pursuit of Happiness," *Logos: Philosophic Issues in Christian Perspective* [1982] 3:61–77).

13. Tracy, *Plurality and Ambiguity*, 93, cf. 10–17, 98–99; David Tracy, "Christianity in the Wider Context: Demands and Transformations," *Religion and Intellectual Life* (1987), 4:7–20; Bernstein, *Beyond Objectivism*, 2, 142–144.

14. MacIntyre, *Whose Justice?* 6–11, 349–359, 389–403, cf. MacIntyre, *After Virtue*, 275–278.

15. MacIntyre, *Whose Justice?* 402–403.

16. Ibid., 8–11, 349–369.

17. MacIntyre, *After Virtue*, 215–216.

18. Stout, *Ethics After Babel*, 286.

19. The ending of *After Virtue*, with its expectation of a new St. Benedict, could be read as such a suggestion. This is also a suggestion some critics see in the writings of Stanley Hauerwas.

20. Tracy, *Plurality and Ambiguity*, 20ff.

21. This attitude is one that H. Richard Niebuhr astutely dissects in chapter 5 of *The Responsible Self* (New York: Harper & Row, 1963). Also relevant is Gadamer's view, reported by Bernstein, *Beyond Objectivism*, 156, "the danger of contemporary *praxis* is not *techne*, but domination [Herrshaft]."

22. Murray, *These Truths*, 13.

23. I wish to thank Richard Collins, Rebecca Kasper, Shawn McCauley, Katherine Thome, and Charles Valenti-Hein, members of the graduate seminar "Pluralism and Moral Norms" at Marquette, for the helpful comments and searching questions they offered on matters discussed in this essay.

10

Destiny and Moral Duty: Which Is Prior?

Clark A. Kucheman

It may well be true, as Philip Rossi says in "Conflict, Community, and Human Destiny: Religious Ethics and the Public Construction of Morality," that "diverse considerations regarding human destiny already function as a central, though implicit, moral reference point for participants in the discourse that constitutes public conversation and civic argument." If so, then it is also true both that "public discourse is better served by making explicit the various considerations that function as such a reference point for all those who participate in it" and that "there needs to be a place within public conversation and civic argument where matters of human destiny can be debated and where the implications these matters have for the well-being of individuals, institutions, society at large, the world community, and the planet we inhabit can be drawn out." If we intend to participate intelligently in the public debate about "the goals and priorities we are to set for political, economic, and social life," then surely we need to be aware of the factors influencing the views of the people who participate in the debate with us.

Granting, however, that "considerations of human destiny" in fact do influence the views of participants in this debate, the question remains as to whether these considerations *should* have a "fundamental bearing upon the goals and priorities we are to set." "What is needed first," before we can determine what our moral duties are, Professor Rossi explains more clearly, "is an articulate presentation of a philosophical and theological vision of what we may hope for in human existence in consequence of the necessity of our going on together; this should be a picture, if you will, of the good to which we

126

are called and to which we are all drawn."[1] But why? Suppose that somehow we are able to determine what is "the final destiny and purpose of our lives" or, as he puts it here, what is "the good to which we are called and to which we are drawn." Do we thereby also determine what actions we ought as a matter of moral duty to do, or what "goals and priorities" for public policy we ought morally to adopt? Does the fact that some end or purpose, some "final outcome," is our destiny, our *telos*, imply that we ought as a matter of moral duty to act in pursuit of it?

We do have a destiny or *telos* to be sure. There is an end or "good" the achieving of which would fulfill our nature as persons, namely, what Hegel refers to as "concrete" or "positive" freedom. But the relationship between this *telos* and moral duty is precisely the reverse. The fact that positive freedom is our *telos*, destiny, or "good" is not by itself what makes it categorically imperative for us to act so as to become and be positively free; on the contrary, positive freedom is our *telos*, our "destiny and purpose," because we ought categorically to pursue it.

Rossi's purpose is to show only that we need *some* understanding of our destiny, *some* conception of what is "the good to which we are called and to which we are all drawn." In consequence he does not go on to propose a specific one. For the sake of discussion, then, let me propose—postponing the explanation of what it is until later—that the aforementioned positive freedom is my (and all other persons') destiny, that positive freedom is what I would achieve if I were to actualize my essential nature as a person. Now if I affirm positive freedom to be my destiny, by virtue of my essential nature as a person, do I thereby also affirm that I ought categorically—as a matter of moral duty—to act so as to become and be positively free? No. Since I cannot validly infer a proposition stating what I ought *categorically* to do from a proposition stating only the fact that positive freedom is my destiny, I affirm only that I ought *hypothetically* to act in this way. I affirm that, *if* I will it as my purpose or end to actualize my essential nature, *then*—as a means to this end—I ought to act so as to become and be positively free. I affirm that I ought to act so as to become and be positively free only on the condition that my purpose—which I am at liberty to change at will—happens to be that of actualizing my essential nature, my destiny or *telos*.

Hence the fact that some "final outcome"—including the one I am proposing here, positive freedom—is my *telos*, or my "good" in the sense of what would fulfill my essential nature as a person, does not

127

by itself imply that I ought categorically, for moral duty's sake, to act in pursuit of it.

Why, then, is it categorically imperative for me (and for all other persons) to act in pursuit of this end? What is positive freedom, and why is it my destiny or *telos*, not merely in the factual sense that achieving it would fulfill my essential nature but also in the morally normative sense that it is what I ought as a matter of moral duty to strive to actualize?

It is crucial to note that as a person, I am not as such the same as I am as an individual human being. "I am alive *in* this bodily organism which is my external existence,"[2] to be sure, as Hegel puts it. Indeed, I depend upon it. But "when I say 'I,' I *eo ipso* abandon all my particular characteristics, my disposition, natural endowment, knowledge, and age."[3] For all of these—including even my strongest desires—are objects about which I think and from which I therefore distinguish myself. As a person or "I" I am that from which I can*not* distinguish myself, namely, the subject or "thinking power"[4] whose activity the thinking is. As a person or "I" I am thus "the ultimate and unanalyzable point of consciousness"[5] in relation to whom everything else is an external object. "The ego is quite empty," as Hegel puts it, "a mere point, simple, yet active in this simplicity."[6]

As an "I," a "thinking power," I am in fact free, then, we now can see, at least negatively and in some degree, in that by virtue of my power of thinking I am capable of willing or deciding what propositions to believe theoretically, and consequently what actions to do practically as well, freely *from* causes external to me. My willing or deciding, whether about what to believe or about what to do, is negatively, contra-causally free. As "mere point" who thinks, as Hegel explains, "anyone can discover in himself ability to abstract from everything whatever, and in the same way to determine himself, to posit any content in himself by his own effort."[7]

In my negative, contra-causal freedom I can decide freely to decide what propositions to believe and what actions to do by submitting my deciding to someone—or to something such as a strong desire I may happen to have—that is external to me as "I." However, as I do if I "ced[e] to someone else full power and authority to fix and prescribe what actions are to be done . . . , or what duties are binding on [my] conscience or what religious truth is, &c,"[8] as Hegel says, I *freely* decide to decide *unfreely*. I am still negatively, contra-causally free if I do this, to be sure, and so I am responsible for the beliefs I hold and the actions I do. It is my free decision to submit my deciding to someone or something external to me. I am nevertheless freely *un*free if I do this, since my free decision is to decide what to believe and what to do by obeying someone or something external to me. I freely will to will unfreely, and so I am negatively but not positively free.

Positive freedom, then, we can see by way of contrast, consists in negatively, contra-causally freely willing to will what propositions to believe and what actions to do freely, that is, by obeying only one's own "I." "Freedom is to will something determinate, yet in this determinacy to be by oneself and to revert once more to the universal [the 'I'],"[9] as Hegel says. Or again, "The will is [positively] free only when it does not will anything alien, extrinsic, foreign to itself (for as long as it does so, it is dependent), but wills itself alone—wills the will."[10] I am positively as well as negatively, contra-causally free if and only if I decide negatively, contra-causally freely to decide what to believe and what to do by obeying myself as "I."

To do this is of course not to decide to believe whatever propositions and to do whatever actions best satisfy the desires I happen to have. My desires are external rather than internal to me as "I," and therefore I freely decide to decide *un*freely, not *freely*, if I freely decide to decide what propositions to believe and what actions to do by submitting to my desires. Instead, I freely will to will in obedience only to myself as "I" and so positively freely—I "will the will"— only if and to the extent that I freely will to will "what is rational."[11] More precisely, I negatively, contra-causally freely decide to decide positively freely if and to the extent that I freely decide to decide what propositions to believe theoretically and what actions to do practically by thinking in obedience to "the necessary forms and self-determinations of thought"—"pure reason"[12]—namely, the laws or principles of deductive and inductive logic. For as person or "I" I *am* the "mere point" who thinks, the "thinking power," and since, in Hegel's words, "in logic a thought is understood to include nothing else but what depends on thinking and what thinking has brought into existence,"[13] I therefore obey myself as "I" if and only if I decide what propositions to believe and what actions to do by deliberating in a logically valid way.

Now, finally, we can see both that and why it is categorically imperative for me (and for all other persons) to do this. "What is right and obligatory is the absolutely rational element in the will's volitions."[14] "Will making itself its own object is the basis of all right and obligation. . . . The freedom of the will *per se* is the principle and substantial basis of all right—is itself absolute, inherently eternal right, and the supreme right in comparison with other specific rights."[15] Why? Because I can deny that I ought categorically to decide what propositions to believe theoretically—and therefore also what actions to do practically—by deliberating in a logically valid way only by affirming at the same time that I ought categorically to do so. Since by affirming any proposition whatever I presuppose that logically valid deliberation justifies me in doing so, I contradict myself if I deny rather than affirm that I ought categorically to decide what propositions to believe by deliberating in a logically valid fashion.

Hence, positive freedom is my (and all other persons') *telos* as person or "I," not only in the factual sense that it fulfills my nature as a "thinking power" but also in the morally normative sense that I ought categorically to will the actualization of positive freedom as my overall purpose or end. It is for me (and for all other persons) a morally imperative "final outcome," one that I (and all other persons) ought for moral duty's sake to pursue.[16] "To such an extent as man acts like a creature of nature, his whole behavior is not what it ought to be. For the spirit [i.e., thinking being] it is a duty to be free, and to realize itself by its own act."[17]

NOTES

1. "Abortion and the Pursuit of Happiness," *Logos: Philosophic Issues in Christian Perspective*, no. 3 (1982): 72.
2. G. W. F. Hegel, *Philosophy of Right*, tr. T. M. Knox (Oxford: Clarendon Press, 1962), para. 46, 43. Hereafter referred to as *PR*.
3. *PR*, para. 4, addition, 226.
4. G. W. F. Hegel, *Logic*, trans. William Wallace (Oxford: Clarendon Press, 1975), para. 28, 49.
5. *Ibid.*, para. 24, 38.
6. *PR*, para. 4, addition, 226.
7. *PR*, para. 4, 21.
8. *PR*, para. 66, 53.
9. *PR*, para. 7, addition, 229.
10. G. W. F. Hegel, *The Philosophy of History*, trans. J. Sibree (New York: Dover Publications, Inc., 1956), 442.
11. *PR*, para. 15, addition, 230.
12. G. W. F. Hegel, *Science of Logic*, trans. A. V. Miller (London: George Allen & Unwin, 1969), 50.
13. *Logic*, para. 24, 39.
14. *PR*, para. 137, 91.

15. *The Philosophy of History*, 443.

16. While I cannot give a full explanation here, suffice it to say that logically valid deliberation requires us to affirm that we ought categorically to act only in ways that treat all persons, all "thinking powers"—including ourselves—always as persons, "I"'s who freely will purposes of their own, and never as mere things, "it"'s which cannot think and so do not freely will purposes of their own. It requires us to "behave . . . toward others in a manner that is universally valid," as Hegel puts it, "recognizing them—as [we] will others to recognize [us]—as free, as persons" (*Philosophy of Mind*, trans. William Wallace and A. V. Miller [Oxford: At The Clarendon Press, 1971], para. 432, 173).

17. *Logic*, para. 24, 44.

11

Personal Responsibility and the Common Good in John Paul II

John Langan, S.J.

During the decade of the eighties Roman Catholic social teaching went through a period of high visibility. This reflects the active involvement of Roman Catholicism (along with other churches) in political and social conflicts in such disparate locations as El Salvador, South Africa, Poland, the Philippines, the United States, Ireland, Brazil, Lebanon, Uganda, and Korea. It also reflects the increased output of the church's two main centers of teaching authority: the papacy and the various national bishops' conferences. This body of teaching, which goes back in its modern form to the encyclical *Rerum novarum* of Leo XIII in 1891, has been a primary locus for the church to elaborate its complex and ambivalent reactions to the modern world and a way for the church to position itself in relation to shifting political and ideological currents. These functions of the church's social teaching are particularly explicit in the pastoral constitution of Vatican Council II on the church in the modern world, which is usually referred to by its Latin title, *Gaudium et spes*. At the same time Catholic social teaching has drawn on both philosophical and religious sources and methods. It has presented itself as the continuation and application of natural law in the conditions of our times and as an expression of the church's proclamation of the good news of salvation in which the church draws on biblical affirmations and symbols and exercises its prophetic function.[1]

ANALYSIS OF ENCYCLICALS

The current custodian and chief expositor of this body of teaching is himself a philosopher, who clearly takes a strong personal interest in

132

the articulation of his own views on a wide variety of social, political, and economic issues and who is concerned both to preserve the continuity of Catholic teaching and to assert the active presence of the church in the contemporary intellectual dialogue. In what follows, I will be engaged in a preliminary analysis of themes from the teaching of John Paul II. If I may put the matter personally, this is my effort to explain to myself why I am simultaneously attracted and disconcerted by this pope's two major social encyclicals, *Laborem Exercens* (LE) and *Sollicitudo Rei Socialis* (SRS). Trying to answer this question is not a matter of purely autobiographical interest, since it seems clear that these documents have puzzled many people in English-speaking cultures in the academic, public policy, and business arenas. They have appeared as signs of encouragement to many on the left who are often out of sympathy with much that the present pope says on moral and religious issues and as signs of contradiction to many on the right who applaud his opposition to Marxism and liberal permissiveness.

Both documents, but more especially, *Sollicitudo Rei Socialis*, which was issued in the early part of 1988, are of more than usual current political interest, since they represent the views of someone who has been deeply interested in getting Europe beyond its once seemingly permanent division into East and West and who leads one of the few institutions that has been a significant (though often silenced and persecuted) actor on both sides of that division. I propose to focus on section 5, "A Theological Reading of Modern Problems," paragraphs 36–40 of *Sollicitudo Rei Socialis*, which begins with a remarkable conclusion: "It is important to note therefore that a world which is divided into blocs, sustained by rigid ideologies, and in which instead of interdependence and solidarity different forms of imperialism hold sway, can only be a world subject to structures of sin" (36).[2] Here is the East-West conflict with its negative consequences for the development of the South, which John Paul II has already described in section III, "Survey of the Contemporary World." He has already made it clear that he regards the ideological bases of this conflict as temporally and historically conditioned and indeed as somewhat archaic. He observes that both the fundamental intellectual conceptions shaping the present conflict—liberal capitalism and Marxist collectivism—are "imperfect and in need of radical correction" and that the church takes a critical attitude to both of these competing world systems.[3] He then proceeds to raise a very interesting and fundamental question about both systems: "In what way and to what extent are these two systems capable of changes and updatings such as to favor or promote a true and integral development of individuals and peoples in modern society?" (21).

All of this is reasonably familiar to students of Catholic social teaching, which has, over the last century, striven to position itself independently as an alternative to both Marxist socialism and liberal capitalism. But John Paul II goes beyond the range of customary platitudes on this subject in characterizing the bipolar world of East-West relations as necessarily a world "subject to structures of sin," as he does here. Here, as the argument of this paragraph makes plain, he is making a double move. On the one hand, there is the move from personal sin to structures of sin, a move that he had already made in the Apostolic Exhortation, *Reconciliatio et Paenitentia* of 1984. There he had insisted that institutions, structures, and societies are not the subject of moral acts, and that social sins are "the result of the accumulation and concentration of many personal sins." In *Sollicitudo Rei Socialis* he maintains that structures of sin are "always linked to the concrete acts of individuals who introduce these structures, consolidate them and make them difficult to remove"(36). The earlier treatment of this theme in *Reconciliatio et Paenitentia*, quoted in the footnote, makes it clear that the pope wishes to accuse of personal sin not merely those who introduce, promote, or defend evil structures but also those "who are in a position to avoid, eliminate, or at least limit certain social evils but who fail to do so out of laziness, fear, or the conspiracy of silence, through secret complicity or indifference, of those who take refuge in the supposed impossibility of changing the world and also of those who sidestep the effort and sacrifice required, producing specious reasons of a high order."[4]

This listing of the factors that lead us to passivity and to sins of omission in the face of grave evils is sufficiently pointed and comprehensive to make most of us at least consider the possibility that our own passivity may lack not merely justification but even excuse. At any rate, it is important to see that the pope's affirmation of personal responsibility and personal sin is not intended to restrict the scope of socially significant sin to a relatively small number of "movers and shakers" who initiate harmful practices or who derive substantial benefits from them. Rather, it seems to apply to almost all who can count as citizens or agents. John Paul II's approach would not allow us to draw a comforting line between a sinful social realm of powerful institutions and a private realm of passive innocents whose lives are occasionally marred by personal vices. Rather the point is that very many of us are guilty of personal sins that help to establish or maintain structures of sin. The pope does admit, however, that the situation confronting ordinary moral agents working in contemporary society is not an easy one: "The sum total of negative factors working against a true awareness of the universal common good, and the need to further it, gives the impression of creating, in persons and institutions, an obstacle which is difficult to overcome" (36). This implies that many people are functioning with a diminished awareness of the social moral demands of their situation. It is clear that for John Paul II personal sin remains the fundamental category, and the notion of structures of sin is secondary and derivative both in terms of our thinking about our situation and our actions to transform it.

The other move that the pope makes in this paragraph is that he defends the appropriateness of speaking of social and political problems in terms of sin. This is a move which puts him at odds with those who on empiricist or naturalistic grounds would reject the application of theological categories to social phenomena. It also puts him at odds with the much larger number of those who, because of a variety of intellectual and non-intellectual factors, prefer to think about social realities in more neutral, value-free, impartial ways. These ways have become the *lingua franca* for political and social reporting and analysis, but even in a secularized milieu it is not easy to eliminate all moral implications and resonances from our language in these areas. As John Paul II observes:

> One can certainly speak of "selfishness" and of "shortsightedness," of "mistaken political calculations" and "imprudent economic decisions." And in each of these evaluations one hears an echo of a moral and ethical nature. Man's condition is such that a more profound analysis of individuals' actions and omissions cannot be achieved without implying, in one way or another, judgments or references of an ethical nature. (36)

In the pope's view, socio-political analysis contains an evaluative element, which may or may not be based on "faith in God and on his law" (36).

Analysis from the theological viewpoint takes the further step of considering social phenomena in terms of "the will of the Triune God" who "requires from people clearcut attitudes which express themselves also in actions or omissions toward one's neighbor" (36). The failure to observe the commandments of the "second tablet," (those that deal with our treatment of our fellow human beings) is both an offense against God and a source of harm to the neighbor. It introduces "into the world influences and obstacles which go far beyond the actions and the brief lifespan of an individual" and also "involves interference in the process of the development of peoples" (36). What we should notice here is not merely the affirmation of the close connection of our attitudes to God and to the neighbor, which is a standard theme in contemporary Catholic moral theology,[5] but also the very strong emphasis on the causal interconnectedness of our actions and the enduring and irretrievable character of their consequences. The emphasis on consequences, especially as these affect the social context, is, interestingly enough, a theme that is common to this pope and to utilitarian moralists.

But the moral atmosphere, the climate of concern which the pope deems appropriate for the making of moral decisions, is clearly more intense, more charged, even more anxious than the neutral and secular climate usually favored by utilitarians. Rather, it seems closer to the more strenuous approaches to the moral life propounded by Augustine and Kierkegaard, in which sin and guilt are inescapable and in which freedom, if not exercised in union with God's will, is more burden than benefit. The decisive step forward from the present sinful situation is not for John Paul II the adoption of a new set of policies which will have better consequences. Instead, it is the recognition of "the urgent need to change the spiritual attitudes which define each individual's relationship with self, with neighbor, with even the remotest human communities, and with nature itself, and all of this in view of higher values such as the *common good*, or . . . the full development of the whole individual and of all people" (38). In Christian terms, he observes, this is a matter of "conversion," which "entails a relationship to God, to the sin committed, to its consequences, and hence to one's neighbor" (38).

ATTITUDES AND SOCIAL CONSEQUENCES

In the presentation of both the moral problem and its resolution, there is a strong emphasis on the movement from attitude through action to consequences and a profound reluctance to adopt a restricted understanding of the moral life that would concentrate exclusively on either attitudes or consequences. This is not surprising in a religious social ethics, which is under the double requirement of looking to the relationship of the believer to God and to the effects of actions on other persons. It is quite appropriate, then, for John Paul II to direct our attention specifically to two attitudes that have easily understood social consequences. These are: "the all-consuming desire for profit" and "the thirst for power" (37). The pope is particularly concerned about these attitudes when they are found in extreme or absolute forms. He recognizes that these attitudes can exist independently of each other; but he resists the temptation to attribute the first of these attitudes to the West and the second to the East in our present bipolar world. Rather, he makes the claim that "in today's world both are indissolubly united with one or the other predominating" (37). He does not offer any specific evidence or arguments for this interesting claim, which seems both attractive and vulnerable to counterexamples. What he does insist on is that these sinful attitudes favor the introduction of "structures of sin" and that they serve as the deep explanation of socially significant decisions even when these are not expressed in moral terms. He affirms that "hidden behind certain decisions, apparently inspired only by economics or politics, are real forms of idolatry: of money, ideology, class, technology" (37). For these are not merely the values of individuals; they can also be found in nations and blocs. In John Paul II's view, thinking in terms of the various "forms of idolatry" rather than in terms of "imperialism" enables us to grasp "the true nature of the evil which faces us with respect to the development of peoples: it is a question of moral evil, the fruit of many sins which lead to 'structures of sin'" (37).

Analysis of the problem of development in moral and theological terms also enables us to "identify precisely, on the level of human conduct, the path to be followed in order to overcome it" (37). This path involves the recognition of moral value and of the necessity for the transformation of spiritual attitudes. More specifically, the pope points to "the positive and moral value of the growing awareness of interdependence among individuals and nations" (38). Interdependence is both a social system determining relationships in the contemporary world and a moral category. The virtue that expresses our new moral and social attitude is the virtue of solidarity, which John Paul II defines in the following way:

> This [solidarity] then is not a feeling of vague compassion or shallow distress at the misfortunes of so many people, both near and far. On the contrary, it is a firm and persevering determination to commit oneself to the common good; that is to say to the good of all and of each individual, because we are all really responsible for all. (38)

137

The pope's language here makes it clear that he sees solidarity as very closely linked to justice; for his definition of it echoes the definition that Thomas Aquinas gives of the virtue of justice, that is, justice as present in the agent or subject rather than as a set of norms for social institutions.[6] Instead of the indefinite and potentially individualistic *unicuique* ("each one"), which figures in Aquinas's definition, John Paul uses "the common good." While the classical definition uses the comparatively objective and restricted notion of rendering to each person what is due (*reddere debitum*), John Paul employs the more personalist notion of self-commitment, a notion which strikes this observer as more open to the future and to the possibility of unspecified demands.

The connection between solidarity and the classical understanding of justice is also apparent if we reflect on the two previously mentioned attitudes that John Paul II sees as most opposed to solidarity: the desire for profit and the thirst for power. For these are attitudes that lead people to take more than their share, to manifest the *pleonexia*, or graspingness, that Aristotle saw as the most prolific source of injustice in social life.[7] To overcome these attitudes, which generate sinful structures, John Paul II commends "a diametrically opposed attitude: a commitment to the good of one's neighbor with the readiness, in the Gospel sense, to 'lose oneself' for the sake of the other instead of exploiting him and to 'serve him' instead of oppressing him for one's own advantage" (38). This of course is what one might call a top-of-the-line form of solidarity, which draws on the heroic sacrifices commended in Christ's teaching and example. There can be little doubt that sustained commitment to such a self-surrendering and serving attitude would remove the typical human agent from the possibility of falling under the dominion of the desires for power and profit that the pope sees as fundamental sources of social evils.

There also seems to be a continuing need for more mundane and less sacrificial forms of solidarity, which are not simply the polar opposites of our desires for profit and power. In fact, John Paul II goes on to specify the exercise of solidarity so that it includes the responsibility more influential people have for the weaker members of society and the responsibility the weaker members have for claiming their legitimate rights. Among the positive developments in the contemporary world that the former archbishop of Krakow wants to commend are: "the growing awareness of the solidarity of the poor among themselves, their efforts to support one another, and their public demonstrations on the social scene which, without recourse to

138

violence, present their own needs and rights in the face of the inefficiency or corruption of the public authorities" (39). In a passage such as this John Paul II acknowledges the necessity and value of self-assertion by the poor, a self-assertion which takes its ethical shape from the needs and rights of the poor and which brings them from passive subjection through to active citizenship. In this regard John Paul II points in the same direction as do liberation theologians when they call for the empowerment of the poor and the United States Catholic bishops when they call for an economy which makes the right to participate effective for all.[8]

CONDITIONS OF SOLIDARITY

We should note that combining the endorsement of an ethic of non-violent self-assertion for the poor and weak with an ethic of generous self-giving for the rich and strong produces a situation of formal asymmetry and practical convergence. Those above the median are urged to accept less favorable outcomes for themselves, and those below it are encouraged to seek more favorable outcomes for themselves. This, I would argue, will only make sense if certain conditions are satisfied.

First, there has to be a clear recognition that the goods necessary for survival and for functioning as free and equal citizens are sufficiently valuable that their absence can be a legitimate basis for social criticism and for broad economic and political changes. The value of these goods is such that it is a serious moral and religious error to urge others to do without them or to acquiesce in social arrangements that deprive significant numbers of people of these goods or of the opportunity to obtain them. *A fortiori*, it is morally and religiously unacceptable, indeed, sinful, to deprive people of these goods. At the same time these goods, some of which we label material (food, clothing, shelter, health care) and some of which we label civic or cultural (civil liberties, education, the rule of law), do not have the ultimate and transcendent worth of moral and religious values. These higher values justify, require, and in some cases facilitate the redistribution and reallocation of the instrumental goods that we need for living as persons and as citizens. More particularly, the goods that we have labeled as material and the wealth that enables us to obtain them have to be understood as goods, not by reason of their correspondence to our ever increasing desires or by reason of the possibilities of indefinite multiplication and maximization that they present but by reason of their instrumental contribution to comprehensive human well-being. Such an understanding of these goods provides a middle ground between the otherworldly depreciation of the goods of "this world," which has marked a great deal of traditional Catholicism, and those excessively avid commendations of material goods which appeal to naive or desperate desires for personal happiness through consumption and which often serve to give a specious legitimation to *pleonexia* in the lives of individuals and societies.

Second, the moral urgency of rights has to be interpreted so that it applies primarily and decisively to those rights that are necessary for survival and for participation in society as free and equal citizens. Thus, rights to private property, rights to goods and services that are not included in this core, take a secondary place and are open to partial restriction and renunciation for the sake of the common good. This is in accordance with the traditional recognition in Catholic social teaching that property rights are not to be absolutized[9] and with the general philosophical view that human or natural rights, at least in their central instances, take precedence over positive rights that arise from particular decisions and historical circumstances.

The underlying issue here is whether the strong and the rich are well off because all their gains are ill-gotten and originate in violations of moral norms and of the rights of others. The view that the correct answer to this question is affirmative has been widely spread by many critics of capitalism, ranging from muckraking journalists who were more interested in good stories than in ideological systems, to liberation theologians who embrace dependency theory with its affirmation that the wealth of the center depends on its exploitation of the periphery. However, given the manifest disparities in human talent and willingness to work and venture, and given the enormous diversity of the ways in which circumstances alter human lives and fortunes, the affirmative answer, while clearly true for a large number of particular cases and while possibly true for many more, is not a sustainable thesis when it is made comprehensive and universal. If at least some of the resulting differences in people's economic and social situations are not the result of morally suspect activity, then we have to deal with a situation of inequality in which people have been exercising their rights to make economically significant decisions and in which they have been acting in accordance with legal and ethical norms such as the honoring of contracts. In Robert Nozick's terminology, they have been observing justice in transfers.[10] So it seems that what gains they have made are rightfully theirs.

At the same time, if the position of Catholic social teaching on these matters is correct, some of their gains will have to be restricted and redistributed. This will require an ordering of rights according to the weight and urgency of considerations which justify their being overridden. Catholic social teaching has registered its disapproval of increasingly inegalitarian outcomes, even while it has never insisted on a strict or leveling equality.[11] Rather than arguing for confiscation of the property of the wealthy on the ground that disparity of wealth is intrinsically unjust or that wealth has been unjustly acquired, it has advocated redistribution, both legally required and voluntary, to meet the needs of those whose well-being is endangered. This advocacy of redistribution goes beyond urging generosity to the poor as a commendable exercise of supererogation and Christian charity. It involves a claim that as a matter of justice the common good requires redistribution to meet the basic needs of the poor. The common good itself has to be understood in such a way that it is both an integral and necessary part of the good of the rich, which they are not free to neglect, and that it includes the basic well-being of the poor (as well as of the rich).

The obligation to promote the common good falls upon all. Yet such a formulation tells us little because the common good is a complex analogical good that cannot be promoted by simple maximization and because the obligation to promote the common good turns out to be a set of more specific obligations to act in ways that will promote the common good. These are obligations that have to be argued for in more specific ways.

Third, there has to be a network of psychological motives and social considerations that will be effective in causing people and groups above the median to accept a diminishing of their prospects, interests, and even rights so that those who are at or below the decent minimum may fare better.[12] It has been common ground to both liberal and Catholic social thinkers that achieving this convergence of prospects by purely coercive methods would require a dangerous concentration of power in the state and would set administrators and regulators a task of enormous complexity that would quickly surpass their capacities for judgment and decision. It would thus be quite likely to produce economic stultification on a grand scale, a phenomenon that has figured prominently in the recent wave of self-criticism within communist regimes. On the other hand, Catholic social thought has been willing to accept and even urge a considerable measure of governmentally imposed redistribution for the sake of those least well-off. So the church has not relied simply on calls to conversion and voluntary giving. It has clearly presented the issue as a matter of justice, and so it rules out complacency and passivity in the face of outcomes which diverge systematically or constantly from the norms it proposes. Once these various points are noted, it may not be possible to go much further, since the proper mixture of appeals to compassion and generosity, of reminders of the stern demands of justice, of legal enactments with proportionate penalties, of macroeconomic policy adjustments and tax incentives, of community activism and personal initiatives, will probably vary with different cultures and with different policy problems. We should not underestimate the difficulties of persuading the rich and the powerful to accept restrictions on their prospects, whether these rich and powerful constitute a small elite or an extensive stratum of an affluent society. Such a task of persuasion is not impossible, but it is normally very difficult and grows comparatively easy only at certain moments of opportunity. I suspect these moments will be found only in times of great economic and political crisis (the Great Depression, World War II, the current wave of economic failures in the Second and Third Worlds) or less often in times of sustained economic expansion (the war on poverty).

CRITICAL QUESTIONS

So far, my remarks on *Sollicitudo Rei Socialis* have been primarily expository and interpretative. These are functions that cannot be taken lightly in assessing the social teachings of the present pope, whose writings are both more abstract and more concrete, more expansive and more demanding than papal social teachings have usually been in this century. Furthermore, this encyclical manifests a high proportion of assertion to argument and frequently crosses with unwarranted facility from analysis to admonition. These are traits that trouble those of us who have been trained in the more modest and more painstaking disciplines of moral and political philosophy as these are currently practiced in the anglophone world. We lack many of the signposts that are familiar to us in the philosophical debates arising from the work of John Rawls and Robert Nozick, and in the broader cultural and policy debates carried on by Daniel Bell, Michael Novak, the United States Catholic bishops, Robert Bellah, and others.

My own conviction is that initially, at least, we should not criticize papal teaching for its failure to speak to American experience in American terms, though we should be sensitive to the real differences in terminology and intellectual outlook that result from this fact. The first task has been to conduct a preliminary reconnaissance to determine what is central in the teaching of this document and what is the structure of the thought and the aspirations that inform it. Still, without feeling any desire to rush to judgment, I want to raise some critical questions.

First, there seems to this reader to be a profound tension between the affirmation of the possibilities for conversion and the recognition of the ways in which people are involved with or enmeshed in structures of sin. Second, I sense an underlying impatience with those historical, technical, and institutional ways of explaining how manifest problems came to have the shape they actually have. Such explanations can dull our sense of the moral urgency of change and may cause us too readily to identify the real and the rational, the contingent outcome of historical events, and the necessary unfolding of historical process.[13] Nevertheless, without them we are likely to lack historical perspective and a sense of the roots of our problems. Third, alongside the reiterated affirmations of interdependence, there is a refusal to come to terms with the interlocking character of our decisions, with the ways in which the freedom of others complicates and frustrates our efforts to resolve the problems the pope indicates. Fourth, there is a persistent reluctance to examine the problems presented by the negative and unintended consequences of those actions that we perform with even the best of intentions and attitudes, as well as to think through the problem of tradeoffs in interdependent systems. If one thinks that something like this set of criticisms is correct, even if they are put in rather cryptic and undiscriminating fashion, then one has reason to suspect that the underlying tendency of this pope's social thought is a utopian and ahistorical moralism.

Sollicitudo rei socialis, with its simultaneous emphases on the influence of human sin on the shaping of social institutions, on the inescapably social character of our actions, on the urgency of personal conversion from egoistic desires for power and wealth to spiritual values, and on the indispensability of solidarity for the attainment of the common good, reads in many ways like a sustained effort to put us all in a box clearly marked for moral laggards and sinners. Such affirmations as "collaboration in the development of the whole person and of every human being is in fact a duty of all towards all" (32) seem to be little more than moralistic exhortations designed to convict all of us of sin, and are likely to produce in many a reaction of defensive or even derisive dismissal. The pope's immensely demanding articulation of our social life and its moral requirements can lead us to several different responses.

One is what I would call the Lutheran reply, which is to affirm that in our social responsibilities and relationships we are bound to be both just and sinners, a condition which cannot in principle be overcome. This reply is at odds with the Catholic conception of sin and justification as well as with this particular pope's strenuous calls for the moral and religious transformation of contemporary society. The Lutheran reply can be developed in either of two directions, one a resigned acceptance of this painful condition of being drawn to the common good and being unable to attain it; the other a meliorist trudging forward in the hope that by endurance and work we will make things somewhat better though we will also dirty our hands in the process.

The second reply is the modernist one, the reply of those who have been schooled by the "masters of suspicion" and who will look for the hidden ideological content of initially attractive and apparently compelling value affirmations. This can become a defensive strategy intended to reassure ourselves and our fellow citizens that we are doing as well as can reasonably be expected and that further moral demands on us are out of place. If successful, this breaks us out of the box; but it is not easy to reconcile with a candid assessment of our various social pathologies and with recognition of extensive areas of failure in our political and economic life as well as with the general Christian acknowledgment of human sinfulness. This reply is likely to be the voice of a "realism" that is more tired than honest.

The third reply is what I would call the Jamesian one, which is the belief that such a demanding reading of our moral situation is a call for us to live the moral life of our society in a more generous and expansive way, rising to the trumpet calls and the mountain vistas offered by a religious conception of morality as the demands of an infinite and loving God.[14] In this view, we are called to do heroic things, and we shall be better even for our occasional or even repeated failures. This view, while attractive, especially to Americans of an optimistic and energetic temperament, is not easy to reconcile with morality as a system of universally binding norms or with the deep social need for a high degree of reliability in our moral endeavors. It may, if it is not balanced by a humble realism about oneself and one's moral limitations, lead to what Christianity has historically rejected as the heresy of Pelagianism.

The fourth reply is akin to the third, in that it expects an optimistic transformation of the box that we are in, but differs from it in that it expects that transformation to come from God's grace altering our social world. It is what I would call the millenarian reply, a view that God will bring about a new social order, a "kingdom of the saints," in which policy will conform to principle, performance will match profession, and "the meek . . . will inherit the earth" (Matt. 5:5). It is always difficult for Christians to affirm confidently that such a change will not occur, much less that it cannot occur. But it is equally difficult for them to make it a reliable basis for personal decisions and social policies; this is a difficulty that has been apparent at least since the time Paul wrote his second letter to the Thessalonians.

All of these replies are, I would argue, unsatisfactory either as responses to the moral burden of contemporary social life itself or as exegeses of the thought of John Paul II. I think that there is a fifth response, a way out of "the box" that is as removed as the previous four from standard forms of political analyses in terms of interests and power relationships. This fifth response also deviates from the customary expectations that we have about ourselves and our fellow human beings as creatures marred by moral frailty and social blindness, even at our best. This is to suppose a situation in which people come to understand the destructive and oppressive character of their dominant social institutions. They aspire to a new order of society in which human rights are guaranteed, new institutions are created, and the virtues of justice and solidarity are practiced. They come to understand that, in order to bring about this new order of society, they must withdraw from their involvement in the sinful structures of the old order (often enough at some risk to their careers, their liberty, and even their lives). They must without resorting to force or relying on the weight of routine, break the hold of sin on their lives and their society. Then there exists for them the real possibility of a considerably better world with the prospect that individuals will meet their responsibilities and that the common good will be realized.

If one looks at events in Eastern Europe in 1989–1990, one can argue that what has been sketched here is not simply a moralistic or utopian fantasy but a very general and not implausible account of a remarkable political and social transformation that has actually occurred. Realists (of the political rather than epistemological variety) may well point to special circumstances in this transformation, in particular, the widespread recognition by the great majority of the participants that resort to force would be counterproductive and would leave nearly everyone worse off. They can also point to the quasi-universal dissatisfaction with the economic performance of the East-bloc countries. Historians can point to the ultimate failure of analogous movements of popular feeling in 1848 and 1968. Observers anxious about the future rightly question the prospects for new institutions in what are bound to be difficult economic times and remind us of the persistence of ethnic hatreds and unresolved grievances. The papal effort to fashion a politics of personal responsibility for and commitment to the common good may illuminate and be illuminated by this one very special moment in European history without proving itself as a universal prescription. Certainly, most contemporary commentators, whether they are conventional realists in their analyses of international relations or ideological cold warriors, are not able to tell us much more than that the course of events in Eastern Europe in 1989 was surprising and did not fit their previously established categories. But these events and the papal interpretation of the situation to which they were a response can suggest to us the possibility of a way out of the box constructed by our lofty moral aspirations and our limited capacity to envision and achieve the good. Even if this possibility, the possibility of a freely undertaken, nonviolent moral renovation of the major institutions of society is only rarely available to us, its very possibility tells against reductive and pessimistic interpretations of the human condition that would minimize the political significance of both personal responsibility and the common good.

NOTES

1. For the changes in the relative weight accorded to these two different sources of Roman Catholic social teaching, see David Hollenbach, *Claims in Conflict: Retrieving and Renewing the Catholic Human Rights Tradition* (New York: Paulist Press, 1979), ch. 2, "The Development of the Roman Catholic Rights Theory."

2. John Paul II, *On Social Concern (Sollicitudo rei socialis)* (Washington, D.C.: U.S. Catholic Conference, 1988), para. 36. The numbers in parentheses after

quotations from the encyclical refer to the numbered paragraphs of the encyclical.

3. In this encyclical, John Paul II observes that "the Church's social doctrine adopts a critical attitude towards both liberal capitalism and Marxist collectivism" (para. 21) and affirms that "the Church's social doctrine is not a third way between liberal capitalism and Marxist collectivism" (para. 41)

4. John Paul II, Apostolic Exhortation *Reconciliatio et Paenitentia* (1984), para. 16; cited in *Sollicitudo rei socialis*, para. 36, footnote 65.

5. For a particularly influential affirmation of the identity of the love of God and the love of neighbor, see Karl Rahner, S.J., "Reflections on the Unity of the Love of Neighbor and the Love of God," in *Theological Investigations*, VI, trans. Karl H. and Boniface Kruger (Baltimore: Helicon Press, 1969).

6. Thomas Aquinas, *Summa Theologiae* II. II, 58, 11c.

7. Aristotle, *Nicomachean Ethics*, V. 1. 1129b1.

8. U.S. Catholic Bishops, *Economic Justice for All* (Washington, D.C.: U.S. Catholic Conference, 1986), paras. 71, 73, 77, 88, 91.

9. Cf. Paul VI, *Populorum Progressio* (1967), paras. 22, 26.

10. Robert Nozick, *Anarchy, State, and Utopia* (New York: Basic Books, 1974), 150–153.

11. Cf. *Economic Justice for All*, paras. 68–76, 183–185.

12. It can be argued that this is the central task that John Rawls sets for himself in *A Theory of Justice*, namely, to show that it is rational for nonaltruistic agents to accept such an orientation of social policy.

13. This has been a line of criticism urged against the philosophical theodicy of Hegel.

14. See, particularly, the essay by William James, "The Moral Philosopher and the Moral Life," in *The Will to Believe* (New York: Longmans, Green, 1896), esp, 210–215.

12

On the Priority of Personal to Structural Evil in Catholic Social Teaching: A Critique

Nancey Murphy

John Langan's essay, "Personal Responsibility and the Common Good in John Paul II," can be divided into two sections: the first is a very interesting exposition of the social teachings of John Paul II. The second part is a critical assessment of those teachings. I shall begin my response with an exposition of the critical part of the essay, exposition and interpretation being functions that are not to be taken lightly in assessing Langan's position.

LANGAN'S CRITIQUE

The focus of Langan's criticisms is the relation between individual sin and social structures in the thought of John Paul II. For our purposes, the most significant aspects of the pope's teachings are summarized in the following quotations from Langan's paper:

> Institutions, structures, and societies are not the subject of moral acts, . . . "social sins are the result of the accumulation and concentration of many personal sins."

> It is clear that for John Paul II personal sin remains the fundamental category, and that the notion of structures of sin is secondary and derivative both in terms of our thinking about our situation and our actions to transform it.

> The decisive step forward from the present sinful situation . . . is the recognition of "the urgent need to change the spiritual atti-

tudes which define each individual's relationship with self, with
neighbor, with even the remotest human communities" . . . this
is a matter of "conversion."

The important factor here is the emphasis on a one-way causal relation: individual action determines social realities.

Langan offers four criticisms of this position: (1) its view of conversion fails to take adequate account of the ways people are trapped
in structures of sin; (2) it does not take sufficient notice of the actual
historical processes that create human problems; (3) it fails to take
account of the ways in which others' choices limit one's possibilities
for response to human problems; and (4) it fails to reckon with unintended consequences of human actions.

After raising these four criticisms, which question the adequacy of
John Paul II's analysis of the relations between human freedom and
structural evil, Langan switches to a different mode of criticism. Here
he questions the pope's intentions in his teachings, suggesting that
since his expectations for personal conversion are unrealistic, the real
motive appears to be more to convict the world of sin than to change
the world. Such teaching, Langan claims, has the effect of putting the
reader "in a box"—one is trapped between high moral aspirations
and social realities that make attainment of those ideals impossible.
There is an obvious connection between this criticism and the pre-
ceding ones in that it is the latter which shows the pope's moral
exhortations to be unrealistic.

Next, Langan surveys four imagined responses the reader might
make to the papal box, which I summarize as follows: (1) the
Lutheran reply—*simul justus et peccator!*; (2) the modernist reply—
what's he *really* up to?; (3) the Jamesian reply—*excelsior!*; and (4) the
millenarian reply—hang on and wait for the eschaton.

Langan's final consideration, which he proposes as a fifth reply or
response to the psychological box in which readers of John Paul II's
teaching are likely to find themselves, is to suggest that evil social
structures can be recognized as such, and that their power over individuals' lives can be broken by a concerted effort to withdraw support from them in a nonviolent manner. As a consequence people
may make significant gains in freedom to choose aright and will then,
in turn, build a better world. As (perhaps ambiguous) evidence for
this possibility, Langan cites recent events in Eastern Europe.

Now, what is the intended force of this section of the essay? Is the
presentation of option five intended to release us from the psycho-

The Good Society

logical box *and* to invalidate the earlier criticisms, thereby vindicating John Paul's position? Or is it only the former, in which case the pope's teaching merits a mixed review?

FURTHER REMARKS

I wish to shift now from analysis to reflection on the substantial issues raised by Langan. In particular, I believe Langan's four critical questions deserve closer attention. As mentioned above, these are directed against a view that stresses personal responsibility (individual free choices) as the source of structures of evil—a view, by the way, that is typical of modern tendencies to reductionism. Langan's four criticisms show this to be an oversimplification at best.

These four criticisms are all consistent with a very different analysis of the relations between personal sin and structural evil—one that gives at least equal attention to the role of social structures in determining personal wrongdoing. This analysis suggests that while structures of sin can come into being through evil choices, they come also through ignorant if well-intentioned choices. Once in place, they drastically limit human freedom. They become forces in the universe beyond the control of the individuals involved, often compelling their collusion. The fact that we need social structures and that we often create them with the best of intentions lends a tragic note to human existence. The pope's social thought, then, is indeed utopian, as Langan suggests. We cannot live without social structures, but ignorance as well as worthwhile motives, such as self-preservation, will (regularly if not inevitably) produce structures of evil, and these in turn limit the possibilities for individual conversion. The pope's position is, in Langan's term, moralistic—or I would prefer to say, overly voluntaristic—because it fails to take account of individuals' enslavement to the given structures.

The foregoing analysis can have a chilling effect on one's optimism and drive for social change. Reinhold Niebuhr's "realism" is to this view as the Lutheran response is to John Paul II's. If I may indulge in speculation for a moment, I imagine that if there is a motive *lying behind* the pope's social teaching, it is exactly to dispel any "realism" that would further paralyze would-be activists or salve the consciences of those in active collusion with the structures of evil. Worthy motives indeed. But if a call for moral reform addressed to the individual *is* unrealistic, then what is the answer?

150

First, if scholars such as Hendrik Berkhof and G. B. Caird are correct, then something like the analysis I have presented goes back to Paul and his disciples.[1] In the letter to the Colossians, especially, the work of Christ is interpreted as the liberation of God's people from bondage to the "principalities and powers." This phrase has long been taken to refer to demonic powers, but Berkhof and others argue that while there are lingering connections with the gods of other nations, these terms refer primarily to fallen social structures. Thus, even if one's worldview rules out personal evil spirits, the Pauline analysis of divine conflict with the principalities and powers is still meaningful and surprisingly relevant to questions of how to address structural evil.[2]

Second, Langan's own fifth response contains, at least implicitly, three ingredients for an effective strategy in the face of structural evil. The response involves (1) recognition of the evil, (2) group solidarity, and (3) nonviolent means. The element of group solidarity is least explicit in Langan's account—it shows only in his use of "people" in place of "individuals," and in the fact that he sees as a possible example the events in Eastern Europe, where organizations such as Solidarity have played such an important role.

If we give due attention to these three requirements for social change, especially to the need to pit structure against structure, then a role for the Christian church is not far to seek. The church at its best is a family, a people, a race, wherein oppression is not to be tolerated—"You know that the rulers of the Gentiles lord it over them. . . . Not . . . so among you" (Matt. 20:25–26). The very existence of the church can be a liberating fact. I quote John Howard Yoder: "For Paul, as interpreted by Berkhof, the very existence of the church is her primary task. It is in itself a proclamation of the Lordship of Christ to the powers from whose dominion the church has begun to be liberated. The church concentrates upon not being seduced by them."[3]

The church's role, then, is to provide an alternative model for human existence wherein domination, ethnic strife, and exploitation are abolished, so that by contrast the world's oppressive structures can be seen for what they are (and here we see that there is some truth contained in the millenarian response). In its opposition to the principalities and powers, it is not to be seduced by the temptation to use the world's means, most particularly, its violence.

Paul's emphasis on the newness of the church consisting in the reconciliation of two races is especially relevant in this season when nationalism and ethnic violence threaten to derail *perestroika*. The fact that much of this ethnic violence is done in the name of Christianity is an especially chilling reminder of the readiness of the church to be seduced.

CONCLUSION

I am in no position to arbitrate between one social analysis and another—Yoder's, for instance, versus John Paul II's. To do so would require, at least, a great deal of the patient historical analysis of social problems that Langan suggests is missing from current discussions.

I do think, however, that Langan's own views are more consistent with a very different analysis of social problems than those based on a reduction of the social to the individual. Have I also shown that Father Langan is a closet anabaptist? Perhaps.

NOTES

1. See G. B. Caird, *Principalities and Powers* (Oxford: Clarendon Press, 1956); and Hendrik Berkhof, *Christ and the Powers* (Scottdale, Penn.: Herald Press, 1962).

2. I am following John Howard Yoder here. See *The Politics of Jesus* (Grand Rapids: Wm. B. Eerdmans, 1972), esp. ch. 8.

3. Ibid., 153.

III

Ethics and Religious Pluralism

13

The Universality of the Golden Rule[1]

John Hick

The basic criterion for judging religious phenomena is soteriological. The salvation/liberation which it is the function of religion to facilitate is a human transformation, which we see most conspicuously in the saints of all traditions. It consists, as one of its aspects, in moral goodness, a goodness which is latent in the solitary contemplative and active in the saint who lives in society, serving his or her fellows either in works of mercy or, more characteristically in our modern sociologically conscious age, in political activity as well, seeking to change the structures within which human life is lived. This stems in each case from a basic ethical requirement; and it is this that provides the criterion for the moral assessment of religious phenomena.

Our task is accordingly to display this common moral requirement. In doing so we must distinguish between ethical ideals and the concrete ways in which these have been applied and misapplied at particular times and places. For such applications involve many factors other than the basic values themselves. Human reason, which is often, as David Hume said, "the slave of the passions,"[2] has regularly been used to twist moral principles in justification of individual, class, and national acquisitiveness and domination. Further, a variety of empirical and metaphysical beliefs, often differing widely between different cultures and historical epochs, enter into our concrete moral judgments.

An example of this worth noting is that of the human sacrifices that were practiced within many of the archaic forms of religion. In many cases these arose from conceptions of the gods as demanding and as

155

capable of being placated by them; and in these cases our modern abhorrence echoes that of critics in the axial age:

> Shall I give my first-born for my transgression,
>   the fruit of my body for the sin of my soul?
> He has showed you, O man, what is good;
>   and what does the Lord require of you
> but to do justice, and to love kindness,
>   and to walk humbly with our God?
>
> (Micah 6:7–8)

But very often also they seem to have arisen in a quite different way, from mistaken magical or primitive scientific beliefs according to which a human death could have objective beneficial effects for the community. J. G. Frazer, in his great compendium of the phenomena of "primitive religion," gives many examples of such beliefs. One comes from ancient Mexico:

> The ancient Mexicans conceived the sun as the source of all vital force; hence they named him Ipalnemohuani, "He by whom men live." But if he bestowed life on the world, he needed also to receive life from it. And as the heart is the seat and symbol of life, bleeding hearts of men and animals were presented to the sun to maintain him in vigour and enable him to run his course across the sky. Thus the Mexican sacrifices to the sun were magical rather than religious, being designed, not so much to please and propitiate him, as physically to renew his energies of heat, light, and motion. The constant demand for human victims to feed the solar fire was met by waging war every year on the neighboring tribes and bringing back troops of captives to be sacrificed on the altar. Thus the ceaseless wars of the Mexicans and their cruel system of human sacrifices, the most monstrous on record, sprang in great measure from a mistaken theory of the solar system.[3]

Various other religio-scientific beliefs also gave point to human sacrifice. One was that the world, having originally been created as the result of a cosmic blood sacrifice, could be renewed by further such acts. "In short, such a sacrifice—a repetition of the primordial divine act—ensures the renewal of the world, the regeneration of life, the cohesion of society."[4] Yet another belief of this kind was that a life sacrificed at the foundation of a new building, especially a temple or palace, would ensure its durability.[5] Thus what Eliade calls "creative murder"[6] arose from a variety of causes, some indeed reflecting conceptions of deity that have to be rejected on moral grounds, but many reflecting pre-scientific understandings of the way in which the world works. And so he warns against a too sweeping judgment upon this very widespread practice of the ancient world:

> in all traditional societies human sacrifice was fraught with a cosmological and eschatological symbolism that was singularly powerful and complex . . . This bloodstained ritual in no way indicates an intellectual inferiority or a spiritual poverty in the peoples who practice it.[7]

The main changes between the ages of ritual human sacrifice and our own day have been in our understanding of the workings of nature, and in the enlargement of moral vision from the tribal to a national and then—very tentatively and insecurely—to a global horizon. But despite these advances, it remains true that our own time has seen human sacrifices on an unprecedented scale in war, holocaust, and avoidable mass starvation. It is safe to say, and perhaps wise to remember, that ancient magical science allied to ancient tribal ethics sacrificed far fewer lives than modern science allied to modern nationalistic values. It is a sobering thought that, almost certainly, many more human beings have been deliberately slaughtered by their fellows in the twentieth century than in all the previous centuries of human history put together.

To select another example of cultural variation in the application of moral principles, the torture and execution of heretics in the late medieval and early modern periods of Christianity presupposed the belief that heretics who die without having recanted will suffer eternal torment in hell, together with the further assumption that a recantation made under duress can have religious value. Today virtually all Christians would agree in rejecting these beliefs. But we can distinguish them from the fundamental moral principle of promoting the good of others—both the good of the heretics who were supposedly being saved from hell, and the good of the church as a whole which was supposedly being saved from dangerous germs of spiritual corruption.

In principle, then, and to a considerable extent in practice, we can separate out basic moral values from both the magical-scientific and the metaphysical beliefs which have always entered into their application within particular cultures. From a religious point of view we must assume the rooting of moral norms in the structure of our human nature and the rooting of that nature in our relationship to the

Real. The central moral claim upon us is accordingly to behave in accordance with our true nature, from which we have fallen into sin or into the darkness and confusion of *avidyā*. The ethical insights of the great teachers are visions of human life lived in earthly alignment with the Real, insights either heard as divine commands or intuited as the truth of the eternal Dharma or Tao or Logos. Implicit within these we can discern the utterly basic principle that it is evil to cause suffering to others and good to benefit others and to alleviate or prevent their sufferings. This is so fundamental and universally accepted a principle that it is seldom formulated. And yet, if all human beings lived in accordance with it there would be no wars, no injustice, no crime, no needless suffering.

One cannot prove such a fundamental principle. It is too basic to be derived from prior premises: the whole of our moral discourse hinges upon it. When, to take an extreme case, we discover individuals who are completely amoral and who see nothing wrong in, for example, inflicting gratuitous terror and pain on a child, society can forcibly restrain them or try to control them by fear of punishment, but it cannot compel them to feel for themselves the morally evil character of such behavior. We regard them either as insane or as lacking in an important human quality. In the end we can only say that it is human to sympathize with others in their miseries and joys and that without this fellow-feeling there would be no morality and therefore no society. The Confucian teacher Mencius (Meng Tzu, 371–289 B.C.E.) expressed this basic insight very clearly:

> I say that every man has a heart that pities others, for the heart of every man is moved by fear and horror, tenderness and mercy, if he suddenly sees a child about to fall into a well. And this is not because he wishes to make friends with the child's father and mother or to win praise from his countryfolk and friends, nor because the child's cries hurt him.
>
> This shows that no man is without a merciful, tender heart, no man is without a heart for shame and hatred, no man is without a heart to give way and yield, no man is without a heart for right and wrong.[8]

The Golden Rule, in its positive or negative forms, is a widespread expression of this principle that it is good to benefit others and evil to harm them. In the Hindu scriptures we read: "One should never do that to another which one regards as injurious to one's own self. This, in brief, is the rule of Righteousness."[9] In the Jain *Kritānga* Sutra we read that one should go about "treating all creatures in the world as he himself would be treated."[10]

The Buddhist scriptures do not seem to have a precise formulation of the Golden Rule, although there are several passages in which the Buddha, rebuking those who are ill-treating others, says such things as "Life is dear to all. Comparing others with oneself, one should neither strike nor cause to strike."[11] But the basic principle of universal compassion is frequently taught: for example, "As a mother cares for her son, all her days, so towards all living things a man's mind should be all-embracing."[12] Confucius, expounding humaneness (*jen*), said, "Do not do to others what you would not like yourself."[13] In the Taoist *Thāi Shang* we read that the good man will "regard [others'] gains as if they were his own, and their losses in the same way."[14] The Zoroastrian *Dadistan-i-dinik* declares, "That nature only is good when it shall not do unto another whatever is not good for its own self."[15] Jesus taught, "As ye would that men should do to you, do ye also to them likewise" (Luke 6:31). In the Jewish Talmud we read "What is hateful to yourself do not do to your fellow man (*haver*). That is the whole of the Torah."[16] And in the Hadith of Islam we read Muhammad's words, "No man is a true believer unless he desires for his brother that which he desires for himself."[17]

It is this principle or ideal that is spelled out and amplified in the moral precepts of the great traditions.[18] The teaching always has a particular historical location, being set in the context of the existing state of society, which was in some cases more "primitive" and in others more "civilized." In terms of a given cultural-economic-political situation the teaching shows how to behave towards neighbors, parents, children, the rich, the poor, slaves, strangers, enemies . . . In each case it begins on the common ground of fair dealing and respect for others' lives and property and leads on towards the higher ground of positive generosity, forgiveness, kindness, love, compassion, where we find the ethical evidence of the transformation of human existence from self-centeredness to Reality-centeredness.

Love, compassion, self-sacrificing concern for the good of others, generous kindness and forgiveness—which we have seen to constitute the basic ethical principle of the great traditions—is not an alien ideal imposed by supernatural authority but one arising out of our human nature (though always in tension with other aspects of that nature), reinforced, refined and elevated to new levels within the religious traditions. This basic ideal has itself been operative in the initial acceptance of great teachers. If, for example, Gautama had preached and lived an Eightfold Path of selfishness, greed, theft, hatred, violence, slander, deceit and sensual self-indulgence, he would not have been able to set the Wheel of Dharma turning for the welfare of many. Again, if Jesus had extolled hatred instead of love, or if his own life and death had not incarnated the ideal of self-giving love that he taught, no one would have accepted him as a true son of God, revealing the heavenly Father's nature.[19] Or again, if Muhammad had not embodied in his own life the submission to God that is the central demand of the Qur'an, or had failed to live in accordance with the ethical requirements which he taught, he would not have been regarded as a true prophet of Allah. Thus the ideal of love, compassion, generosity, mercy has always been a basic factor in the recognition of someone as an authentic mediator of the Real. And having been recognized partly by their embodiment of this ideal, such persons have then by their lives and teachings deepened and clarified our understanding of the ideal itself.

It is this basic norm enshrined in the great traditions that provides the broad criterion by which we can make moral judgments in the sphere of religion. In one sense its application is comparatively easy, but in another sense extremely difficult. It is easy in the sense that we can readily list actions and patterns of behavior which are good and evil respectively under this criterion. Nazism, for example, appears somewhere within the outskirts of the spreading network of overlapping phenomena covered by the concept of religion. But whereas the other "secular faiths" of Marxism, Maoism and Humanism contain important elements of good as well as of evil, Nazism taken as a whole appears retrospectively as unambiguously evil: for in conceiving and carrying out the Jewish holocaust it gave vent on a vast scale to the darkest and most destructive distortions of human nature. It is the common criterion of true *Menschlichkeit*, expressed in *agape* or *karunā*, that makes this so immediately evident to us. And as contemporary examples of evils that are identified by the same criterion we can list the continuing (although officially abolished) outcaste status within Hindu society, and the (also illegal) burning of brides because of an insufficient dowry; the cutting off of a thief's hand under the *shariah* law in the Muslim-dominated Sudan and the savage persecution of the Bah'ais in Iran; the direct involvement over several generations of the dominant Christian churches in massive racial oppression in South Africa and in grossly oppressive regimes in South America; the failure to accord proper human recognition to the Palestinian people by the state of Israel. Again, one can list Hindu-

Muslim and Hindu-Sikh violence in India, Catholic-Protestant violence in Northern Ireland, Christian-Muslim violence in Lebanon; and so on in a virtually endless count of religiously validated and intensified evils.

We can equally readily list religiously related activities that are admirable under this basic criterion: the provision of a basis for social cohesion for human societies, large and small; the creation of schools, universities and hospitals and the nurturing of literature, philosophy and the arts; innumerable works of mercy and charity . . . Again the list is virtually endless. But when we seek to go beyond the identification of particular phenomena as good or evil to make ethical judgments concerning the religious traditions as totalities, we encounter large complicating factors which must give pause to any project for the moral grading of the great world faiths.

The largest of these historical cross-currents has been the rise of modern science. For it is this that has made possible the rapid development of the western and northern hemisphere, lifting it out of a relatively primitive technological state and out of the generally feudal social and political conditions of the pre-modern period. This part of the world is predominantly Christian and post-Christian, so that Christianity has during the last three hundred years come to be associated with the economic affluence, the expansion of education and the intellectual ferment and political democratization that have come in the wake of the scientific revolution. In contrast, the eastern and southern hemisphere, dominated by the Muslim, Buddhist, Hindu and African primal traditions, has been generally associated until very recently, as still today in many areas, with continuing pre-modern social, economic and political conditions.

Not only has modern science made possible the present relative affluence of the western and northern hemisphere, but it has had equally important effects on its intellectual and ethical climate. It undermined, in the seventeenth and eighteenth centuries, the generally dogmatic and superstitious mentality of medieval Europe by giving birth to the more open, critical and questioning outlook that characterizes modernity. This has now become an aspect of the "Christian West" in distinction from the still relatively medieval ethos, largely unaffected by the canons of scientific thinking, of many millions in the Islamic, Hindu, Buddhist and primal worlds. Again, as another aspect of the development of western science-based civilization, there has been a humanization of values producing what we may call the modern liberal ethical outlook. From this standpoint, in its ideal form, all human beings are seen as having an equal intrinsic value, and evil is accordingly discerned not only at the personal level but also in political and economic arrangements by which one group exploits another, whether the lines be drawn in terms of color, gender, caste, class nationality or religion. Likewise moral value is seen not only in individual acts of compassion and mutual aid within the existing social structures but also in political movements seeking to transform those structures; and the expansion of human freedom is welcomed in recognition of the equality of the sexes, in liberal education, in democratic forms of government, in life-preserving and life-enhancing applications of science, in rehabilitation as the aim of a penal system . . . And once again these liberal values have had their main development within "Christian civilization," though they are also now exported as secondary influences to much of Asia and Africa. Thus it seems to many that Christianity is both the source and the inspiration of a contemporary ethical outlook which matches more nearly than any other the common ideal of the great traditions.

However, this comfortable assumption quickly begins to crumble under historical analysis. Modern science is not a product of Christianity as such but of the impact on Christian Europe of the Greek spirit of free enquiry during the vast cultural transformation known as the Renaissance, stimulated by a rediscovery of classical literature and thought that was rapidly spread by the new invention of printing. It is no doubt true that, as A. N. Whitehead and others have argued, the theological belief in an orderly and unitary world ordained by a rational creator provided a milieu within which this could happen.[20] But that Christianity did not bring forth modern science simply from its own resources is shown by the fact that it had presided unchallenged over the life of Europe for more than a thousand years before the scientific spirit began to stir within it. And when this spirit did emerge, rapidly developing its own momentum, its most powerful foe was the church, which saw much of the new knowledge as a dangerous challenge to its established dogmas. The Copernican revolution in astronomy, dethroning humanity from a central position in the universe; the discovery that the earth is enormously older than the biblical dating had allowed; and the Darwinian theory of evolution, entailing that the human species was not created ready-made but has gradually evolved out of lower forms of life, were felt at the time as hammer blows against the Christian revelation. The late nineteenth century saw the bitter retreat of theology before the advancing forces of science;[21] and it has only been through prolonged debates, much personal agonizing and traumatic schisms between "fundamentalists" and "liberals," that Christianity has for the most part come to accept the new scientific picture of the world, reinterpreting many of its doctrines accordingly.

Accordingly Christianity should not be credited with the achievements and benefits of modern science—nor debited with its nuclear dangers. Modern science originated in the Christian West and could not have arisen at the same time elsewhere. But once launched, it rapidly developed into an autonomous human enterprise with its own methods and outlook, owing allegiance only to the ideal of objective truth. It is not tied to the region where it first appeared and is in fact rapidly spreading throughout the world by being grafted onto the Hindu, Buddhist, Muslim, Marxist and other cultures. Christianity is the first religious tradition to have been influenced by the scientific enterprise and to be largely transformed by its new outlook and knowledge. But the same process has begun within the other great civilizations of the earth, and has been limited by material and educational resources rather than by religious backgrounds. We may surmise that the Hindu and Buddhist traditions will be able to assimilate the scientific outlook as relatively easily as post-Confucian China, whereas Islam may perhaps find the process as traumatic as Christianity has done. But to compare a West which has emerged from its medieval phase with an East which is now in the throes of emerging, attributing the wealth and productivity of the one to Christianity and the poverty and economic backwardness of the other to Hinduism, Buddhism and Islam, is to ignore the immensely important non-religious factors in history. What we see is a difference in stages of modernization under the influence of a religiously neutral science and technology which have transformed the western and are now in the process of transforming the eastern civilizations. Thus the special relationship between Christianity and modern science, with all its good and bad effects on human life, is a contingent and temporary connection.

A second critical comment concerns the modern liberal moral outlook. This does indeed accord ideally with the basic value of generous kindness, love, compassion taught by all the great traditions and mediated to the West by Christianity. But it does not represent simply a flowering of Christian teaching. The love commandment of the Sermon on the Mount by itself, without the insistent promptings of humanist and rationalist voices, did not end slavery[22] and has not ended exploitation. Nor did it even, by itself, bring the perception that freedom and equality are ideals to be sought after. On the contrary, for more than a thousand years the application, or misapplication, of Christian ethical principles produced and validated strongly hierarchical societies in which power was narrowly concentrated in kings and emperors as God's vice-regents on earth; in which the inherited stations of "the rich man in his castle and the poor man at his gate" were accepted as divinely established; in which women were emphatically subordinated to men;[23] and in which individual freedom of thought and action were narrowly circumscribed and punishments were brutal in the extreme. It was the fertilization of the medieval Christian ethos by the humanistic ideals of ancient Greece, recovered in the Renaissance and consolidated in the Enlightenment of the eighteenth century, that produced the contemporary liberal moral outlook. As in the case of the rise of science, this has resulted from an interaction of cultural influences—a religious influence deriving from the Bible and another influence generated by the complex of forces creating the modern scientific world-view.

It must be added that the liberal morality pervading modern western societies has another side to it which is feared rather than envied from within the more traditional Islamic, Hindu, Buddhist, primal and also Marxist cultures. This is a combined result of the stress of dehumanizing urban environments and the individualistic "permissiveness" reflected in the divorce explosion, the resulting prevalence of one-parent families, the high rates of abortion and suicide and the widespread use of hard drugs. All this meshes with a pursuit of individual possessions and pleasure in a consumer society seeking an ever higher material standard of living through increasingly sophisticated luxuries that consume the world's resources, thereby depleting its basic non-renewable wealth. Further, as the first civilization to have at its disposal the immense new powers of modern technology, the West has also been the first to encounter the dangers which these powers bring with them. Nuclear armaments mean that western nationalism, intensified by the capitalist-communist ideological struggle, could lead to a massive thermo-nuclear exchange creating a "nuclear winter" in which civilization as we know it comes to a painful end. All these factors together have created a dark shadow accompanying the bright promise of our contemporary science-oriented culture.

NOTES

1. From John Hick, *An Interpretation of Religion* (London: The Macmillan Press, and New Haven: Yale University Press, 1989), 309–315 and 325–342. Reprinted by permission of Macmillan Publishers and Yale University Press.

2. David Hume, *A Treatise of Human Nature* (1739), ed. L. A. Selby-Bigge (London: Oxford University Press, 1968), 415.

3. James G. Frazer, *The Golden Bough* (1922) abridged edition (London: Macmillan & Co., 1941), 79. I do not think that it is possible to accept Wittgenstein's view that these beliefs recorded by Frazer lacked factual content; see Ludwig Wittgenstein, "Remarks on Frazer's Golden Bough," trans. A. C. Miles and Rush Rhees, in *The Human World* (1971), no. 3. On this issue see Chapter 12.3 above. Frazer also gives numerous examples of the killing of divine kings (Frazer, *The Golden Bough*, ch. 24). According to him these arose from the mixed religio-scientific belief that the safety of the people, and even of the world itself, was bound up with the health and strength of the sovereign regarded as an incarnation of deity. Because he must not be allowed to grow old and feeble he was executed either when he began to fail or whilst his strength was at its height and could be channelled into his successor. This particular group of examples has however been questioned, for example, by E. E. Evans-Pritchard, *The Divine Kingship of the Shilluk in the Nilotic Sudan* (Cambridge: Cambridge University Press, 1948), 20–21, 34–35, and I mention it here only as a rather famous item in the literature that has now become dubious. For a recent criticism of Frazer's general approach, see Jonathan Z. Smith, "When the Bough Breaks" in *History of Religions* (1973), vol. 12, no. 4.

4. Mircea Eliade, *A History of Religious Ideas*, vol. II (1978), trans. Willard R. Trask (Chicago and London: University of Chicago Press, 1982), 156.

5. Eliade, *History of Religious Ideas*, vol. II, 91.

6. Ibid., 134.

7. Ibid., 152.

8. Leonard A. Lyall, trans., *Mencius* (London and New York: Longmans, Green & Co., 1932), III:6.

9. *Mahabharata*, Anushana parva, 113:7, see Pratapa Chandra Roy, trans., *The Mahabharata* (Calcutta: Bhārata Press, 1893). Taken out of context the sentence is ambiguous and could be read as an injunction to selfishness: do not do anything to injure yourself. But the context makes it clear that the intention is the opposite.

10. Hermann Jacoby, *Jaina Sutras* (1895) (Delhi: Motilal Banarsidass, 1968), bk. I, lect. 11:33, 314.

11. *The Dhammapada*, 2d ed., trans. Narada Mahathera (Colombo: Vajiranama, 1972), 10:2, 124. Compare 10:1 and *Udāna*, V:iv.

12. *Sutta Nipāta*, 149, in E. M. Hare, *The Woven Cadences of Early Buddhists (Sutta Nipāta)* (London: Oxford University Press, 1945), 24.

13. Confucius, *The Analects of Confucius*, trans. A. Waley (London: George Allen & Unwin, 1938), XII:2.

14. *Thai Shang* 3 in James Legge, *The Sacred Books of China: The Texts of Taoism, Part 2* (Oxford: Clarendon Press, 1891), 237.

15. *Dadistan-i-dinik* 94:5, in E. W. West, *Pahlevi Texts* (Oxford: Clarendon Press, 1882), 271.

16. *Babylonian Talmud*, Shabbath 31a.

17. This saying of Muhammad is well attested in the Hadith corpus, for example in *Muslim*, chapter on *iman*, 71–72; Ibn *Madja*, Introduction, 9; *Al-Darimi*, chapter on *riqaq*, 29; *Hambal*, 3, 1976.

18. That charity, loving kindness, forgiveness, mercy, and justice are enjoined by all the great traditions is argued and illustrated by Peggy Starkey, "Agape: A Christian Criterion for Truth in the Other World Religions," in *International Review of Mission* (1985), vol. 74, no. 296. On the other hand, Stewart Sutherland, "Religion, Ethics, and Action," in *The Philosophical Frontiers of Christian Theology*, ed. Brian Hebblethwaite and Stewart Sutherland (London and New York: Cambridge University Press, 1982) has questioned whether people with different religious or metaphysical beliefs can properly be said to share the same ethical principles, arguing that their different beliefs will entail their having different intentions even when they perform phenomenally similar actions. However it seems to me more correct to say that (in many cases) their different beliefs lead to their acting ethically in the same way. See also Peter J. Donovan, "Do Different Religions Share Common Moral Ground?" *Religious Studies* (1986), vol. 22, nos. 3–4.

19. There is a striking recent example of the priority of moral judgment in the recognition of authentic religion in the statement of the Christian archbishop Desmond Tutu, opposing racial oppression in South Africa, "If anyone were to show me that apartheid is biblical or christian . . . I would burn my Bible and cease to be a Christian." See Desmond Tutu, *Hope and Suffering* (Johannesburg: Skotoville Publishers [1983], London: Fount Paperbacks, and Grand Rapids: Wm. B. Eerdmans, 1984), 155.

20. Alfred North Whitehead, *Science and the Modern World* (Cambridge: Cambridge University Press, 1926), 17–18.

21. There is a classic account of this in A. D. White, *A History of the Warfare of Science with Theology in Christendom* (1896) (New York: Dover Publications, 1960), 2 vols.

22. In the New Testament Christian slaves are exhorted to obey their master (1 Timothy 6:1–2; 1 Peter 2:18–20; Colossians 3:22; Ephesians 6:5).

23. In the New Testament Christian wives are exhorted to obey their husbands (Ephesians 5:22; Colossians 3:18; 1 Peter 3:1) and to be obedient to men (1 Corinthians 14:34). See also James A. Brundage, "Prostitution in the Medieval Canon Law," in *Signs: Journal of Women in Culture and Society* (1976), vol. 1, no. 4.

14

Buddhism and Dialogue Among the World Religions: Meeting the Challenge of Materialistic Skepticism

Bhikkhu Chao Chu

The great religions of the world are today facing a common challenge from the forces of materialistic skepticism. Both material-reductionist science and modern philosophies, which reduce moral teachings to meaningless nonsense, contribute to the erosion of traditional moral values. Systems of morals and ethics have customarily been the product of religious traditions, the truth of which is increasingly called into question. Most of the great religious traditions claim to have the sole and final truth, revealed to humankind in the form of a sacred scripture. But when two or more of these great traditions come face to face, it is evident that their revelations are not the same. If claims of divine revelation are to be taken seriously, then not all revealed traditions can be true. Only one of them can be right. Naturally the followers of each particular tradition insist on the truth of their own tradition. They are, in a sense, quite right to do so, as their revelation is the only basis they have for morals and ethics. Yet, such attachment to one's own revealed tradition continues to be a serious source of conflict in the world.

However, a possible basis for consensus does seem to exist. Most societies that base their morals and ethics on revealed traditions share basic prohibitions against such acts as killing, stealing, and lying. Even in a secular society that no longer believes in revelation, a belief in such prohibitions tends to survive the loss of faith in the revelation upon which they were formerly based. It seems possible that there is in all people an innate inclination toward certain basic values. People tend to believe that it is wrong to kill, steal, or lie; yet the supposed revealed basis for such a belief may differ from society to society or may be altogether absent in a secular society. We may well ask why people universally tend to believe in such values.

From the Buddhist perspective, the answer is not far to seek. Knowledge of moral values is considered to be like knowledge of other natural laws. Relations of cause and effect observed throughout the natural world are understood to extend into the realm of human volition and action. All normal human beings agree that happiness is preferable to suffering. The Buddhist ethical system is based on this universal understanding. No commandments are made, but suggestions are offered, based on the knowledge of the natural laws of moral cause and effect that lead away from suffering to the greatest possible happiness for all beings. The reason why different people, whose respective revelations disagree in various ways, nonetheless tend to agree about prohibitions against such actions as killing, stealing, and lying is because they all perceive, however dimly, the same universal laws inherent in the world itself.

A human being who has reached full spiritual perfection has direct knowledge and insight into the impermanence and subtle interconnectedness of all phenomena. Such a one has a perfect understanding of the natural moral laws of cause and effect, and teaches others for the good of all. This is what is meant by a Buddha, or awakened one. The appearance of such a fully perfected spiritual teacher is understood as a natural event, which occurs from time to time when causes and conditions are right. Within historic times we know of the appearance of a Buddha in India over twenty-five hundred years ago. It is from this fully achieved being that our present Buddhist teaching descends.

It should be understood that nothing in the Buddhist teaching depends on faith. The many contradictory conceptions of god held by various revealed traditions have no place in the Buddhist teaching. Likewise, the absolute truth of any scriptures—including Buddhist ones—is denied by the Buddhist teaching. Faith in a particular god or scripture—to the exclusion of others—is a weak and insupportable basis for a system of ethics. It may be objected that a Buddhist is expected to have faith in the former existence of the Buddha and the truth of his teachings. This is true in much the same sense that many persons have faith in the former existence of Kepler and have faith in the heliocentric theory of the planetary system. No one can know Kepler in person, but his theories can be verified by any person who wishes to make the effort. The Buddhist teaching is much like science in this respect. Enlightenment is understood to be a reproducible result. Any person who wishes to may make the sufficient effort to attain Buddhahood, and directly know the truth. Even if the further objection is made that it is unlikely that some person may indeed do so, the fact remains that the attitude of Buddhism is entirely scientific in the sense that it does not require faith, but understanding. One is encouraged to follow experience and reason as far as one can. It is only when one reaches the limit of one's own abilities that one may wish to turn to the guidance of another of greater spiritual insight.

This brings us to an urgent contemporary issue faced by all the world's great religious traditions. Applied science or technology is increasingly influential in the lives of everyone. Great economic and ecological imbalances are being brought about because of the unwise use of scientific discoveries. Many people who have lost faith in their traditional religions believe in the truth and power of science, and many of religious faith still acknowledge science to one degree or another. But it cannot be denied that science contradicts some claims of revealed religions. One result of this is the powerlessness of the revealed religions to provide any credible moral guidance for the uses of applied science. Here again the Buddhist perspective has something to offer. There is nothing in the Buddhist teaching that can possibly contradict the findings of natural science. The Buddhist position is that the rational interrogation of nature is as true as it can be. There may be other truths, suprasensible truths beyond quantification and physical experiment, but these can only compliment and complete the scientific world-view and can never contradict it. As science advances, it wholly confirms, as far as it can, the teachings of Buddhism. Simple examples are the development of the science of ecology and systems theory, both of which are natural applications of the Buddhist teaching of interdependent origination of phenomena. It should be recognized, then, that the possibility of giving moral guidance to applied science exists, but only outside the closed circles of mutually exclusive revealed traditions.

In general, the Buddha's teaching encourages personal effort. One is responsible for one's own moral development. "By oneself is one defiled, by oneself is one purified: No one being can save another." One is not asked to have faith in a supernatural being to be forgiven. Human beings are regarded not as basically sinful, but as potential Buddhas. One cultivates love for all, starting with oneself. This is a healthy psychological attitude that can cut across all barriers. One beneficial consequence of this attitude is that it is more difficult to build an autocracy on a way of life built on individual responsibility.

Revealed religions, on the other hand, requiring as they do an absolute faith in a higher authority, have more than once lent themselves to despotism, and continue to do so. It should be noted in this regard that the scriptures of the major revealed traditions have historically shown themselves capable of being interpreted in support of oppression, violence, and atrocity. Although there have been monarchs and individuals calling themselves Buddhists who have done horrible things, it continues to be impossible to find scriptural support for such acts.

Buddhism is an open tradition that encourages interfaith dialogue. The Buddha teaches us not to be overly attached to particular groups, whether family or religious tradition. We must cultivate an open heart of unbounded love for all beings alike, including not just our friends and enemies, but all beings known or unknown to us, including animals. We can therefore end all needless suffering and killing that is a product of our foolish attachment to any particular group, political body, or religious tradition. The problem with interfaith dialogue is that while there may be some resemblances in ethical values amongst various revealed traditions, the roots of their respective beliefs—their differing scriptures and conceptions of god(s)—can never be the same. A truly open dialogue, in which one openheartedly considers the beliefs of another, can only result in the mutual destruction of these beliefs, which is not necessarily a bad thing as they are the cause of so much trouble. Buddhism therefore vigorously encourages a truly open and thoroughgoing interfaith dialogue in which one shows no undue attachment to any particular group or tradition. It must be noted that this teaching of nonattachment is meant also to apply to Buddhism itself. The Buddhist teaching is not regarded as absolutely true, but instead like a finger pointing to the moon. Many different fingers, long or short, might point to the moon. The relative angle of the pointing fingers will differ slightly depending on where they are located geographically. Only a very little child or an animal will look just at the finger and not at the moon beyond. Thus the spiritually mature persons will not attach any absolute value to a tradition or a teaching, but will recognize that such things will vary according to causes and conditions and are only useful tools. It is like the man who wishes to climb a high mountain but must first cross a great river. The exact shape of the raft that carries him across the river is not really important. Likewise, when he has reached the other shore, it would be foolish of him to carry the raft on his back as he ascends the mountain. Thus a wise humanity will cultivate nonattachment toward particular groups and an open heart toward all. A truly open interfaith dialogue cannot occur until people are willing to do this. The moral result would be the dissolving of barriers and the cultivation of openheartedness. Buddhism freely offers this insight to all who can understand it. Thus, the only real Buddhism, the fulfillment of Buddhism, is no Buddhism at all; it is not a faith, but a way of life that promotes unity within diversity, harmony within plurality. We look to openhearted interfaith dialogue as one means of dissolving barriers that divide persons of good will, so that they may all be guided not by artificial divisive traditions, but by their own sublime original nature.

15

The Virtues of Listening: Some Buddhist Perspectives on the Role of Ethics in the Dialogue Among World Religions

Bruce C. Hall

"The Role of Ethics in the Dialogue among Religions"[1] has at least two senses. Ethics is an item on the agenda, an area to be discussed. Buddhist ethical teaching is profuse and rich and can usefully contribute topics to that discussion. On the other hand, ethics has a role in the interreligious dialogue itself. Ethical grounds are involved in distinguishing genuine dialogue, open conversation, from other rhetorical projects such as converting the unbelievers, winning a debate, restoring threatened feelings of superiority, or engaging in purely academic comparative study. I will address this second sense of the role of ethics, ethical considerations that apply when we try to turn the interreligious dialogue into what Professor Gordon D. Kaufman means by "conversation."[2] Buddhism, in particular the scholastic tradition of Indian Buddhism, can help define the ethical requirements for conversation among religions. I will raise some general points on the position of ethics in the system of Buddhist discourse, then consider two specific sets of virtues, one Theravada, the other Mahayana.

The Buddhist fondness for numerical lists is well-known, even infamous. A traditional device of Buddhist discourse is to articulate a subject into lists—the four this and the five that—then comment on the items. This habit may reflect an originally oral tradition or a basically analytical frame of mind. In any case, to locate the realm of ethics in the geography of Buddhist discourse, we begin with a master list which organizes the whole of Buddhist teaching in terms of the Four Holy Truths—the Truths of Suffering, the Arisal of Suffering, the Cessation of Suffering, and the Path to the Cessation of Suffering.

This formula gives a Buddhist diagnosis of the human condition, an analysis of its causes, the possibility of its transformation, and a system of practice leading to that transformation. In Buddhist tradition ethics falls under the heading of the Path. That is, ethical questions are not approached by theoretical inquiry but belong to the discussion of practice, and usually appear as teaching about specific sets of precepts or virtues.

How Buddhist ethics is inseparably part of Buddhist practice should become clear when we examine the nature of this Path. The formula of the eightfold path is familiar to many, but a more fundamental, and briefer, articulation of the path is the threefold training: in *śīla, samādhi,* and *prajñā. Śīla,* the closest Buddhist equivalent to "ethics" or "morality" in general, also means specific sets of precepts, often in restrictive form: the Buddhist "thou shalt nots." *Samādhi* means meditative concentration or mental focusing, as goal and technique. *Prajñā,* often, I think misleadingly, translated "wisdom," means "understanding" as faculty and act. The whole threefold training makes up *bhāvanā,* "meditation" in its broadest sense. Despite great inconsistency in the use of the English word, meditation is not here identified with one item of the three, but rather each of the three involves specific types of meditation, and all three together are aspects of a whole system of meditation practice.

Śīla, moral training, is both a preliminary foundation for meditation practice proper, and a continuing strand in that practice. That is, striving to live by the precepts is a precondition for a viable meditation practice; practice includes specifically moral meditations, precepts and virtues can be topics for meditation, and continuing, integrated practice of *samādhi* and *prajñā* meditations deepens the ability to live the precepts. This system, in general and in its ethical components specifically, is valued as training conducive to attaining enlightenment and the cessation of suffering.

Some examples may clarify this abstract discussion. As noted above, moral practice begins in attempting to live by precepts—not to kill, not to steal, and so on—as something itself conducive to spiritual progress and as a foundation for further meditation. The next stage is a variety of preliminary meditations, antidotes to the passions that obstruct further practice. For example, in *Theravada* practice manuals, people especially subject to the distraction of hatred are advised to cultivate the so-called "four unlimited": friendliness, compassion, sympathetic joy, and impartiality. These four are a list of social virtues and a description of ideal behavior, but they are also specific and detailed practices—contemplative moral exercises with a specific "text."

The first "unlimited," often translated "love," derives from a word for friend, and friendliness suggests an appropriately Buddhist moderation. As an exercise it means projecting specific wishes for well-being onto various persons. Friendliness must first be cultivated toward oneself. From a Buddhist viewpoint this is natural and healthy; those who cannot feel friendly toward themselves never feel genuinely friendly toward others. These thoughts of friendliness are then directed, successively, toward persons to whom one feels regard, indifference, and hatred, until the feeling of friendliness gradually becomes truly unlimited. Friendliness can lack detailed content, so compassion—that is, empathizing with pain without passing judgment—is next cultivated and extended in the same way. Compassion may subtly promote feelings of superiority, which are countered by the third "unlimited," the cultivation of sympathetic joy, empathizing with joy without passing judgment. Buddhism considers it harder for the ego to abide other people's smiles than their tears. All three of these are kept from mere sentimentality by cultivating the fourth "unlimited"—impartiality, equanimity, or detachment—also directed at oneself and the whole range of others.

The "four unlimited"—a Buddhist ethical ideal for human relations, and a specific contemplative exercise as an antidote to hatred—can also suggest qualities needed for a genuine conversation among religions. How does conversation differ from dialogue as a model for what we want to do? It seems to me that dialogue presupposes at least two people talking, and following certain basic rules of talking. For example, at the minimum we cannot both talk at once. We tend to focus on talk, and exactly what rules apply to it. I think we also tend to assume that we, as rational philosophers, know how to talk, and the problem is what rules do *they* have to follow so that *we* can have a dialogue. On the other hand, let us take seriously Professor Kaufman's model of ordinary conversation. What is the minimum requirement for there to be conversation *at all*? A one-sided dialogue is a contradiction in terms, but we do speak of one-sided conversation. The minimum requirement for having a conversation at all is that there must be at least one person *listening*. Two people talking in certain ways are needed to initiate a dialogue, but one person deciding to listen can create a conversation. If what initiates conversation is our own decision to listen, then we really do not need to set any preconditions for others. The depth and mutuality of the listening will determine how wide open the conversation will be, but we can begin it by simply doing something ourselves rather than setting conditions for others. One can, after all, listen to anyone, even to fanatics. If, with Professor Kaufman, we assume that the compelling reason to have this conversation among religions at all is to reduce fear, hatred, and conflict, then it becomes clear that listening is always the first thing we need to do, often the best thing, and sometimes the only thing.

Now, these "four unlimited" are in fact qualities of real listening. Listening begins with a general attitude of relaxed friendliness. Obviously hatred, mistrust, deceit, arrogance, and so on preclude listening. It is less obvious that love can do so too. I do not mean false love, condescension mascarading as love, or the like. Taking love at face value, I would still say that if I love people intensely, if I want passionately to save their souls, I will probably be incapable of listening to what they have to say. It is a common experience that true conversation can be most difficult with those whom we most love. When we really can converse with a lover or parent or child we are likely to say, with some surprise, that we are also friends. I suggest that this example of Buddhist ethical practice helps define the listening needed for genuine conversation among religions. Listening requires a relaxed attitude of friendliness and a sympathetic interest in each others' pains and joys, and it needs to be tempered by conscious cultivation of detachment and impartiality.

Let us next consider a contribution from Mahayana tradition. Among Mahayana ethical lists there are many formulas for the virtues of *bodhisattvas*, beings working toward buddhahood. These lists too are both ideal descriptions of qualities and practices to be cultivated by those who follow this path. These qualities are called *pāramitā*, which can be translated as "perfection" (or something to be perfected), but which is often etymologized as "that which carries one across to the other shore," across the ocean of delusion to the far shore of enlightenment. A common list of six *pāramitās* consists of three pairs: charity and precepts, patience and courage, concentration and understanding. It is significant that charity (literally, "giving") comes first. The basis of ethical and spiritual life is charity, not following moral rules, but following the rules is also necessary as a balance. Patience and courage are passive and active poles of persistent and energetic effort. The term translated as patience is especially rich in meanings. It means sustained, patient effort and forbearance under trial. It means tolerance of circumstances and people, others and oneself, and toleration of ideas, even those at present inconceivable—something which also requires courage. The third pair are meditative concentration (*samādhi*) and understanding—both intellectual and intuitive (*prajñā*). The perfection of understanding implies the understanding of "emptiness," perhaps the "fullest" concept in the whole of Buddhist philosophy. Here suffice it to say that "emptiness" includes understanding the conventional, limited, dependent nature of all concepts and viewpoints, including any conceptualization of emptiness itself. Understanding emptiness raises the six *pāramitās* from conventional virtues to qualities which carry one across to the other shore.

What relevance does this example of peculiarly Buddhist ethical and spiritual discourse have to the nature of interreligious conversation? Again, the Buddhist formula can suggest analogies to the listening required for conversation. Listening is based on a spirit of giving—giving attention, respect, space to other traditions, and specifically to their otherness. In listening we are abiding by rules: our own precepts and the rules of conversation itself. It requires moral courage to take seriously ideas that contradict one's own deepest beliefs. Really listening requires every form of patience and toleration, especially the patience that accepts the otherness of the other and refuses easy retreat into either ranking traditions or dissolving their distinctness in the warm mush of "all religions are one." Meditative concentration in the strict sense may not be needed for listening and conversing, but some element of concentration is, according to Buddhist psychology, a necessary aspect of any moment of consciousness. Listening seriously to other traditions requires its own form of sustained concentration.

Finally, understanding is both a precondition for conversation and its goal. The concept of emptiness also has its parallel here. I do not see how one can truly listen and converse without clearly understanding one's own limitations and lack of absolute knowledge. This does not require discarding the *contents* of belief as all empty. It does require understanding that *as individuals* our knowledge is conventional, limited, and dependent. Real conversation does not require that, for instance, Buddhists or Christians give up special faith in Buddha or Christ. It does require that Buddhists and Christians forgo the arrogance of presuming to *speak for* Buddha or Christ. Such arrogance, conscious or unconscious, precludes conversation. The humility needed for conversation is itself a virtue in the several traditions.

The recollection of humility may be the best lesson to be learned from the attempt at conversation.

Actively cultivating humility is part of the specific practice of the several traditions. The conversation among religions can be most fruitful if participation in the conversation is continuous with the individual religious practices of the participants. In this way, the conversation itself can be a matter of practice for participants, not only as conversation partners, but as Buddhists and Christians, Muslims and Jews, Hindus and even Humanists.

NOTES

1. This was the title of the panel discussion at the 1990 Claremont Graduate School Conference in Philosophy of Religion at which this paper was first presented.

2. Gordon D. Kaufman, "Religious Diversity and Religious Truth," forthcoming in a *festschrift* in honor of John Hick, edited by Arvind Sharma (London: Macmillan Press).

16

Global Ethics and Dialogue Among World Religions: An Islamic Viewpoint

Muzammil H. Siddiqi

I believe that religious dialogue is a supremely ethical enterprise. The objective of such dialogue is not only to learn the facts about other people, their faiths and traditions but also to clear the world community of prejudice and misunderstanding and to establish human fellowship based on fairness, justice, and goodwill. Religious dialogue should help us take practical steps toward establishing a global ethics that will bring about social, economic, and political justice as well as ecological balance and responsibility.

S. Cromwell Crawford, in his recent edited work, *World Religions and Global Ethics*, has rightly pointed out that

> Global ethics starts with the assumption that as human beings we are *already involved* in global society, whether we know it or not; whether we like it or not. Biologically, we all belong to "a single, common species of life," and therefore we all partake in several common features. Ecologically, we are part of the planet's biosphere and are rooted in the earth's material and energy system. Historically, in matters of language, religion, arts, and technologies, the separate wells from which we drink are all fed by subterranean streams. Culturally, we are multinational and the whole world is becoming a melting pot. Spiritually, increasing numbers are embarked on a journey of self-discovery through interreligious dialogue.[1]

It is my understanding that Islam upholds and strongly advocates this global vision. Its emphasis is that all human beings share the same origin and are moving toward a common destiny and goal. Here

178

I shall briefly outline the worldview of Islam and its relevance for global ethics and interreligious dialogue.

ISLAMIC WORLDVIEW

Islam is a monotheistic faith. It strongly holds that there is only one God. God is the Creator, Nourisher, and Sustainer of the whole world. Allah is the Arabic name that means "the God." Allah is not an Arab God or a Muslim God. In the *Qur'ān* He is not called "God of Quraish" (the tribe of Muhammad), or "God of Arabs." He is repeatedly called "God of the worlds" (*rabb al-'alamīn*). The very first verse of the *Qur'ān* begins with the words:

Grateful praise belongs to God, the Lord of the Worlds. (1:1)

The last chapter of the *Qur'ān* is called *al-Nās* (humankind), and God is addressed there as:

Nourisher of humankind, Sovereign of humankind, God of humankind . . . (114:1–3)

The most basic and fundamental assertion of Islam is its declaration of *tawhīd*, that is, the unity, uniqueness, and universality of God. "There is no god but Allah" is not only the credal formula of Islam but also its soul and spirit. It is the bedrock for all Islamic ethics, culture, and civilization. Indeed, there can be no Islam without *tawhīd*.

Tawhīd has three basic dimensions in Islam. It has a spiritual and devotional aspect which manifests itself in Islamic worship and rituals that declare the unity of God and call one to devote and submit oneself to Him in such a way as to bring about the voluntary union of the human with divine. The second dimension of *tawhīd* is moral and cultural. Here it works for the integration of human self. *Tawhīd* here means that a Muslim must strive to unify all varied and variegated aspects of her or his life under one principle, namely, the Divine guidance. Religion thus does not mean only "the flight of the alone to the alone" or "what one does with one's solitude," but it carries with it social, economic, and cultural aspects as well. The third dimension of *tawhīd* is ecumenical, meaning the unity of humankind under the sovereignty of God.

Islam also teaches that for the spiritual, ethical, and social guidance of humankind God has doubly favored all human beings without any distinction of race, color, or gender. On the one hand God provided every human being with *al-fitra*, the wholesome nature that can distinguish between right and wrong, truth and falsehood, good and bad, harmful and useful, and so on. *Al-fitra* is a universal natural standard that is given to all human beings. *Al-fitra*, however, is not enough to keep a person on the right path. It can be influenced and can be subjected to social, environmental, and other pressures and temptations. It is for this reason that God gave humanity a second source of guidance. He appointed from amongst all human beings some individuals to whom He communicated and revealed His will and command. These are known as prophets and messengers of God who were teachers and guides of human beings throughout history. Prophets came to all people. God says in the *Qur'ān:*

> We indeed sent among every people an apostle. (16:36)
> . . . .
> There was never any people without a warner having lived among them. (35:24)

God's message came to all people. There are no people, country, or region which were neglected by God. God loved all people. He gave every human being the gift of *al-fitra* and sent among all people His guides and reminders.

Human beings are the honored creation of God (17:70). God made humans as the stewards (*khalīfa*) and trustees of the resources of the earth and heaven. The *Qur'ān* says: "We offered the trust unto heavens and the earth and the hills, but they shrank from bearing it and were afraid of it. And man assumed it. Lo! he proved a tyrant and a fool" (33:72).

The implications of this worldview are deeply ecumenical and universal. Here we have one God, one Creator, one humanity, and one source of guidance and moral values. Religions are the repositories of this divine knowledge and moral and ethical guidance. The universality of religious phenomenon proves that there has always been a universal desire among humans to know the ultimate reality. Islam does not only accept this but goes a step further and claims that God has spoken to *all* people through His prophets and messengers.

Historically speaking, however, it would be wrong to say that all religions remained in their pristine purity, that prophetic messages did not undergo any changes, and that other human factors did not contribute to the development, growth, decline, or distortions in religions. The story of religions is not all beautiful and rosy.

Nevertheless, the question we have to ask is this: how would the Islamic worldview affect our global ethics? And what role would such an ethics play in our interreligious dialogue and relations?

GLOBAL ETHICS OF ISLAM

There are two interesting ethical terms of Islam that frequently occur in the *Qur'ān: Ma'rūf* (good, virtue, etc.) and *Munkar* (bad, evil). *Ma'rūf* literally means that which is known and recognized. It means an action that is generally recognized and known to people as acceptable, good, and hence virtuous. *Munkar* on the other hand means that which is unrecognized and unacceptable. It is an action that is generally unacceptable to people and hence bad and evil. Thus the *Qur'ān* seems to have recognized a general common standard of virtue and evil. This of course does not mean that good and evil are left to be decided by the general conventions of the people. No, it means that there is a general standard of goodness and evil recognized by the humanity at large. Just as there is a common reason and common sense among people, so there is also a common sense of virtue and goodness that is universal in all times, places, and peoples.

A modern Muslim theologian interpreted these terms in the following way:

> The term *ma'rūfāt* [plural of *ma'rūf*] denotes all the virtues and good qualities that have always been accepted as "good" by the human conscience. Conversely, the word *munkarāt* [plural of *munkar*] denotes all the sins and evils that have always been condemned by human nature as "evil." In short the *ma'rūfāt* are in harmony with human nature and its requirements in general and the *munkarāt* are just the opposite.[2]

The Islamic law classifies the *ma'rūfāt* into three categories: those that are mandatory (*farḍ* or *wājib*), those that are recommended or supererogatory (*mustaḥab* or *mandūb*) and those that are acceptable (*mubāḥ*). The *munkarāt* are also classified in two categories: those that are prohibited or forbidden (*ḥarām*) and those that are disliked (*makrūh*). Islamic law and ethics work under these five categories.

This is a particularly Islamic scheme of things. I am not suggesting that everyone must adhere to this scheme, or unless all humankind accept this scheme there cannot be any dialogue. I am, however, suggesting that this could be a basis for a dialogue on global ethics, at least from a Muslim perspective. It would mean that Islam provided a basis for working out a global ethics which could inspire, at least Muslims and, one hopes, others to work toward the achievement of a world community based on justice.

ETHICS IN INTERRELIGIOUS DIALOGUE

The role of ethics in interreligious dialogue is to emphasize this commonality of human vision for good, right, truth, justice, beauty, freedom, and love. At no other time were we human beings in need of these values as much as we are today. Technical civilization has brought global interdependence. Now, either we can help each other and live and let live, or we can easily destroy each other. Global interdependence can also bring global annihilation. Martin Luther King's potent phrase, "Injustice in any place is a threat to justice in everyplace," is being realized by many today. It is strange that those who are talking today so much about ecological responsibility, concern for the environment, and preserving the ozone are willing to do very little for economic justice, have no concern about political oppression, and care very little to preserve human dignity. We often hear the complaint that the ecological movement has found little response from the third world countries. But the question is, "Where is the motivation, for the oppressed, to work to preserve a world in which opportunities and choices are determined by skin color and/or gender? For most of the world's population, there is no clear and qualitative distinction between ecological destruction and their slow death through poverty."[3]

It is important that world religions engage in dialogue and bring to service their theological resources and ethical and moral values to help humanity achieve human fellowship and world community based on a comprehensive global ethics.

NOTES

1. S. Cromwell Crawford, *World Religions and Global Ethics* (New York: Paragon House, 1989), xiii–xiv.

2. A. A. Maudūdī, *Islamic Way of Life* (Lahore: Islamic Publications, 1950), 19.

3. Anthony Pinn, "African-Americans and Eco-Justice: Not Just a 'White-folks' Issue,'" *Harvard Divinity Bulletin*, vol. 19, no. 3 (Fall 1989): 9.

17

Ethics and Dialogue Among the World Religions: Some Observations on Gender-Based Dialogue

Tova Meltzer

> The idea that there are distinct moral languages, disparate con-
> ceptualities within which to understand and appraise conduct,
> character, and community, has become a commonplace in recent
> humanistic scholarship.[1]

Recent studies in psychological theory and education, notably the work of Carol Gilligan and her colleagues, have shown us that we can no longer speak simplistically of *"the* ethical system" or *"the* morality" of a society, as if there were a single agreed-upon definition of such key concepts as "self," "relationship," and "morality." Rather, just as with every other dimension of human experience, the ethical aspects are gendered. That is, there is no such thing as a neuter, or neutral, ethical system in which all humans, men and women, participate. Ethical experience is the experience of men and women, and it is not the same. It is, therefore, not sufficient to delineate a structure for, or definition of, the ethical system of a society. We must also ask *for whom* in the society are these meanings operative? In other words, we must now consider pragmatics as well as semantics. Long-held assumptions about the universality of moral doctrines are thus being challenged by studies which look at the socially constructed nature of reality. A common finding in many of these recent studies points to the existence of two voices and perspectives: one of justice and the other of care. The justice perspective includes a morality of rights and formal reasoning; universal, fundamental moral rules are discovered and applied by use of what is regarded as a universal logic. The care perspective is based on a morality of responsibility and the maintenance of harmony; morality is found in how one responds to others—caring, protecting, and relationship-maintaining activities.

In her preface to *Mapping the Moral Domain*, Carol Gilligan begins by describing an observation of a recent children's essay contest in Memphis. The children were asked to write about how to improve their city. The boys wrote about the expected aspects of urban renewal—physical property alterations and additions. The girls, however, wrote about improving and strengthening relationships between people. This association of moral voice with gender is controversial and raises important questions. What are we to make of the apparently gender-based differences in the ways of experiencing oneself in relation to others? Are the differences in the ways people *speak* of themselves and others also evident in how they actually *interact*? Carol Gilligan raises even more important questions: "Why do the same words (such as 'improving the city') have different meanings for different people? Whose meanings will prevail and be taken as 'right' or definitive? What are the implications of seeing or speaking in what is considered to be the 'right' language?"[2]

In assessing the role of ethics in the dialogue among the world religions, discourse considerations are foundational. Whose voice and perspective are we hearing when confronting such statements as "Islam says this . . ." or "Christianity says that . . ."? Carol Gilligan and colleagues, in their North American studies, have identified a justice perspective and a male voice as normative, at least within the fields of psychology and education. This is not to equate male voice and the justice perspective, but rather to make an observation on dominance and power structures within societies. The details of many of the psychological studies indicate that both care and justice perspectives are at least recognized by, if not operant within, most individuals. Granting this point, however, still leaves us with the necessity to recognize that it is largely a matter of power and hierarchy which conditions whose voice will be acknowledged and heard at any historical moment.

We have been taught that a society's ethical system is normally deeply rooted in a religious tradition—and now, that that religious tradition is not neutral, but gendered, the experience of men and women. It is incumbent upon us to recognize the gendered and polysemic constructions of the world religions. These recent psychological studies are not directly concerned with the normative ethical statements emanating from any particular religious tradition, yet the im-

185

plications cannot be ignored. Do Carol Gilligan's "justice voice" and "care voice" represent the two basic ethical perspectives in Christianity (the dominant religious base of the society of her research subjects), or perhaps, even more broadly, general perspectives within monotheistic traditions? Are other voices present in other traditions? Would the same research conducted in a polytheistic society (among Hindus for example) yield similar results? These questions are approaching the problem from *within* each tradition. The close connection between the "justice voice" and "care voice" research findings and the ethical perspectives in the dominant Western monotheistic faiths needs to be acknowledged and further scrutinized. Are we learning more about men and women in general, or about how men and women at a given point in time in a Western society have variously integrated religious ethical perspectives and how this integration is perpetuated through socialization?

The complexity of the issue of voice becomes yet greater when we begin with the basis for our own understandings. Our thinking, like all of our experience, is gendered. It would be most interesting to divide a representative group from several of the world's religious traditions into a men's group and a women's group, to have these two smaller groups discuss the topic of the role of ethics in the dialogue among the world religions, and then to compare the perspectives of each group. Not only is the self-understanding of each of us a gendered understanding, but our understanding of the other is equally gendered. My own observations from attendance at numerous interfaith dialogue sessions in the United States is that male-dominated meetings focus on the formulation of universal, general principles, yielding a morality of rights and abstract reason; whereas female-dominated sessions rely on narratives in depicting a morality of care and responsibility. When put together, which group's mode of discourse would dominate? Well, we already have the answer to that question; just reflect on the nature of most meetings and conferences in which men and women participate together. Such a tendency (not too strong, I hope) to follow the norm may also be observed in my own comments.

The issue of voice in our assessment of how we imagine ourselves and others in relationships, while gendered, however, is not simplified by an *a priori* division into women's and men's perspectives. As Carol Gilligan has said, "The fact that a person adopts one approach in solving a problem does not mean that he or she does not know or appreciate others."[3] Recent studies point to a tendency for people in situations of moral ambiguity to opt either for considerations of justice or considerations of care.[4] Men opted more often for justice, and women more often for care, but the details of these studies prevent one from hasty assumptions about "male behavior" versus "female behavior." A broader perspective sees justice and care as two ideals in human relationships, two different ways of thinking that must be taken together to account for the similarities and differences we observe in the West between the moral reasoning of men and women.

If there were not tensions within individual ethical systems, we would probably not have devoted so much time and attention to the study and discussion of ethics. Recognition of gender-based voices provides an important dimension for our consideration of the nature and origin of ethical systems, and one way to account for observed tensions. It also enables us to ask in which voices do we perceive similarities or differences in our dialogues with the other. Carol Gilligan has contended that there are (within a single tradition) two moral systems, operating independently but with equal adequacy, and incapable of being synthesized. If we proceed to accept this as a possibility, we must then ask which are the voices of communication in a religious dialogue. And realizing that we cannot synthesize, we cannot simultaneously understand a situation from more than one perspective (although we can and frequently do move between perspectives), the nature and relationship of the voices will achieve greater clarity. Scholars, historians, and philosophers of religion must recognize the multivocality within religious traditions as essential for increased insight and understanding of the incredible richness and complexity of human experience. The "independent" operation of the systems is best understood as an ontological discreteness; for the more we study any particular experiential setting, the more we become aware that functionally the systems operate in a continuous dialectic in which the one could not exist without the other.

The historical dimensions of gender-based voice in religious discourse must not be overlooked. Feminists and non-feminists alike have often been too hasty to ascribe the universal qualification of "male" or "female" to particular behavioral patterns. This not only pays insufficient attention to cultural constraints, but it does not recognize the ever-changing nature of human cultures and the processes by which phenomena are continually resignified. As an example drawing upon highly familiar terrain in my own mental geography, I would like to call to your attention one possible interpretation of ethical perspectives during the first two thousand years of recorded history, specifically that of the early writings from ancient Mesopotamia and Egypt. Those of us who spend a great deal of time reading the original documents from these cultures are strongly impressed by the overwhelming, almost excessive, concern with human relationships, especially in texts such as proverbs, admonitions, or other wisdom literature. Even in texts purportedly about justice, such as the so-called law code of Hammurabi, the conception of justice is not an abstracted set of general principles, but rather, justice is that which is observable in proper human relationships. The relationships are always primary. If we accept Carol Gilligan's distinction between a justice perspective and a care perspective as at least a testable hypothesis, then what we are seeing in these early ancient texts, are examples of cultures where the care and responsibility perspective is normative. This finding runs counter to the position that the domination of men's thinking as we understand it today in our culture, that is, the justice perspective, is a necessary correlation of a patriarchal social structure (and I do not question the patriarchal structure of the early societies). Evidence such as this from the ancient past presses us to question the origins of the justice perspective. Is it not likely that this justice perspective arose as the ideology of a dominant class, rather than as the universal truth it claims to be? One of the few cross-cultural studies exploring Carol Gilligan's hypothesis compares Western moral thought with African worldviews.[5] Significant parallels are noted between the Western feminine, that is, the care and responsibility perspective, and the African view. These parallels are all seen to originate in a common source—oppression. This study, then, provides an additional stimulus for our thinking.

The recognition that women's thinking, women's moral reasoning, is not necessarily the same as men's changes radically the approach we must take to seeking new understandings of the other, and calls for a questioning of the established forms for dialogue among the world religions. The consideration of voice and perspective, of gender-based discourse, in our seeking for increased understanding of other traditions must not be allowed to become sidetracked by the academic issues of universality or origins. In dialogue among world religions all voices within each tradition must be heard. Only in this way will we be enabled to advance in understanding and improving the life of all humans—men and women.

NOTES

1. Jeffrey Stout, *Ethics After Babel: The Language of Morals and Their Discontents* (Boston: Beacon Press, 1988), x.

2. Carol Gilligan, *In a Different Voice: Psychological Theory and Women's Development* (Cambridge, Mass.: Harvard University Press, 1982), i.

3. Ibid., iii.

4. Ibid.; Carol Gilligan, Janie Victoria Ward, and Jill McLean Taylor, eds., *Mapping the Moral Domain: A Construction of Women's Thinking to Psychological Theory and Education* (Cambridge, Mass.: Harvard University Press, 1988); Eva Feder Kittay and Diana T. Meyers, eds., *Women and Moral Theory* (Savage, Md.: Rowan & Littlefield Publishers, 1987).

5. Sandra Harding in *Women and Moral Theory*, 296–315.

Index

Index

Bunyan, John, 54–55
Burns, Robert, 62

Caird, G. B., 151
Calvin, John, 102, 111
Calvinism, 102. *See also* Scottish
  Covenanters
Camus, Albert
  The Plague, 13
capitalism, 133–134, 140–141
care, ethics of, vs. ethics of justice,
  184–188
categorical imperative, 127, 129–130
Catholic Worker Movement, 66
The Catholic Worker (newspaper), 62,
  66
Chodorov, Nancy
  Reproduction of Mothering, 112
Christian humanism
  deficiencies of, 77–83
  defined, 87
  other monotheistic traditions and,
    89n23
Christianity
  modern science and, 161–163
  relationships among varieties of
    goodness within, 10–12
  varieties of goodness within, 4–
    10
church, as model for human
  relations, 151–152
code of Hammurabi, 188
collective good
  personal responsibility and,
    132–146
  sacrifice of, 30–34
communitarian ethics, 124n11
community, search for, 104–105,
  107
community life. *See also* social life
  Day's farming commune and,
    18–21
  forms of, 8–9

comparative religious ethics, 12,
  13–15
compassion, 174
conflict resolution, and limits on
  public discourse, 115–118, 121,
  122, 123
Confucianism, 158, 159
consequences
  attitudes and, 136–139
  Catholic vs. utilitarian emphasis
    on, 135–136
  unintended, 143
conversation vs. dialogue, 174–175
conviction-civility problem, 97–99
Crawford, S. Cromwell
  World Religions and Global Ethics,
    178
crisis, stories of, 114, 116–117, 121
Cuddihy, John Murray, 96
cultural constraints, and care vs.
  justice perspective, 187–188
cultural difference, 8–9, 10. *See also*
  otherness and difference
Cupitt, Don, 72, 74, 75–76, 77–83,
  85, 87
  The Leap of Reason, 90n42
  The New Christian Ethics, 75
  Taking Leave of God, 75
cynicism, 106

Day, Dorothy, 18, 62–67
  The Long Loneliness, 66–67
"decisionism," 70
delight
  assumptions about, 54
  authenticity and, 60–62
  centrality of, 67–70
  difficulties with ethics of, 55
  Dorothy Day and, 62–67
  grading and, 69–70
  as intrinsic to good life, 60
  Sarah Pierpont Edwards and,
    57–60

192

Index

responsibility. *See also* personal
  responsibility
  ecological, 74, 182
  ethics of care vs. justice and, 186
  for non-human good, 47–48
  of the rich, 138, 139
  for self-assertion by poor,
    138–139
revisionism, 75, 76
Roman Catholic social teaching,
    132–146, 148–152
Rossi, Philip, 126–130
Rousseau, Jean Jacques, 97,
    103–104, 107, 111
Russell, Bertrand
  "A Free Man's Worship," 80

sacrifice. *See also* human sacrifice
  of collective good for non-human
    good, 30–34
  for common good, 138, 156–157
sainthood, 4–5, 6. *See also*
  perfection; supererogation
Sartre, Jean-Paul, 11
Sayers, Dorothy
  "Dilemma," 82
Schafer, Thomas, 57
Schleiermacher, Friedrich, 29, 36
Schweitzer, Albert, 6, 12, 20
science. *See also* technology,
  dangers of
  Buddhism and, 168–169
  Christianity and, 161–163
  discernment of divine purpose
    and, 38
  ethical response and, 36
  existence of God and, 45
  inferences from ethical beliefs
    and, 40–41, 42n7
  moral guidance for, 169
Scottish Covenanters, 95–96,
    101–102

secular humanism
  as account for moral life, 87
  vs. Christian humanism, 77, 80
  sexism and, 84
  varieties of goodness and, 12–
    13
secularization, and public discourse,
    114–115
self-deception
  in Christian humanism, 77, 80
  public civility and, 107
  theological realism and, 86
Sennett, Richard
  The Fall of Public Man, 99, 100,
    101, 110
senses, 25, 27, 29–30, 40
sexism, 84, 85. *See also* gender
sexuality, 58, 59–60
Sheppard, Dick, 11
sin. *See* personal sin, and structures
  of sin
social issues, and theological
  categories, 135
social life, 68–69. *See also*
  community life
social order, need for change in,
    145–146
solidarity, 151
  conditions for, 139–142
  definitions of, 137–138
  justice and, 138–139
South Africa, 160, 166n19
South America, 160
Spinoza, Baruch, 46
spirituality. *See also* relation to
  God
  sexuality and, 58, 59–60
  in theological non-realism, 90n42
Starkey, Peggy, 166n18
Stoicism, 26, 27, 28
subjectivity, 30
summum bonum, 3, 4, 20. *See also*
  ideal life, notion of; perfection